LIBERTY AND

CONSCIENCE

LIBERTY AND CONSCIENCE

A Documentary History of

the Experiences of Conscientious Objectors

in America through the Civil War

Edited by

PETER BROCK

UNIVERSITY PRESS

2002

OXFORD

UNIVERSITY PRESS

Oxford   New York

Auckland   Bangkok   Buenos Aires   Cape Town   Chennai
Dar es Salaam   Delhi   Hong Kong   Istanbul   Karachi   Kolkata
Kuala Lumpur   Madrid   Melbourne   Mexico City   Mumbai   Nairobi
São Paulo   Shanghai   Singapore   Taipei   Tokyo   Toronto

and an associated company in Berlin

Published by Oxford University Press, Inc.
198 Madison Avenue, New York, New York 10016

www.oup.com

Oxford is a registered trademark of Oxford University Press

Library of Congress Cataloging-in-Publication Data
Liberty and conscience : a documentary history of the experiences of conscientious
objectors in America through the Civil War / edited by Peter Brock.
p. cm.
Includes bibliographical references.
ISBN 0-19-515121-6; ISBN 0-19-515122-4 (pbk.)
1. Conscientious objection—United States—History—17th century—Sources.
2. Conscientious objection—United States—History—18th century—Sources.
3. Conscientious objection—United States—History—19th century—Sources.
I. Brock, Peter, 1920-
UB342.U5 L53 2002
355.2'24'09730903—dc21   2001036671

1 3 5 7 9 8 6 4 2

Printed in the United States of America
on acid-free paper

Preface

The experiences of American conscientious objectors (COs) in the two world wars of the twentieth century as well as under the Selective Service Act of 1948, which governed military obligation during the Vietnam War, are fairly well documented and relatively easy for students, teachers, and others interested in the subject to access. The present volume covers the earlier period of conscription, which ran uninterruptedly from the colonial era to the conclusion of the Civil War. For this period, documents on conscientious objection to military service and related forms of compulsion, although in one form or another quite extensive, are less accessible to the reader.

In 1968, during the Vietnam War, Lillian Schlissel published a pioneering collection of documents on conscientious objection entitled *Conscience in America*. But, understandably in the circumstances, her work concentrated on the twentieth century, with the earlier centuries treated somewhat perfunctorily. Over thirty years have elapsed since her book appeared, but so far no one has attempted to provide more adequate coverage on conscientious objection during the first era of American conscription. I have tried here to fill this lacuna.

In contrast to the twentieth century, when objectors not infrequently drew their inspiration from humanist or political motives or from a non-Christian religion, during the period covered by this volume conscientious objection was almost exclusively religious in inspiration and contained within the Christian tradition. The documents presented here should therefore be of interest to students of American religion in addition to readers concerned with various aspects of peace studies. They shed light, too, on the development of civil liberties in the United States and in colonial and revolutionary America. Even the military historian may perhaps discover, in the interplay between army authorities and conscientious objectors to militia conscription or Civil War draft, fresh materials for reflection on the role of militarism in the United States.

To round off the picture, I have included a few documents on conscientious objection in the colonial West Indies and Upper Canada, thus supplementing the bulk of the contents, which is drawn from the area that became the United States. For the first two areas also formed part of a broader transatlantic social and economic community.

Printed primary sources form the core of my documentation; in several cases these sources are embedded in a secondary work. There are also some manuscript materials. I would like to thank Christine Chattin for her careful typing of the original manuscript. I would also like to thank Cynthia A. Read, Executive Editor, Oxford University Press, for her encouragement of my project; Theo Calderara, Assistant Editor, for his assistance; and Ellen Guerci, Production Editor, for her able guidance of my manuscript through the various stages of production.

Toronto   P. B.
December 2001

Acknowledgments

The following acknowledgments are gratefully made for permission to print:

to Professor Richard K. MacMaster, Elizabethtown College, Elizabethtown, Pennsylvania, for Document 10;

to the Newmarket Historical Society, Newmarket, Ontario, for Document 16;

to the Friends Historical Library of Swarthmore College, Swarthmore, Pennsylvania, for Document 20;

to the Dutchess County Historical Society, Poughkeepsie, New York, for Document 25 ("Imprisonment of Four New York Quakers, Spring 1839");

to Harvard University Press for Document 27; Reprinted by permission of the publishers from *Letters of William Lloyd Garrison*, edited by Walter W. Merrill, Cambridge, Mass.: Harvard University Press, Copyright © 1979 by the President and Fellows of Harvard College. The Letters of William Lloyd Garrison are held by the Boston Public Library, Boston, Massachusetts;

to Western Reserve Historical Society, Cleveland, Ohio, for Document 29;

to the Brethren Press, Elgin, Illinois, for Document 35.

Contents

PART VI
CIVIL WAR AMERICA

LIBERTY AND

CONSCIENCE

I

⸺ ⸺

C O L O N I A L   A M E R I C A

America's first conscientious objectors (COs), so far as we know, were Quakers.[1] Quakerism reached America in the second half of the 1650s and soon took root in the existing colonies of Massachusetts, Plymouth, New Hampshire, Rhode Island, New York (then New Netherlands), Maryland, Virginia, and the Carolinas, as well as in the West Indian islands under English rule. In 1682 the Quaker William Penn founded Pennsylvania to serve as a refuge for his persecuted brethren at home. The new province, which then included Delaware, together with neighboring New Jersey, soon became a center of Quakerism. In colonial Pennsylvania, even after the official withdrawal of Quakers from government in 1756, citizens remained free from the obligation to bear arms until after the outbreak of the Revolution. Everywhere else, however, "colonial draft legislation provided that every male citizen between certain ages, usually 18 to 50, would keep himself armed and be subject to call as a member of the colonial militia force. Private and general musters were ordered and penalties provided for those who willfully refused or neglected to muster.[2]

Quakerism had arisen in republican England around 1650 under the inspiration of a prophetic cobbler, George Fox. Though Fox himself seems to have maintained from the beginning a personal testimony against bearing arms, there were many Quakers in the Commonwealth army and at the outset the question of peace did not figure prominently among Quakers. The

Quakers were eventually to establish a Society of Friends, which in due course set up an ecclesiastical discipline, enforced rigorously by the threat of disownment of members who did not abide by its rules. After the restoration of the monarchy, British Quakers issued a *Declaration* in January 1661 in which inter alia they stated unambiguously "that the Spirit of God . . . will never move us to fight and war . . . with outward weapons, neither for the Kingdom of Christ nor the Kingdoms of this world."[3] Henceforward what became known as the Quaker peace testimony included the refusal of at least personal participation in any form of military service.[4]

With respect to militia service, which was the most frequent—but by no means the only—military obligation imposed by the authorities on both sides of the Atlantic, the Society of Friends required its members not only to refuse to bear arms but to refuse to pay the—usually small—fine exacted from draftees unwilling, for whatever reason, to appear at a muster. A person should not have to pay for doing what he or she considered to be right: thus Friends argued. Delinquency in paying a militia fine almost inevitably entailed distraint of property, often in excess of the amount owed, or brief imprisonment if the man did not possess property of his own on which a distraint could be made. But Friends considered these "sufferings" a small price to pay for maintaining a clear conscience.

The Society frowned even more severely on members ready to hire a substitute to appear in their place: a second alternative for those not wishing themselves to serve. Hiring a substitute indeed remained a temptation when the call-up was for prolonged service during a military emergency or actual war. The "enemy" in the American colonies might be hostile Indians or the French or Spanish imperialist rivals of the English.

In seaports or on the high seas, young Quakers might fall victim to impressment into the Royal Navy. This was the fate of John Smith and Thomas Anthony in 1705 (Document 4).

The first recorded cases of Quakers being penalized in America for their stand as COs to the militia come from Maryland and date from around 1658. Their treatment was often fairly severe (Document 1). Though conditions were eased in this respect early in the next decade, Quaker "militia sufferings" continued for a long time to come (Documents 3B and C). Eventually some provinces attempted to make provision in their militia laws for Quaker scruples against fighting: the Society of Friends, after its turbulent beginnings, had after all settled down into comparative respectability. But because, whatever individual Quakers might think, the Society of Friends as a collective body continued to uphold an "absolutist" position and reject any alternative to unconditional exemption, the conditional exemption provided by sympathetic provincial legislators, in fact, brought no relief to the Society's hard-pressed objectors—unless indeed they were prepared to risk disownment for breaking their Society's rule. Some COs in fact did so—and some of them got away with it.

The most generous CO legislation framed by a colonial legislature (except Pennsylvania, which did not have militia conscription) came from Rhode Island, where, in an act passed in 1673, it was declared that "persons [were] not to be compelled to train, fight or kill against their consciences" (Document 2). This step need not surprise us. For not only was Rhode Island the home province of the great protagonist of civil liberty, Roger Williams (d. 1683), but its government at this time had a large Quaker component. Alongside Quaker COs there were a few Baptist pacifists, though that denomination as a whole did not share Quaker views on war. The act of 1673 was withdrawn several years later; still, Quakers in Rhode Island remained comparatively untroubled by military obligation. A striking feature of the CO clauses in the act of 1673 is the provision there for alternative civilian service in case of an enemy invasion of the province. However, that part of the act does not ever seem to have been put into effect; indeed, it is doubtful if strict Quakers would have complied with this requirement, despite its humanitarian intent, for they opposed compulsion even for a good deed in exchange for not doing something they considered to be wrong.

Among other military requirements that American Quakers refused were compulsory labor to build or repair forts (Document 3A) and the digging of ditches for army use. In 1711, for instance, during the War of the Spanish Succession, a clash occurred between Alexander Spotswood, the governor of Virginia, and the province's Quakers, now organized into a Virginia Yearly Meeting. Governor Spotswood wrote angrily to the authorities at home:

> I have been mightily embarrassed by a set of Quakers who broach doctrines so monstrous as their brethren in England never owned, nor, indeed, can be suffered in any government. They have not only refused to work themselves, or suffer any of their servants to be employed in the fortifications, but affirm that their consciences will not permit them to contribute in any manner of way to the defence of the country even so much as trusting the government with provisions to support those that do the work, tho' at the same time they say that being obliged by their religion to feed the enemies, if the French should come hither and want provisions, they must in conscience supply them. . . . I have thought it necessary to put the laws of this country in execution against this sect of people . . . and impose fines and penalties upon their disobedience."[5]

After the Treaty of Utrecht of 1713 a long period of peace ensued. War came again in 1739. The brief War of Jenkins' Ear led into the War of the Austrian Succession (1740–1748), followed by the Seven Years' War, known on this continent as the French and Indian War (1755–1763). This war brought about a condition of great tension in Quaker Pennsylvania. In the frontier areas of the province the inhabitants, mostly non-Quakers, demanded defensive measures against the attacks of hostile Indians, backed by the French. Combined with pressure from the home government, such demands eventually prevailed on the Quaker majority in the provincial Assembly to grant sixty thousand pounds "for the king's use" (until then the Assembly had stubbornly refused to do this) and to set up a voluntary militia. Only seven Quaker deputies voted against granting money for war. But Quaker control of the legislature—"the holy experiment"—now ended, even if members of the Society of Friends continued to sit in the Assembly in a private capacity.

Quaker pacifist radicals, led by the saintly tailor John Woolman, now led a campaign to refuse payment of taxes that were clearly destined for war purposes. Civil disobedience, they urged, was the proper Quaker response in the existing situation in Pennsylvania: a stance that conflicted indeed with that of George Fox and his generation of Friends during the previous century. Some Pennsylvania Quakers followed the advice of the radicals and refused to pay the tax recently imposed by the Assembly, thus risking distraint on their property and even imprisonment. But more paid, even though Philadelphia Yearly Meeting had eventually thrown its support behind the radicals on this issue.

Everywhere outside Pennsylvania the new war situation meant renewed hardship for Quaker COs. This applied even to New Jersey, where John Woolman resided—though in a Quaker meeting that came within the confines of Philadelphia Yearly Meeting (Documents 5A and B). Nevertheless, the military authorities not infrequently showed understanding of these men's scruples. When, for instance, young George Washington, then a colonel in the Virginia militia and later president of the United States, was faced with seven Quaker conscripts who stubbornly refused to handle a weapon or accept any alternative such as paying a fine or having a substitute, he treated them courteously. On releasing them from bondage he humorously "asked of them . . . that if ever he should fall as much into their power as they had been in his—they would treat him with equal kindness" (Document 5C).

We have been concerned so far with Quaker COs. Apart from several very small groups like the Rogerenes or the German Baptist Brethren (in 1908, by now greatly increased in numbers, they became the Church of the Brethren), the anabaptist Mennonites represented the other major peace sect of the colonial era. Still entirely German speaking, they had emigrated from Central Europe beginning in 1683, and settled in Pennsylvania and Virginia. Their doctrine of nonresistance (*Wehrlosigkeit*) dated back to 1527. True Christian discipleship, they believed, demanded renunciation of war and participation in government. Yet "the sword" was "ordained of God outside the perfection of Christ" to punish the wicked and defend the good.

American Mennonites did not possess an intellectual elite as the Quakers did, and apart from their pastors, whose book learning was confined to the Scriptures, they were in this period still almost exclusively farmers or rural craftsmen. They left far fewer documents for posterity than those diligent record-keepers, the Quakers. In response to military obligation Mennonites willingly paid a fine in lieu of bearing arms. In acting thus they believed they were only rendering to Caesar what was already his. But they were opposed to hiring substitutes, since a transaction of that kind merely transferred to another—and hitherto innocent—man the sin of shedding human blood. In colonial Pennsylvania, of course, like the Quakers they were free of the burden of militia conscription. But in the smaller Mennonite community of Virginia they were required to serve. However, by paying their fines, even during the alarms of the French and Indian War, they avoided trouble with the authorities over this issue (Document 5D).

🌿 1 🌿

The First Quaker Conscientious Objectors in America, 1658

Maryland

Anno 1658. The beginning of our account of sufferings in this province may appear somewhat abrupt, because we find not, among our papers collected, any exact account of the first settlement of the people called Quakers here, and the earliest sufferings we meet with are without any particular dates. Only in general the reader may observe, that such of them as are so, appear to us to have been transacted in or before the year 1658, *viz.*

William Fuller and Thomas Homewood, for their conscientious refusal to obey the orders of court made by the officers of Cecilius Lord Baltimore,[1] respecting the militia, had taken from them goods to the value of £8.15s.6d.

Richard Keene, for refusing to be trained as a soldier, had taken from him the sum of £6.15s. and was abused by the sheriff, who drew his cutlass, and therewith made a pass at the breast of the said Richard, and struck him on the shoulders, saying *You Dog, I could find in my heart to split your brains.*

From Joseph Besse, *A Collection of the Sufferings of the People called Quakers, for the Testimony of a Good Conscience* (London, 1753), 2:378–80.

This sheriff's name was Coarsey. At another time one John Odber a captain, and a justice of the peace, named Ashcomb, with many rude associates attending them, having heated themselves by drinking out several casks of wine, came to the houses of Richard Keene and others to take away their goods, under pretence of defaults in appearing at arms, but indeed to raise money to pay for the wine they had drank; and when Richard Keene's wife reproved the said justice for his drunkenness, his answer was as sottish as his practice, *viz. A man is never drunk if he can get out of a cart's way when it is coming towards him.* Thus even the magistrates did glory in the commission of those vices, which it was the duty of their office to have punished.

William Muffit, for refusing to be trained, was fined £6.15s. and the officer gave orders to the sheriff, *if he could not get his goods, to take his chest, and if not his chest, his shirts.*

John Knap, for refusing to be trained, had goods taken from him to the value of £7.10s. with a chest. He was also fined £3.10s. for not swearing. These distresses were a great suffering to a poor labouring man, above sixty years of age, being a considerable part of the small remains of many years' pain and industry. . . .

Michael Brooks was fined £7.10s. because he could not swear, and £4.10s. for refusing to bear arms under the command of John Odber Captain, a man so profane as to affirm in the hearing of many persons, that *They were not fit to be soldiers who could not swear, be drunk, and whore.* To such men as these the properties of sober and conscientious men stood exposed, and were often sacrificed to their unruly passions and domineering tempers. Edmund Hinchman was also fined £4.10s. for not bearing arms under the said Capt. Odber. . . .

Thomas Mears had also taken from him by John Norwood sheriff goods worth £5 because his son had refused to bear arms. . . .

Susanna Elliot, for default of her servant's appearing in arms, had goods taken away worth 16s. . . .

Hugh Drew being fined £4.10s. for refusing to bear arms, but being very poor and in debt, he sold his cow with intent to pay his debt, but the officers understanding it, seized the money the cow was sold for, being £5.5s. for the said fine.

William Davis, a poor man, fined £4.10s. for refusing to be trained, and for that fine had goods taken from him worth £5.11s.

William Cole, for refusing to bear arms, had a servant, who was an apprentice bound to him for seven years, taken from him, and though the said servant's time was really worth £16 yet the officers valued him at no more than £5.5s. . . .

Robert Dunn, for refusing to bear arms, had goods taken from him worth £18.5s.

Francis Barnes, for refusing to be trained, had taken from him goods worth £6.5s.

John Ellis, for refusing to train, had goods taken from him worth £6.5s.
. . .

Taken also for not bearing arms, from William Elliott, goods worth £4.17s.6d. From Edward Coppedge, goods worth £5.7s. From Henry Carline, a cow and a calf, and a yearling heifer, undervalued at £5.13s.6d. From John Walcott, goods worth £5.5s. And from William Read, a servant worth £7.10s.

The aforesaid Edward Coppedge was also whipt by order of the military officers.

Ishmael Wright, William Stockden, and Guy White, for not training, had taken from them by the sheriff Coarsey, by order from Capt. John Odber, to the value of £7 and the Sheriff threatned to turn them out of their house and plantation, John Ashcomb justice being then present. . . .

ꙮ 2 ꙮ

Rhode Island, 1673: "None to be compelled to train or fight against their consciences"

Proceedings of the General Assembly held for the Colony of Rhode Island and Providence Plantations at Newport, the 13th of August, 1673.

Voted, that Mr. John Easton, Mr. William Harris, Mr. John Tripp, Mr. Peter Easton, and Lieut. William Cadman are chosen a Committee[2] to prepare matters for this Assembly, concerning the Indians' drunkenness, encouragement of the militia, the danger we are in by the late enterprise of the Dutch taking New York, and such other public matters relateing to this Assembly, and make their return to this Assembly. . . .

[Concerning the militia,] seeing the King's Majesty is pleased to forbear to compel such to war who are persuaded in their consciences they may not fight to kill, how much less may such compel them that have consciences that need and receive a toleration from the King, even in the highest temporal things [and] how much more ought such men to forbear to compel or endeavor to compel their equal neighbours against their consciences, to

From John Russell Bartlett, ed., *Records of the Colony of Rhode Island and Providence Plantations, in New England* (Providence, 1857), 2:488, 497–99.

train to fight and kill by force of any bylaw of theirs, but rather consider, that if the King's Majesty indulge us all even in temporals, how much more ought his subjects to indulge one another.

Be it therefore enacted, and hereby it is enacted by his Majesty's authority, that no person nor persons (within this colony), that is or hereafter shall be persuaded in his, their conscience or consciences (and by him or them declared), that he nor they cannot nor ought not to train, to learn to fight, nor to war, nor kill any person or persons.

That neither he nor they shall at any time be compelled against his or their judgment and conscience to train, arm or fight, to kill any person nor persons by reason of, or at the command of any officer of this Colony, civil nor military, nor by reason of any by-law here past or formerly enacted; nor shall suffer any punishment, fine, distraint, penalty nor imprisonment, who cannot in conscience train, fight, nor kill any person nor persons for the aforesaid reasons expressed with many more implied, and others for brevity concealed, such aged men of such said understandings shall be exempt from trainings, arming, rallying to fight, to kill, and all such martial service as men are by any other debility; as said lame, sick, weak, deaf, blind, or any other infirmity exempteth persons in and by law, so the aforesaid men have no ability to fight, having no knowledge so to do, nor capacity so to learn, they taking themselves forbidden of God to learn war any more.

Provided, nevertheless, that all those who are persuaded in their understandings and consciences, that it is lawful, and no offence against God, to fight, to kill enemies in hostility against the King and his subjects, that such said persons of lawful age, and not exempted by any other debilities, may be compelled and ought to obey, and not to deny obedience to such said service, as if the aforesaid act by which the aforesaid exempted had never been made.

Provided, nevertheless, that such said persons who cannot fight nor destroy men, it [not] being against their conscience to do and perform civil service to the Colony, though not martial service, and can preserve (so far as in them lies) lives, goods, and cattle, &c., that when any enemy shall approach or assault the Colony or any place thereof, that then it shall be lawful for the civil officers for the time being, as civil officers (and not as martial or military) to require such said persons as are of sufficient able body and of strength (though exempt from arming and fighting), to conduct or convey out of the danger of the enemy weak and aged impotent persons, women and children, goods and cattle, by which the common weal may be the better maintained, and works of mercy manifested to distressed, weak persons; and shall be required to watch to inform of danger (but without arms in martial manner and matters), and to perform any other civil service by order of the civil officers for the good of the Colony, and inhabitants thereof; and the aforesaid or bylaw to stand in full force and every clause therein (in this Colony), any other former bylaw, act or acts, clause or clauses in them or either of them, to the contrary hereof in anywise notwithstanding.

⚛ 3 ⚛

Witnessing to the Quaker Peace Testimony

A. Letter to the Governor of New York, 1672

To the Governor of New York:

Whereas it was desired of the country that all who would willingly contribute towards repairing the fort of New York would give in their names and sums, and we whose names are under written not being found on the list, it was since desired by the High Sheriff that we would give our reasons unto the Governor, how willing and ready we have been to pay our customs [and] county rates and needful town charges and how we have behaved ourselves peaceably and quietly amongst our neighbours, and are ready to be serviceable in anything which doth not infringe upon our tender consciences. But being in measure redeemed of wars and stripes we cannot for conscience' sake be concerned in upholding things of that nature as you yourselves well know. It hath not been our practice in Old England since we were a people; and this in meekness we declare. In behalf of ourselves and our Friends, love and goodwill unto thee and all men.

John Tilton   Samuel Andrews
John Bowne   Matthew Pryer   Samuel Spicer
John Underhill   John Richardson   John Feke
Flushing, the 30th of the 10th month 1672.

From Rufus M. Jones, *The Quakers in the American Colonies* (London, 1911), 249.

B. From the Minutes of New England Yearly Meeting, 1712

4/12/1712—At our General Yearly Meeting held at Portsmouth. Peter Varley and John Kenny were imprisoned on the 8th day of 7th month 1711 to go in the expedition to Canada, and remained under confinement until the 8th month 1711 being under the command of Sydrach Walton who suffered them not to be abused during the time of their voyage as per account brought into this meeting.

John Terry and Moses Tucker were likewise imprisoned to go on the said expedition to Canada, and being in hopes of getting discharged went to Boston, and after much labour thereabouts were nevertheless sent as prisoners to the castle at Boston, and from thence conveyed by force on board transport under the command of Major Roberton, whose hard usage was such that one of the above Friends (John Terry) died within twenty-four hours after their return to Boston, as may be seen by a particular account thereof presented to this Meeting.

C. Hatsell Okelley, 1748

To the yearly meeting Committee of friends at Boston and elsewhere:[3]

Friend[s] these are to inform for that where as Hatsell Okelley[4] of Yarmouth in the County of Barnstable in Colonel Silvanus Bourns Regiment is made prisoner in the County Gaol at Barnstable for Refuseing to take up arms in the Kings service when imprest by Captain Ralph Chapman on order. Now the said prisoner is desirous application should be made by said Committee where they may think proper for his Relief and it being some time before there will be a monthly meeting where he belongs these are to testifie the Committee above said that the above said Hartsell Okelley is one under the Care of the monthly meeting at Sandwitch where we the Subscribers do Belong

Dartmouth the 31 of the 8th month 1748

Zacheus Wing, Nicolas Davis, Edward Wing, Seth Killey

* * *

Barnstable SS

[seal] To the keeper of His Majesties Gaol

In Barnstable for the County of Barnstable

Whereas Hatsell Okelley of Yarmouth in the County of Barnstable Husbandman is this day brought before me the Subscriber John Otis, Esq one of

From Rufus M. Jones, *The Quakers in the American Colonies* (London, 1911), 150.

From Henry J. Cadbury, *Friendly Heritage: Letters from the Quaker Past* (Norwalk, Conn., 1972), 138–40.

his Majesties Justices of the Peace for the County of Barnstable aforesaid on the Complaint of Ralph Chapman of Yarmouth in the said County of Barnstable, Gent. and Captain of the second foot company of Militia in the town of Yarmouth in the said County of Barnstable in Colonel Silvanus Bourns Regiment setting forth that at Yarmouth aforesaid he Received orders from his said Colonel upon the 25th day of June last to Impress or cause to be Impressed Four able Bodied efectivemen out of his said Company to attend his Majesties service Eastward on that frontier and accordingly hes caused to be Impressed for said Service on the 5th of July following Said Hatsell Okelley who was then a Soldier In his said Company to attend the said Service. Yet notwithstanding the said Hatsell did not attend the said service by himself or other meet person in his Room to the acceptance of his said Capt at time and place appointed within Twenty four hours next after such impressment neither hath he paid the Sum of Ten pounds for his said neglect nor can the said Capt by whose warrant he was impressed find any estate of the said Hatsell Okelleys whereby to make Distress upon for said Ten pounds (as he saith) To which complaint the said Hatsell Okelley pleaded he was not Guilty upon hearing and Examining the Evidences in the case it appeared to me that the said Hatsell Okelley is guilty and he being convicted thereof I do sentance him to be committed to his Majesties Goal in Barnstable in the County of Barnstable and there to be safely kept without Bail or Mainprize for the full space of Six months from this day and to pay costs of prosecution taxed at Thirty six shillings and ninepence in bills of credit on the Province of the Massachusetts Bay in New England of the last Emision.

You are therefore in his Majesties Name hereby Required to receive the body of him the said Hatsell Okelley into his Majesties said gaol and him there safely keep without Bail of Mainprize the full Term and Space of Six months as aforesaid and untill he pay the above Costs and your own fees. Hereof you may not fail. Dated at Barnstable aforesaid this 10th day of October In the 22nd year of his Majesties Reign Annoque Domini 1748

> John Otis
> A true copy of the originall Examined
> per Joseph Dimoc Jr keeper of his Majesties Gaol
> A Copy of Hatsell Okelleys mittimus [Endorsed][5]

❧ 4 ❧

Quakers and Naval Impressment, 1705

INTRODUCTION. As the writer of the following narrative (being personally known to and well esteemed by a number among us,) was enabled to bear a faithful and upright testimony to the peaceable government of Christ, and against the spirit of war, we think the Publication of it may afford strength and encouragement to others to follow his worthy example; we therefore recommend its perusal to the members of our religious society and others, hoping it may have a tendency to advance our peaceable testimony.

A NARRATIVE, &c. The following narrative was taken from a manuscript left by our friend John Smith, which appears to have been written in the early part of his life, in order to preserve some account of his experiences, trials, &c.

I John Smith of Marlborough in Chester County Pennsylvania, was born in the township of Dartmouth and county of Bristol in New England, on the 22d. of the 4th. month 1681; my parents professed the truth in their latter years; and as I grew to years of understanding the Lord was pleased to favour me with the knowledge of his blessed truth, and the work and operation thereof in my own heart, that by the virtue of it I came to be very much weaned from the vanities and delights of the world, and perishing pastimes that are therein, and those things that I was inclined to by nature.

And as I came to be acquainted with the discipline of the cross, and the divine light shining in my heart, about the 22d. year of my age, I was called to bear my testimony against wars and fightings, as being contrary to the doctrine of Christ, and the nature of his kingdom, and could not join with those that were for bearing arms for the defence of the country, against the French and Indian enemy; and accordingly, on the 15th. of the 6th. month 1703, I was notified by one William Hart, called a corporal, to appear at the town house in Dartmouth, in order to engage in the service proposed, under Benjamin Church, called captain, but refusing for conscience sake to comply, I was summoned on the 14th. of the 1st. month 1704, to appear before Nathaniel Byfield and Ebenezer Brenton, two magistrates of said county of Bristol, and examined concerning my said refusal, in which I still persisting for the reasons above said, I was fined in the sum of five pounds, and one pound three shillings charges. But having a months time to consider

From *A Narrative of Some Sufferings, for His Christian Peaceable Testimony, by John Smith, late of Chester County, Deceased* (Philadelphia, 1800), 10–18.

whether to pay said fine or not, I found most peace in refusing, for which I was sentenced to prison till payment thereof, where I remained till the general sessions in the second month following, and was then required to pay said fine and charges: but still refusing for the reason aforesaid, proclamation was made in court that I should be hired out to work to any that wanted a hand, for any time not exceeding four years, in order to satisfy said fine &c. but none offering to accept my service as above, I was sent to prison again, there to remain till an order was procured from the governor to remove me to Boston castle, there to work as a prisoner till said fine was satisfied.

Here I continued in great peace of mind about two weeks, often being made sensible of Divine kindness in this my confined condition: at the end of two weeks, the above said Benjamin Church came and commanded me out of prison, which I refused to comply with, without the governors order agreeable to the judgment of Court, which order he never produced, but forcibly took me out of prison, and I was ordered on board a vessel to be sent to Boston castle; and on our way through the town we met two of our friends, who in a friendly manner asked the person who commanded me, what art thou going to do with our friend? he answered he was going to take him to Boston castle: the friends remarked to him, how some people in such cases had been disappointed in their expectation and their vessels in danger of being lost: but notwithstanding this precaution, he persisted in his resolution till it had like to have been our case, for being put on board a vessel which had but little ballast in her, and sailing on our way to Boston, being about twenty leagues by water, there came a squall of wind and laid our vessel on one side, on which I ran and loosed the sails, so that she got righted before any of the hands came to my assistance, which the hands on board seeing were glad of my company, and I was thankful to our great preserver for this merciful deliverance. Being got to Boston we met said colonel Church, for he was both colonel and captain; I was allowed the liberty of the town, only to meet at a certain inn about the sixth hour every evening (which liberty I thought was a trial to me, whether I would get away from them or not, but I was their true prisoner, truth's testimony being more precious to me at that time than my outward liberty,) which order I punctually obeyed, so that I had time to see my friends in the town, who shewed great kindness and respect to me.

Thus I continued a prisoner at large in the town of Boston about a week, for the master of the vessel that brought me there, being sensible of the danger he was in at that time, could not be prevailed with to take me to the castle, nor be concerned further with me as a prisoner, but afterwards on the fifth of the third month, I was conveyed to the castle where I remained a prisoner four months and four days, being a prisoner from my first confinement seven months and two days. And notwithstanding some pains were taken to obtain my liberty, particularly by our friend Thomas Story[6] who was travelling in New England at that time, in truth's service, yet it had not the desired effect; during which time the people behaved civilly towards me, as believing I acted from a religious principle, but finding they could not make me submit to them they set me at liberty. On my mother's application to the governor, and making my case known to him, he ordered his clerk to write to the captain of the castle, an order for me to be released, which was done accordingly. During the time of my confinement in the castle, there came a kinsman of mine to see me, he was of some considerable note. . . .

[Early in 1705] I shipped myself on board the brigantine[7] Matthew Eastow commander, bound for London. It proved a very stormy voyage, so that divers times we expected to be cast away, but the merciful hand was our preserver. I had many times with true thankfulness of heart to bless and magnify his great and holy name, in a sweet sense of his mercy and goodness to me.

In about eight weeks sailing, we made Kingsale harbour in the west of Ireland, where we tarried about eight days, and then weighed anchor and sailed for London. We came to the landsend of England on the 13th. of the 4th. month 1705, and next day near Plymouth, a man of war met us, and took me and two more of our hands; but the captain sent us on board our own vessel again that night. There lay seventeen sail of men of war in Plymouth harbour at that time, one of which sent their boat with some hands, and took my companion Thomas Anthony, who came with me from New England and myself on board their ship, leaving but three hands in the vessel with our master, although he was very weak, and not capable of any business. The ship we were taken on board of lay about five leagues off, and the next day went out a cruising: the lieutenant was very envious, and swore divers times that he would run us through with his sword; the captain seemed more moderate, although not inclined to set us at liberty. The day after we sailed, the ship we were in took a French prize with fifty English prisoners on board: when they were going to engage, they placed us to a gun, and commanded us to fight, but we told them we could not, for Christ and his apostles spake to the contrary; but they not regarding what we said, hauled us about the deck to make us work, but we signified we could not on any such account: now expecting our trials likely to increase, we thought it necessary to be constantly upon our watch both inwardly and outwardly, with strong cries to the Lord that he would be near to support us under our exercises; also we thought it not safe that both of us should lie down together.

So it happened on the 18th. of the month that Thomas Anthony being gone to lay down, I being uneasy in my mind had a concern to go upon deck, for what reason I knew not at that time, but being faithful I went upon deck, and therein I found peace; upon which I went between decks again, but growing uneasy in my mind, a concern arose to go upon deck the second time, and when there, seemed quite easy; then fearing lest I was out of my place I went down a third time, and growing very uneasy, it was said in the secret of my heart, thou knowest where to get relief; upon which I went the third time upon deck, and being there some time, the lieutenant who was walking on the quarter deck, said to the boatswain who was on the main deck, have you made the Quaker work yet? he answered no. The lieutenant asked why? was answered, it is for want of your order; on which the lieutenant threw him his cane, saying, there is my order, then the boatswain took the cane and laid on my head with such violence, that he beat my hat to pieces, on which the lieutenant said, take him to the geers, and bring the cat and nine tails, at which time I was freely given up to suffer what they might be permitted to inflict on me; and being at the geers on my knees, it arose in my mind to pray for my persecutors, for they knew not what they did; and if it pleased the Lord, to take me to himself from amongst them, for their wicked conversation was a burden to my life; and indeed my life was not dear to me at that time, to lay down for truth's testimony if required; but through the Lord's mercy they were not suffered to strike me any more. Soon after the captain sent for me and Thomas Anthony into the cabin, where being come he talked much with us, and on seeing my hat he asked how it came torn so, was answered it was done at the boatswain's pleasure. There was the captain of another man of war with him, who swore he would kill us, as soon as he would kill a Frenchman, with many such expressions. The boatswain's mate seeing how I was used, took me by the shoulder, and asked why I did not stay below decks as he would have me, adding you have been beat enough to kill an ox; which expressions of his shewed some respect he had to me, though otherwise bad enough in his conversation; but the sweet peace and satisfaction of mind, that I enjoyed in this time of my suffering, is scarce to be expressed in words, and far exceeded their show of kindness.

Now there being upwards of twenty sail of the English together at that time, in a few days they sailed to Brest, a place in France, to fight the French fleet, but they not coming out, and our fleet meeting with a storm that several ships lost their top masts, we sailed for England, and went into Torbay, and lay there three days, in which time I desired the captain to set us at liberty; but he said if we would work, we should have our liberty, purposely as we thought to ensnare us; but through the Lord's mercy and goodness to us, we were preserved from their snares, and found his pure peace and presence, to be with us in a large manner, that in the greatest of our sufferings and trials, he was near, and in his comfortable presence we did rejoice, that we were counted worthy to suffer for truth's testimony. The 3d. of the 5th. month we sailed for Plymouth, but came not to an anchor: the captain went on shore, and we sent a letter to a friend of ours at Plymouth, but received no answer.

The next day we sailed for Brest again, being more than forty sail in company, and the ship we were in, and another, went to the mouth of the harbour, and took a ship going in loaded with salt, and lay off from Ushant waiting for the French fleet, until our hopes of getting clear from them was almost spent. At another time they sent for me to make points for reefing the sails, which I refusing to do, some mocked and scoffed, while others filled with envy and malice, could scarce keep their hands from me: and thus we passed through many deep exercises, looking every day when we should receive stripes, and sometimes could see nothing but death before us, but the Lord wrought deliverance for us in his own way and time, beyond our expectation, and hath been near for our preservation, blessed be his great name therefor.

The 14th. of this month we sailed to Brest to spy what shipping there was in the harbour, and we went so near in, that the French fired many guns at us from the castle. I and my companion Thomas Anthony sat then between decks, not knowing how soon it might be our lots to be shot; my companion not being well at that time nor for several days before, the doctor sent his mate in kindness to enquire if he wanted any thing he had that he should have it, but he refused taking any thing from him, altho' he acknowledged his kindness. The 20th. of this month we sailed for Brest again, and being becalmed, we thought we must come to an anchor, which if we had it might have gone hard with us; but after some time there sprang up a breeze of wind, and we got away from the French, and a few days after we sailed for England again, and got into Plymouth harbour.

So on the 27th. of this month as soon as we came to an anchor, the captain sent for us into the cabin, and being before him, he said he would let us go on shore, to see our friends, and refresh ourselves, which he did: so being on shore, and it being meeting day we went to the meeting, although in a poor dirty condition by reason of our lying on board so long, and no clothes to shift us, having been on board about six weeks. Friends were glad to see us on shore, and kindly received us into their houses. The first Friend's house we went to was Henry Cane or Crane who was very kind to us, and provided things necessary for us. And Daniel Zachary the owner of the vessel we were pressed out of, had written to a Friend of Plymouth to take care of us when we came on shore, also a Friend of London that was appointed by their mornings' meeting sent a letter to a friend of his at Plymouth, to help us to what necessaries we stood in need of, and he would pay him again, which he did; also said friend spoke to the captain twice about setting us at liberty. Since we were not men for his purpose, the captain said he gave us leave to go on shore, but said nothing of our coming on board again, saying he could not answer discharging us, because he was under the command of the flag.

So having well refreshed ourselves, and were provided with necessaries we travelled through several towns, as Exeter, Bristol, Bath, and divers others, till we came to London, when there we lodged at our friend Thomas Lurting,[8] and having tarried near four weeks in London, also attended meetings as they came in course pretty constantly. We got a passage to Philadelphia in a vessel commanded by one Joshua Guy, there were divers Friends going in her, as John Salkeld and wife, with other passengers. About the 9th. of the 7th. month 1705, we left London, and the vessel fell down to Deal, where my companion Thomas Anthony being taken sick of the small pox, he was put on shore at Deal.

⚜ 5 ⚜

Conscientious Objectors in the French and Indian War

A. From Joshua Evans's *Journal*, 1756

Although I was thus led by precept and example, I was much reproached by some on account of my testimony against war, because I could not pay my money in a way which I believed was to defray, in a measure at least, the expenses of shedding human blood. This exercise came on me in the year 1756; at the time a bloody war subsisted between France and England.

A number of our young men being drafted as soldiers to go on an expedition, some of the inhabitants concluded to open a subscription for money to hire volunteers in their stead. This seemed plausible even to some under our profession, and a number were taken therewith: but when it was proposed or demanded of me, I felt a scruple, and told them, if on considering the matter, I could be free to pay money for such a purpose, I could hand it forward. On this occasion I had none to confer with; but it was opened clearly to me, that to hire men to do what I could not, for conscience's sake, do myself, would be very inconsistent. This led me, in deep humility, to seek for wisdom to guide me rightly; and I found it best for me to refuse paying demands on my estate, which went to pay the expenses of war: and although my part might appear but as a drop in the ocean, yet the ocean, I considered, was made up of many drops.

Thus I had to pass through reproach, because I had enlisted under his

From *Friends' Miscellany*, vol. 10, *Journal of Joshua Evans* (Philadelphia, 1839), 19–21.

banner who declared his kingdom was not of this world, or else his servants would fight. When my goods were taken to answer demands of a military nature, (which I was not free to pay voluntarily) and sold perhaps much under their value, some would pity me, supposing it likely I should be ruined. Others would term it stubbornness in me, or contrary to the doctrine of Christ, concerning rendering to Caesar his due. But as I endeavoured to keep my mind in a state of humble quietude, I was favoured to see through such groundless arguments; there being nothing on the subject of war, or favourable to it, to be found in that text. Although I have been willing to pay my money for the use of civil government, when legally called for; yet have I felt restrained by a conscientious motive, from paying towards the expense of killing men, women and children, or laying towns and countries waste. Through all my trials in these cases, my wife encouraged me to be faithful, saying, "If we suffer in a right spirit, we shall obtain that peace which the world can neither give, nor take away."

... After these trials, some of my greatest opposers in time came to own my testimony, and great was my peace in having attended to my tender scruples; yet I had still many baptizing seasons to pass through.

I cannot see how to reconcile war, in any shape or colour, with the mild spirit of christianity; nor that devouring disposition, with the peaceable, lamblike nature of our blessed Saviour. It seems to me we might as well suppose, theft and murder do not contradict his royal law, which enjoins the doing unto others as we would have them do unto us.

Whilst these storms on account of my peaceable principles were permitted to continue, I endeavoured to keep close to the heavenly Light within. But afterwards, I was told, it was concluded, that as I gave myself up very much to the service of truth, it was not proper I should be troubled on account of military demands; and I understood my name was erased, or taken from their list.

B. From John Woolman's *Journal*, 1757

Ninth of eighth month, 1757.—Orders came at night to the military officers in our county (Burlington), directing them to draft the militia, and prepare a number of men to go off as soldiers, to the relief of the English at Fort William Henry, in New York government; a few days after which, there was a general review of the militia at Mount Holly, and a number of men were chosen and sent off under some officers. Shortly after, there came orders to draft three times as many, who were to hold themselves in readiness to march when fresh orders came. On the 17th there was a meeting of the mil-

From *The Journal of John Woolman*, Whittier edition (Boston and New York, 1871), 129–31.

itary officers at Mount Holly, who agreed on draft; orders were sent to the men so chosen to meet their respective captains at set times and places, those in our township to meet at Mount Holly, amongst whom were a considerable number of our Society. My mind being affected herewith, I had fresh opportunity to see and consider the advantage of living in the real substance of religion, where practice doth harmonize with principle. Amongst the officers are men of understanding, who have some regard to sincerity where they see it; and when such in the execution of their office have men to deal with whom they believe to be upright-hearted, it is a painful task to put them to trouble on account of scruples of conscience, and they will be likely to avoid it as much as easily may be. But where men profess to be so meek and heavenly-minded, and to have their trust so firmly settled in God that they cannot join in wars, and yet by their spirit and conduct in common life manifest a contrary disposition, their difficulties are great at such a time.

When officers who are anxiously endeavoring to get troops to answer the demands of their superiors see men who are insincere pretend scruple of conscience in hopes of being excused from a dangerous employment, it is likely they will be roughly handled. In this time of commotion some of our young men left these parts and tarried abroad till it was over; some came, and proposed to go as soldiers; others appeared to have a real tender scruple in their minds against joining in wars, and were much humbled under the apprehension of a trial so near. I had conversation with several of them to my satisfaction. When the captain came to town, some of the last-mentioned went and told him in substance as follows: That they could not bear arms for conscience' sake; nor could they hire any to go in their places, being resigned as to the event. At length the captain acquainted them all that they might return home for the present, but he required them to provide themselves as soldiers, and be in readiness to march when called upon. This was such a time as I had not seen before; and yet I may say, with thankfulness to the Lord, that I believed the trial was intended for our good; and I was favored with resignation to him. The French army having taken the fort they were besieging, destroyed it and went away; the company of men who were first drafted, after some days' march, had orders to return home, and those on the second draft were no more called upon on that occasion.

C. Colonel George Washington and the Quaker Conscientious Objectors, 1760

[Stephen B. Weeks in his account of Southern Quaker history refers briefly to the sufferings of several young Virginia Friends conscripted into the mili-

From Peter Brock, *Studies in Peace History* (York, England, 1991), 38–42.

tia in the spring of 1756 to serve under Colonel George Washington at Winchester, then situated on the Western frontier. "This," writes Weeks, "was probably the severest trial through which Virginia Friends were called to go" on account of their peace testimony. Weeks based his account mainly on the manuscript records of Virginia Yearly Meeting. Further information on the subject can be found in the published papers of Governor Dinwiddie and of Washington himself. The story as it appeared to the young men themselves is told in the manuscript "Narrative" printed below.

The outbreak of the French and Indian War in 1755, the subsequent defeat of General Braddock by the French, and the exposure of the province's Western frontier to the attacks of hostile Indians had caused the Virginia Assembly to pass more stringent militia regulations than had existed hitherto. Section X of its act of May 1756 laid down that, if the quota for the state militia could not be filled by voluntary enlistment, a ballot should be held among single able-bodied males to choose every twentieth man for active service within the boundaries of the province. Exemption could be obtained on payment of the sum of ten pounds or by providing a substitute, both of which alternatives were against Friends' peace principles and practice. Though this was not specifically stated in the act, the intention of the Assembly was to send the new recruits to reinforce twenty-four-year-old George Washington, who in the previous year had been promoted to the rank of colonel and put in command of the provincial militia with headquarters at Winchester.

The approach of hostilities and the passing of new and more exacting militia legislation by the Assembly had aroused apprehension among Virginia Friends that a new period of persecution was at hand. At their Yearly Meeting, held early in June 1756, a committee was appointed to watch the situation and to take what steps might be necessary in dealing with the authorities. Already, barely a week before Yearly Meeting had assembled, seven young members belonging to Cedar Creek Monthly Meeting had been placed under arrest for refusal to comply with the new militia regulations. (Their fate forms the story related below.) Equally serious was the division that had arisen among the membership as to whether Friends, in view of the severe penalties now likely to result from adopting an absolutist position, might not take advantage of the alternatives offered by the act without unduly compromising their peace stand. A letter, therefore, was dispatched to the Meeting for Sufferings of London Yearly Meeting asking for its opinion on the issues involved, and a decision taken, too, to collect money for the Quaker conscripts to assist them "in case of need." Robert Pleasants, Thomas Pretlo (also spelled Pritlo or Pretlow), David Terril and any other Friends who cared to join the group were requested to "go and visit them [i.e., the arrested conscripts] and carry the money collected, and let them know this meeting sympathises with them and ardently implores the divine assistance to be their support, and bearer up above all fears and frowns of men, and to give them strength of body and mind to go through what may be their lot 'tho it be death itself, and if they stand in need, that this meeting will send them money from time to time upon their advising of Friends therewith, in order that if they do not the service is required of them, not to be chargeable if they can be supplied for money, and that they write unto us as oft as may be in order to let Friends know what steps to make for their relief."

*   *   *

Next month, the special committee appointed at Yearly Meeting dispatched a further epistle to the Meeting for Sufferings in London, emphasizing the growing dissension among members as to the proper course to adopt in face of the demands of the military. Whereas the earlier letter had reassured London that, despite differences of opinion, "Friends are pretty generally faithful in their Testimony against bearing arms," now the spirit of compromise had gained ground. "As Friends pretty generally concurred in paying taxes on our estates intended for the support of war," this second epistle explained, "some have been induced to think a compliance with the . . . Act differs not materially from that, therefore have cleared themselves by drawing [the lot], and others by paying the fine, but others have seen the thing in a very different light and could by no means join with it." The fact that the call-up only affected bachelors and that, therefore, most of the maturer married men were not liable had had an unfortunate result. It meant, the epistle continued, that an opportunity to prove their strict adherence to the peace testimony by a personal witness was not open to "the elders, who may reasonably be expected to have come to a greater degree of experience in the work of true religion, and consequently be more likely to undergo the hardships of cruel sufferings, which in all probability may be the lot of those who are taken in consequence of not complying with the said Act, and be the better qualified to strengthen and encourage the youth being seven in number who are already carried to the frontiers." "All endeavours of Friends with those in authority towards their discharge," the report went on, "have hitherto proved ineffectual and we apprehend their case will be much the harder on account of the part which others have acted, 'tho we have reason to hope they will stand faithful."

The adventures of these seven, "a remnant amongst us who have their dependance on the Lord alone for protection" (so they were described in the second epistle to London), from the time of their arrest towards the end of May to their arrival on 12 June at Colonel Washington's headquarters at Winchester, can be read in the "Narrative" printed here. All attempts to force them to perform military or other official duties were to prove ineffectual. And so we find the perplexed young commander writing back to Williamsburg for the Governor's advice in the matter. On 25 June Colonel Washington reports to Dinwiddie: "There remain now in confinement six Quakers who will neither bear arms, work, receive provisions or pay, or do any thing that tends, in any respect, to self-defence. I should be glad of your Honour's directions how to proceed with them." An angry reply came back promptly from Governor Dinwiddie: "If the six Quakers will not fight you must compel them to work on the forts, to carry timber, &c., if this will not do confine them with a short allowance of bread and water till you bring them to reason."

The threat, however, was seemingly never carried out, partly because of the intervention of Edward Stabler with Washington on behalf of the Quaker prisoners and probably, too, because of the genuine understanding the colonel appears to have gained fairly soon of the real motives of the men's stubbornness. On 4 August he told Dinwiddie: "I could by no means bring the Quakers to any terms. They chose rather to be whipped to death than bear arms, or lend us any assistance whatever upon the fort, or any thing of self-defence. Some of their friends have been security for their appearance, when they are called for; and I have released them from the guard-house until I receive further orders from your Honour, which they have agreed to apply for." Meanwhile, a delegation of leading Quakers had gone to see Governor Dinwiddie and had persuaded him to relax his severity towards the objectors. On 19 August, therefore, we find the Governor writing to Washington "A great body of Quakers waited on me in regard to their friends with you, praying they may not be whipped; use them with lenity, but as they are at their own expence I would have them remain as long as the other drafts."]

A Narrative of the Conduct and Sufferings of Some Friends in Virginia, 1760

On or about the 24th of the 5th mo. a captain was sent with the Governor's warrant attended by a company of armed men,[9] as tho' they had been going to apprehend thieves or murderers, took us from our honest employments, our dear and tender parents, relations and friends and carried us before one called Major Wilstone of the said county of Hanover, who tendered the oath of allegience to us which we all refusing to take, a mittimus was forthwith made out and we were sent by the constable to prison, where we were kept closely confined for about eight days, having no better lodgings than the floor for our beds, and bricks for our pillows. Yet he who permitted us to suffer was graciously pleased to make it both easy and pleasant by giving us a sense of his goodness and mercy, which caused humble thanks to arise in our hearts with earnest desires that we might be preserved in faithfulness and true submission to his will in respect to the discouraging prospect of greater approaching trials.

The last day of our continuance in Hanover county gaol being court day, we were had thro' the crowd up to the justices' bench without any disturbance about our hats,[10] and again had the oath tendered to us, who being all young it was thought many of the people expected to have seen us act something to the dishonour of our christian profession. But the God for whose righteous cause we stood preserved us faithful to what we believed to be our duty. Then being taken into another room our hats were civilly taken off and the Lieutenant Colonel said, as you are Quakers, I suppose you'll not take the oath so you must take the affirmation and read after me. We answered no, lest we should read what we cannot stand by, but told him we were free and willing to comply with the substance of the laws, which were not repugnant to our consciences, but to bear arms or fight we could not. Then said he you must work at the forts which we also refused, so he read on. The next day being the 4th of 6th mo. we were conducted by the Major to Fredericksburg which being about fifty miles took us near two days' travel, and were delivered to an officer there, who asked our name, trade and country, and took an account of our complexions, stature, &c. and then was the Militia Act read, which makes desertion death. We were then told we had liberty to go anywhere in town so that we appeared there at the beating of the drum. Our Friends John and William Ellyson being there before us and put into the guard-house, we asked whether we were not to be put with them, at which they seemed startled and asked whether we were Quakers. We answered that we were so called, and said they, and won't you fight? We replied we never had, and hoped not to begin then. O! then what rage and revilings got up and seemed to be carried as far as they had words to express them.

So after some time had been thus spent, some men were ordered to take us to the guard-house where about twelve or fourteen men were set as a watch over us and so apprehensive were they of our going away that we were not allowed to go out on any occasion without two men with drawn swords in their hands to attend us.

On the 8th of the month we were ordered to march for Winchester under a guard of about one hundred men of whom one Woodward was captain. On the long and fatiguing march we suffered considerable hardships as well for want of provisions and suitable accommodations as the length of the journey which was about 90 miles. For as we could not do any service, we had not freedom to eat of the King's victuals and . . . depended to a great measure on buying on the road, where provisions proved so scarce and the demand from our company so great that we being under some restraint had not an equal chance, so were obliged sometimes to go with empty stomachs.

The first night we were thrust into a little nasty hut which before had been the residence of horses, hogs and fowls; but disagreeable as it was, in it we must go nor could we get provisions for our money. It was a usual custom for the officer to call over the names of the men under charge three times a day, and as we judged our answer to such a call was in some measure an acknowledgement of being soldiers, we could not find freedom to do it, which put the captain into so great a rage he ordered two men to come and strip one of us saying that he would have him flogged for an example to the rest. So he was stripped from the waist upwards, tied to a tree and switches prepared for the execution, when just at the same time one of the soldiers from seeing in what a manner we were to be used for not acting in violation to our tender scruples of conscience, or from some other cause, was taken with a shivering, so as that it seemed as if his legs were not able to support his body, which the captain observing asked him what was the matter. He said he did not know, was told to go to the house and lie down, and at the same time the captain ordered our Friend to be loosed, adding that he would forgive us that time. We let him know that if he called us on any other occasion we were ready and willing to answer, but not as soldiers which we would not submit to be.

After this matter was settled and we got on our march several of the company expressed their sorrow for us, saying they had never wept since they were children but, thro' pity for us, they could not then help it, nor did any of the common people reflect on us, but would tell us, to stand to it as we had begun and never comply.

The next night we reached one Hardings where we got some refreshment, which seemed very palatable, could we have got a sufficient quantity of it. But notwithstanding we paid our money before it was cooked there were so many to partake of it that we poor prisoners got but a short allowance. Indeed we could get but a little till we got to Winchester, which was on the 7th day of the week and 12th of the month, having been part of five days on the journey.

We were conducted to the guard-house which was indeed very nasty, as well as otherwise disagreeable by having the company of a parcel of dirty lousy wicked and profane creatures who were confined on account of desertion and other misdemeanours. The next day we were taken to the magazine to receive arms according to custom, which we refusing were again conducted to our prison where we were kept upwards of 5 weeks. Yet so much confidence did our guard place in us that after a while they seemed to have no apprehensions of our deserting, and sometimes would indulge us to take the air a little (tho' contrary to their orders and without the knowledge of the officers). And [they] were ready and willing to fetch provisions of what other necessaries we had occasion for.

* * *

Thus while we were detained from our dear friends and outward enjoyments we were tried many ways. Sometimes the officers would use arguments to persuade us to act, and when they could not prevail with us to bear arms, they endeavoured to get us to work on the fort. At other times they would endeavour to force us to compliance by threats saying that in case of refusal, we should have 500 lashes and be sent to Fort Cumberland; however they were not permitted to accomplish either. Yet while we were thus confined, one of us was taken very ill with a pleurisy and, as we had nothing to lodge on but the floor, he was removed to a Friend's house at some small distance from town by consent of the officer till he might recover. We were however comforted by sundry epistles, and sometimes the company of several Friends who visited us while under these afflictions, particularly Isaac Hollingsworth and wife. John Hough of Fairfax also came to see us, and about the same time our Friends Edward Stabler and Thomas Pritlo by whom we received a collection from Friends at their late Yearly Meeting at Curles; such is the love of the true begotten children one unto another that neither time nor distance can obliviate it. By the force and virtue of this they were moved to visit us, and by the same we were made to rejoice together in silence, and therein had a sense of divine favour removed to us. They were frequently with us for the space of about ten or twelve days, when Thomas Pritlo, their guide, and Robert Ellyson who came to see his son all returned. Edward Stabler, who had a desire to see Colonel Washington then at Fort Cumberland, could not be free to leave the place till he had used some endeavours with him on our account and accordingly when the colonel returned, which was in a few days, he was applied to by our said Friend and answered in a rough manner that he had orders from the Governor to whip them till they were made to work on the Fort, and said that he gave us that night to consider of it, and in case of refusal, he intended to put it in execution.

Next day our said Friends Isaac Hollingsworth and Edward Stabler came to see us, and sitting together in awful silence our souls were replenished in an acceptable manner by the power of that matchless arm, who can set bounds to the raging waves of the sea, and say thus far shalt thou go and no farther. So after we were comforted together in silence Isaac was concerned for us in prayer, that the Lord who had been with us in six troubles would not forsake us in the seventh and concluded in humble thanksgiving and praise for that comfortable opportunity. As an additional favour after this they went again to see Colonel Washington, who seemed to be in the disposition of mind as before respecting us. They told him if the Governor's orders were such, they believed it was for want of knowing our principles and desired him not to inflict the punishment he proposed till some had been with the Governor on our account. So after some pause he said if any of your Friends will be bound for their appearance when I may call for them, I am willing for the present to discharge them from confinement till the Governor's pleasure may be known. They let him know that he need be under no apprehensions of our going away. But if he doubted it, and would accept of them they would stand as sureties. Accordingly they prepared a writing and presented [it] to him for his approbation, which he observed mentioned no penalty, but on being desired to say what sum he required and seeing they were ready to comply, he replied that would do. So [he] gave orders to the sergeant to let us go; thus we were at liberty again in some measure but not to return home. So we got some business among our

Friends and by that means supported ourselves without further expense to any.

After Edward Stabler returned home several Friends went to the Governor on our account and prevailed so far with him as to have his promise to write to Colonel Washington to favour us as much as possible. But [he] said it was out of his power to dispense with the laws so far as to order our discharge till the expiration of the time for which we were taken, of which we were informed of by a letter from two of our Friends. And accordingly we were never called on afterwards till the expiration of the time fixed by law for the discharge of such who were taken away by virtue thereof. When we waited on the Colonel who in a friendly manner readily gave us discharges we took that opportunity of acknowledging the favours we had received at his hand; so taking our leave of him, he wished us a good journey home. Next morning we set out and in about 5 days we reached our several habitations, where we were gladly received by our dear relations and friends, after an absence of about————with the answer of peace in our own hearts, the————of the 12th month 1756.[11]

Among other trials they were obliged to stand close by a deserter who was shot, the officer hoping that might shake their constancy, but the criminal behaving with an uncommon degree of fortitude and resignation it had quite the contrary effect.[12]

When they made their acknowledgements to Colonel Washington as abovementioned he told them they were welcome, and all he asked of them in return was that if ever he should fall as much into their power as they had been in his—they would treat him with equal kindness.[13]

D. Virginia Mennonites
and the Militia, 1755–1761

At a court martial held in the County of Frederick on Tuesday the 2nd day of September 1755.[14]

The Rt. Honble. Thomas Lord Fairfax County Lieutenant. . . .

Ordered that David Coffman [Kauffman] of the foot company commanded by Capt. William Bethel be fined ten shillings or one hundred lbs. of Tob[acc]o for absenting himself from one private muster within twelve months last past.

Ordered that Samuel Beam [Bohm] of the foot company commanded by Capt. William Bethel be fined ten shillings or one hundred lbs. of Tob[acc]o

From Richard K. MacMaster et al., eds., *Conscience in Crisis: Mennonites and Other Peace Churches in America 1739–1789—Interpretations and Documents* (Scottdale, Penn., 1979), 156, 157.

for absenting himself from one private muster within twelve months last past.

Ordered that Henry Histand of the foot company commanded by Capt. William Bethel be fined ten shillings or one hundred lbs. of Tob[acc]o for absenting himself from one private muster within twelve months last past.

At a court martial held for Frederick County on Friday the 9th Day of October 1761.

Ordered that Jacob Stover of Captain John Funk's Company is fined forty shillings for absenting himself from three private and one general muster within twelve months last past.

Ordered that John Funkhouser, Jr. of Captain John Funk's company is fined ten shillings for absenting himself from the last general muster.

Ordered that Christian Craebell of Captain John Funk's company is fined twenty shillings for absenting himself from one private and one general muster within twelve months last past. . . .

Ordered that Christian Hockman of Captain John Funk's company is fined forty shillings for absenting himself from three private and one general muster within twelve months last past.

NOTES

Text

1. It is difficult, for instance, to know what to make of the case of the Virginian Richard Bickley, who in 1627 was tried for "denying to take up arms and discharge his public duty" as a militia draftee. For this offense the court ordered that, in addition to paying a fine of one hundred pounds of tobacco, "he shall be laid neck and heels 12 hours." Bickley's "offence" may have been nonconscientiously motivated. On the other hand, it is possible that he had acquired pacifist views through the influence of English Baptists, some of whom at this time adhered to Mennonite nonresistance. See "Decisions of Virginia General Court, 1626–1628," *Virginia Magazine of History and Biography* 4, no. 2 (October 1897): 159.
2. R. R. Russell, "Development of Conscientious Objector Recognition in the United States," *George Washington Law Review* 20, no. 4 (March 1952):412.
3. The declaration has been reprinted in *The Journal of George Fox*, ed. John L. Nickalls (Cambridge, England), 398–404.
4. "Because of their personal experience and convictions, [early] Friends did not deny the reality of evil and conflict. Nor did they equate conflict with evil. They were well aware of the suffering which a non-violent witness could bring in an imperfect world. This is in contrast to those who identify peace with the absence of conflict and value that above all things." Wolf Mendl (1974), in *Quaker Faith and Practice: The Book of Christian Discipline of the Yearly Meeting of the Religious Society of Friends (Quakers) in Britain* (London, 1994), sec. 24, no. 22.
5. Letter dated October 15, 1711, *The Official Letters of Alexander Spotswood*, ed. R. A. Brock (Richmond, Va.), 1 (1882): 120, 121. As we see in Document 7, Quak-

ers in England sometimes took a less radical line on such issues than Quakers across the Atlantic did.

Documents

1. Cecil Calvert, second Lord Baltimore. At this time the Catholic Calverts were proprietors of Maryland; they sought to provide a refuge there for their coreligionists, with freedom of religion for other dissenters, too.

2. In 1673 the administration of Rhode Island was largely in the hands of the Quakers, who carried on government even though the colony was then in a state of war. John and Peter Easton, mentioned here, were active members of the Society of Friends. Another prominent Quaker, Nicholas Easton, was governor of the colony. True, Quakers collectively bore a testimony against bearing arms. But some of them, like the Eastons, for instance, certainly did not object—in their official capacity—to participating in military defense, at any rate providing that it did not mean they would themselves have to fight. This very personal variety of early Quaker pacifism is discussed perceptively in *Walking in the Way of Peace: Quaker Pacifism in the Seventeenth Century* by Meredith Baldwin Weddle (New York: Oxford University Press, 2001).

3. "The documents explain themselves and are quaint enough to copy," writes Henry Cadbury in his brief introduction. I have retained the two items in their original form as transcribed by Cadbury from a private manuscript collection in Harvard University Library. Indeed, to modernize the spelling and punctuation in this case would surely deprive the text of a quality I would be sorry to see lost.

4. "The name sounds odd," writes Henry Cadbury, but "the surname is well attested in that Cape Cod area (in a dozen different spellings), and Hatsell (Hatsul) also occurs as a Christian name." Okelley was a member of Sandwich (Massachusetts) Monthly Meeting, one of the oldest Quaker meetings in America.

5. Cadbury writes: "The Monthly Meeting minutes indicate that money was raised for 'Hattel Kelly, a prisoner at Barnstable for not bearing arms' in September and October, 1748." And he continues: "Cases [of Quakers in prison for refusal of military service] two centuries ago existed uncollected and unlisted. A mere accident brings now one or another to our attention. A few years before—in 1742—a minute of this same Sandwich Monthly Meeting complains of 'a cowardly spirit about training' on the part of some of its members [,i.e.,] they acquiesced in military requisitions. But [as we see] not all Friends were delinquent."

6. Thomas Story (1662–1742) was a prominent member of the English Society of Friends active on both sides of the Atlantic. His *Journal* became standard reading among Quakers.

7. The whole of Smith's *Narrative* has been reprinted in my *Records of Conscience: Three Autobiographical Narratives by Conscientious Objectors, 1665–1865* (York, England, 1993), 31–46. John Smith (1681–1766) was the child of Presbyterian parents; he had converted as a youth to Quakerism, along with his parents.

8. Lurting, an ex-sailor, had suffered repeated impressment during the 1660s. See his often reprinted autobiography, *The Fighting Sailor turn'd Peaceable Christian* (London, 1710).

9. In a letter dated October 20, 1756, a leading Virginia Quaker (Edward Stabler) wrote: "In the spring [of 1756] there was an act made for drafting the militia by lot, in which Friends were not exempted." Those on whom "the lot fell . . . . were obliged to go as soldiers or pay £10 to hire another man in their stead . . . . I am

sorry to say the generality of Friends complied with it, except seven young men who would not comply . . . nor hire another in their stead." The seven were John and William Ellyson from New Kent County, and Cornelius and John Harris, and Archalaus, William, and Zechariah Stanley from Hanover County.

10. From the early days of Quakerism Friends had refused to take their hats off in court, believing that such "hat honour" was due only to God.

11. Gaps in the original manuscript.

12. Esmond Wright, *Washington and the American Revolution* (New York, 1957), 32: "By the summer of 1756 and with Dinwiddie's tacit support, Washington was becoming stern. He insisted that a deserter and a sergeant who had shown cowardice, and who had been condemned by court-martial, be put to death before the eyes of the newly drafted men." Colonel Washington had encountered disciplinary troubles with his troops, many of whom were recruited from criminal elements.

13. Note added in a different hand from the main narrative—probably not long after the composition of the latter.

14. The editors of *Conscience in Crisis* write (p. 156): "Virginia, like most of the colonies . . . had a militia law obliging men of military age to turn out on muster days . . . or pay a fine for their failure to do so. Few records of military fines have survived. The Clerk of the Frederick County Court preserved a complete record for this Shenandoah Valley county [where Mennonites were already plentifully settled], when he copied deeds into a book that had been used between 1755 and 1761 for the sessions of the court-martial that levied fines on reluctant militiamen." The nonconscientious resisters figure here alongside those whose objections to militia service were based on their religion, for, "even in a frontier county, militia duty was never popular." Kauffman, Bohm, Histand, Funkhauser, and Craebell can be identified from other sources as Mennonites, while I presume from their surnames that Stover [Stauffer] and Hockman were Mennonites, too.

BACKGROUND READING

Brock, Peter. *Pacifism in the United States: From the Colonial Era to the First World War*, 3–66. Princeton, N.J., 1968.

———. *The Quaker Peace Testimony 1660 to 1914*, 47–61, 87–141. York, England, 1990.

Bronner, Edwin B. "The Quakers and Non-Violence in Pennsylvania." *Pennsylvania History*, 35, no. 1 (January 1968): 1–22.

MacMaster, Richard K., et al. *Conscience in Crisis: Mennonites and Other Peace Churches in America, 1739–1789—Interpretation and Documents*, 25–212. Scottdale, Penn., 1979.

II

ENGLISH WEST INDIES

The islands of the West Indies under English rule provided in the second half of the seventeenth and during the early eighteenth century a home for a community of Quakers. Some were tobacco planters; others were urban craftsmen or shopkeepers or domestic servants. The Quaker message had been brought to the islands during the second half of the 1650s by missionaries from the homeland, who succeeded in converting a few of the local settlers. The Quaker meetings now established indeed remained small, for the existence of Quakerism in this area was precarious. Threatened by England's imperialist rivals, France and Spain, and menaced, too, by attack from pirates, the white islanders were faced internally by the dangers of black slave revolt.[1] By the middle of the eighteenth century Quakers had disappeared from the Caribbean after a long struggle to keep Friends' peace testimony alive in this harsh environment. They would not return for over a century.

Military service, the requirement to bear arms, formed only one of several causes leading to a confrontation with the island authorities. Quakers clashed with the latter also over such issues as the payment of tithes to the established church ("church dues") and taking oaths for various official purposes. But the military question certainly remained, throughout, the most sensitive among such issues. The authorities genuinely feared the impact of Quaker pacifism, if it were to spread, on the islands' defensive position. This accounts for the severity (not always so extreme as we might have expected) with which COs were treated, in contrast to the frequent mildness shown Quaker COs in Britain or the mainland colonies.

The late Henry Cadbury discovered in the archives of Jamaica documents relating to conscientious objection. Other finds may lie as yet uncovered in the archives of other Caribbean islands. But for the military question we have to rely mainly on the materials published in the middle of the eighteenth century by the Quaker annalist Joseph Besse (Document 6). In reference to the Quakers of Barbados, which constituted the center of Caribbean Quakerism, Besse points as a chief cause of their "sufferings" to "their refusal to bear arms or fight, the laws of the country requiring the personal service of the inhabitants, their servants, and horses, and inflicting severe penalties in case of default."[2]

One of the most intriguing episodes in the history of Quaker pacifism occurred late on in the course of Caribbean Quakerism. Early in the eighteenth century the small Quaker community on the island of Antigua was rent by a controversy on the military question. Older Friends wanted to take up an offer made by the local authorities that would have allowed Quaker draftees to perform certain auxiliary services in lieu of bearing arms. Younger Friends, however, wished to reject the proposal, regarding it —with some justification—as contrary to Quaker principles. To accept such service, they argued, would be in essence "all one" with compliance in the demand to bear arms. In 1708 Antigua Friends appealed to London Yearly Meeting, regarded throughout the transatlantic Quaker fellowship as the guardian of Quaker doctrine and practice. Communication across the Atlantic was slow, and London's reply, which came out decisively in favor of such an accommodation with the island authorities as the older Quakers desired, did not reach Antigua until 1709. Margaret Hirst has described this reply as "a temporising document . . . instinct with that spirit of timidity and caution, combined with a genuine loyalty to the tolerant English government, which marked Quaker leadership in the first half of the eighteenth century" (Document 7).

Evidence as to what ensued after Antigua Friends received the letter from London has not survived. In any event, the first phase of Caribbean Quakerism was nearing its end.

❦ 6 ❦

Militia "Sufferings" among Quakers

A. Barbados, 1678–1686

Barbados, 1678 "Sufferings and Death of Richard Andrews"

Richard Andrews, a sober virtuous youth, servant to Joseph Borden, was several times taken out of his master's shop by soldiers, and had to their place of exercising, where they endeavoured to make him bear arms, but he stedfastly refused, saying, *He durst not break Christ's command.* On the 4th of the Third Month 1678, the soldiers carried him to Needham's Fort, and the next day, being the first-day of the Week, their captain, John Burrows, ordered him to be tied neck and heels, in which manner he lay about a hour; after which the captain struck him a great blow with his cane, and threatned him sorely. He was kept at the Fort a week, his lodging being mostly on the cold stones. When he came home his countenance was much altered, his appetite much impaired, and his body very poor and thin. Nevertheless on the 25th of the same month, the aforesaid officers fetcht him out again, and carried him to their place of exercising, where the said captain ordered him to be tied neck and heels again, which was done, and he was tied so strait, that he could hardly speak. Some of the soldiers were troubled at his cruel usage, while others scoffed at and derided him. Within a few days after this usage, he was taken with the bloody-flux, whereof he died in a little time. He expressed during his sickness great satisfaction of mind for having stood faithful to his testimony against fighting, and with much joy and assurance of a future well-being, departed his life in the nineteenth year of his age, leaving behind him this character, *viz.*

> Many that well knew his life and conversation are well satisfied that he is at rest with the lord, for though he was but young in years, he was very diligent in those weighty matters that concerned salvation and the wellbeing of his soul with God for ever. He had been four years and upwards in this island before he fell sick of this sickness which was his death, and never had one days sickness before in this island. . . . He was very understanding and diligent in his outward business to discharge a good conscience towards all with whom he was concerned,

From Joseph Besse, *A Collection of the Sufferings of the People called Quakers, for the Testimony of a Good Conscience* (London, 1753), 2:322, 314–18, 333–35, 388–91.

and finished his testimony joyfully, and his change is blessed, and his memorial shall live among the righteous.

A Summary Relation of the SUFFERINGS . . . comprehending the space of the first four years after Governor Atkins's arrival, and concluding at the 13th of the sixth month 1678,[1] *viz.*

Taken from

William Jones, for not appearing in arms, 1000 lb. of sugar. To raise this they took away the man's bedding, he being a very poor man, and having a wife and five small children, who subsisted only by his labour.

Francis Gamble, for not sending to the militia, 3684 3/4 lb. and for not paying priest's wages, 2007 lb. In all 5691 3/4 lb.

Thomas Richards, for not sending to the militia, 1300 lb.

John Swinstead Sen., for not sending to the militia, 2650 lb.

William Molineux surgeon, for not appearing in the militia, from which his profession should have exempted him, 790 lb. and for not paying the priest's demands, 1200 lb. In all 1990 lb.

William Hutchins, for not appearing to serve in the troop, 230 lb. and for not paying church-dues, so called, 131 lb. In all 361 lb.

Benoni Pearcy, for not sending into the troop, though his horse was judged unfit for service, and he had not land chargeable with sending any, 1220 lb.

James Thorpe, who had formerly been a captain and a justice of the peace, for not appearing to serve in the troop, 900 lb. and for not paying church-dues, so called, 1800 lb. In all 2700 lb. . . .

Lewis Morris, who had formerly been a colonel and one of the council, for not sending horse and men to the militia, 9220 lb. and for not paying church and priest's demands, 973 lb. In all 10193 lb. . . .

Elizabeth and John Gay, for not appearing or sending horse and arms to serve in the troop, 4107 lb. and for not paying church-dues, so called, 715 lb. In all 4822 lb.

Matthew Matthews, for not appearing in the militia and at the guard, 390 lb. and for church and priest's claims, 200 lb. In all 590 lb.

Anthony Pinke, for not appearing in the militia upon summons, 400 lb. and for not paying church-dues, so called, 240 lb. In all 640 lb.

James Mings, for not appearing in Colonel Lambert's troop, 300 lb.

Basil Newton, for not appearing to serve in the company and upon guard, 655 lb. and for not paying church-dues, so called, 140 lb. In all 795 lb. . . .

Philip Collins, formerly a lieutenant and a coroner, for not appearing in the troop, and for not sending men in arms, 3020 lb.

John Savory, for not appearing in the troop, and for not sending men to serve in arms, 8138 lb.

Joseph Borden, for not bearing arms, though upon summons to ride on the patrol he went with his horses several times, and rode with the rest, 6880 lb. . . .

Joseph Walker, for not appearing to attend the governor in arms, 500 lb. and for opening his shop on days called holy-days, 920 lb. In all 1420 lb. . . .

William Cope, for not appearing in arms to attend the governor to his worship on Sundays, so called, 524 lb. and for refusing to take an oath to execute the office of a constable, 1300 lb. In all 1824 lb.

Edward Scott, a poor boat-man, for not appearing in arms, 268 lb. At another time they took away his boat, and made use of it to carry stones for the fort, and kept it so long before they returned it him, that the use of it, and the damage done thereto, was to his detriment to the value of 600 lb. In all 868 lb. . . .

Roger Ellis, for not appearing at the patrolling in arms, at several times, 1900 lb. and for opening his shop on the days superstitiously esteemed holy-days, 2000 lb. In all 3900 lb.

Besides which he suffered, for the last mentioned cause, six months imprisonment. . . .

Ralph Weekes, surgeon, for many defaults in not appearing with horse and man in the troop, 6294 lb.

Mary and Emanuel Curtis, for defaults of not providing man and horse, with arms, to ride in the troops and to lie in the forts, 9623 lb. and for church-dues, so called, 400 lb. In all 10023 lb.

John Braithwaite, for defaults of appearing in the troop, 6817 ½ lb. for not sending men to the forts, 1500 lb. and for not paying church-dues, so called, 1600 lb. In all 9917 1/2 lb. . . .

Richard Sutton, formerly a captain, for . . . defaults of sending to the troop, 1566 lb.

Thomas Rouse, formerly a lieutenant-colonel, for default of an horse and man in the troop, 600 lb. . . .

Elizabeth Piersehouse, widow,[2] for defaults of sending men in to the militia, 2360 lb. . . .

Dermot Croning, a very poor labouring man, for defaults of not appearing in the militia, 1080 lb.

Jasper Codd, a very poor man, for not appearing to serve in the militia, 300 lb. . . .

Winifred Whitehead, for not sending a man to exercise, and another to work at the fortifications, 750 lb.

John Chace, for defaults of sending men in to the militia, 1250 lb. The said John Chase was also committed to prison, and detained there about a month, for refusing to take the oath of a juryman.

Samuel Carpenter, for defaults of appearing, or sending men in arms, 1110 lb. . . .

Together with the particular account of their sufferings, they presented a memorial to the governor, shewing how the penalties inflicted on them had been increased from time to time, *viz.* that

From 1670 to 1671, the penalty was 50 lb. for default of each foot-man, and 100 lb. for each horse and man.

From 1671 to 1675, for each horse and man 270 lb. and sometimes 290 lb.

From 1675 to 1677, for a foot-man 200 lb. and for an horse-man 400 lb. of sugar.

That those severe penalties were inflicted on many of them every month, there being so often a general exercising through the whole island. And that in the exercising week some of them had been charged with the penalty for absence of a foot-man for each day.

After Sir Richard Dutton, the next succeeding Governor was Edwin Stead, to whom also the people called Quakers made representations of their sufferings; shewing with what extreme severity the Militia Act was executed by some rapacious marshals and others, as appears by the following address to him, dated the 17th of the twelfth month, called February, 1686, *viz.*

Sundry particulars relating to the Militia Act, briefly touched, and presented to Edwin Stead, our King's Lieutenant-Governor of the Island Barbadoes, and Council, from the People called Quakers, inhabitants there.

"Humbly Sheweth,   ·
The extreme severity of the said act, with the marshal's illegal abuses in executing the same, to be very grievous and oppressive unto us the king's loyal and peaceable subjects called Quakers, ancient inhabitants in the said island, more than to any other inhabitants of the same, or in any other part of our king's dominions, no not in Jamaica (a place in imminent danger among the Spaniards, in a manner invironed by them, from whom it hath been taken), which we have often complained of to authority here, but find little or no redress to this time, to our great discouragement and hindrance, both planters and handicraftsmen; and that also considerable danger thereby accrues both to the king and country. And inasmuch as we understand something of our king's mercy and clemency extended to us in this case in this his foreign plantation, we likewise hope and request our said governor and council will be pleased, in their serious and Christian moderation and prudence, to help forward so good and gracious a work, which doubtless will be acceptable to God and the king, and future welfare of us his honest and peaceable subjects.

I. We intreat you would be pleased to consider the vast quantity of goods that has been taken from us, on the account of our consciences to God, amounting to above 1,400,000 lb. of sugar, as may appear by account thereof lately delivered to the present governor, to near the end of the Governor Dutton's time, besides what has been taken from us since, most of which has been on the account of the militia, notwithstanding the payment of the King's customs and public taxes of this island, as well as in England, wherein according to proportion we are as great sharers as any, the whole, with the additional severity of the said Militia Act, we are scarcely able (at least some of us), notwithstanding all our providence and industry, to subsist and maintain our families under the same, as by what follows may appear.

II. In that a man to the exercising of the fort may be hired for 7 1/2d. a time, for which by this act is taken from us 20s. a time, that's thirty two for one.

III. In that a man and horse may be hired for 2s. 6d. a time, and from us is taken 40s. a time, that is sixteen for one, and that about sixteen times in the year.

IV. In that the said act enjoins exercising once in eight weeks, and not oftner (unless the governor's special order), yet over and above that, there are many other times, both for horse and foot, to which for non-appearance the whole fine of 20s. and 40s. a time is taken; as general musters, and general sessions, the interment of some great person, alarums, although sometimes false, guarding the governor to worship, and governor Dutton, twice to a play-house, their going off, or coming on the island. In most of which cases no damage, as we understand, can be, or is liable to happen unto the king or country by an omission therein, neither doth the law, as we remember, expressly enjoin the same, the preamble of which imports quite another thing, *viz. For preservation and defence of it, &c.*

V. In that patrollings are lately become constant, once in eight weeks also, as well as exercisings, which by that means makes the above severe law of 40s. a time to be twice as much for the horse within the said time, although the makers of it thought it sufficient to be once in eight weeks, therefore it saith, *and not oftner*, beside many other of the forenamed causes.

VI. In that the said act requires all apprentices, called *supernumeraries*, to appear in arms, many of whose masters being honest, industrious handicraftsmen, have suffered on their accounts very unreasonably, and that's not all neither; for by that means it's thought, that some hundreds of the youth of this country are spoiled, and lost through the evil courses they betake themselves to, for want of masters to teach them better things.

All which, we intreat you seriously to weigh and consider, in order to our relief and encouragement for the future . . . we believe all our said long continued and unparalleled sufferings to this very day have very little added to the benefit of either [king or country], nothing, we believe, thereby increasing the King's revenue, but rather to the damage of both. For as the Israelites could not easily make brick without straw, no more, as you well know, can we manage well our estates, when the best of our negroes and draught-cattle are taken from us, and that not for our debts, or wronging of any man, but only for conscience sake to God as aforesaid.

Thus much, touching the law itself, wherein we might enlarge. We intreat you likewise to consider, that the extremity of our sufferings ends not there neither, by reason of the marshal's cruel and inhuman abuses in executing of the same, which is not only in the taking our negroes and cattle, &c. when other effects are before them, and in our absence had been shewn them, but also that which aggravates the matter (and others would never endure) is their abusive language and deportments still continued unto us as formerly, if but in the least contradicted or opposed, when we know they proceed illegally, as *Quaking-dogs, rogues, sons of whores, lying troublesom fellows*, and drawing their swords, sometimes drawing blood, *viz.* . . . .

The 17th of the twelfth month called February 1686.

RICHARD FORD,	JOHN WHITE,
THO. PILGRIM,	JOS. HARBIN,
FRANCIS GAMBLE,	PHILIP COLLINS."
THOMAS ROBINS,	

B. Jamaica, 1683–1691

Jamaica

ANNO, 1683. William Davis, of Port-Royal, because he refused to appear in arms, and also to provide his servants with arms and ammunition had taken from him by George Carter, serjeant to Henry Molesworth's Company, by virtue of a warrant granted by Robert Phillips, ensign, several quantities of pewter and other goods worth £4 for only £1. demanded. The said William Davis had a few weeks before been robbed by pirates, and at the time of taking away these goods the sergeant said, *He would not leave him a dish to eat on*; and accordingly never returned any of the goods, but told him, *If he would pay the sum demanded, he might have them again*. But as he could not in conscience do that, he suffered the loss of the whole.

ANNO 1684. On the 5th of December, a serjeant with a party of musquetiers, authorized by warrant from Captain Joseph Jennings, came and demanded 10 s. of the said William Davis for not appearing in arms, which he refusing to pay, they took away an iron boom for a mast, weighing 38 lb. which they offered to sale, but finding nobody that would buy it, they brought it again, and the said William was free to receive it, the property of it not being altered. The same day they took away a jack with a line and weight, which he had before sold for 25s. but they sold it for 15s. of which, when they would have returned him 3s. he refused to receive it, because the goods sold were not his property.

ANNO 1685. On the 28th of the Second Month Robert Newman, a serjeant, with a corporal and some soldiers, came and demanded of the said William Davis 10s. for not buying arms, and not sending his servant to exercise military discipline, which he refusing to pay, they took away an hammock, the property of another person who had left it with him, which they sold in the market-place for 15s. and offered to return him 5s. which he would not receive, the goods sold being none of his property. This was done by force of a warrant granted by Thomas Barratt, ensign to the company.

ANNO 1686. On the 3d of the fifth month William Neate, corporal, and others, with a warrant from Joseph Jennings, a captain of the militia, came and demanded of the said William Davis 10s. for not appearing personally in arms, and 10s. more for not accoutring and sending his servant to the muster, which he refusing to pay, they took from him six silk handkerchiefs and other shop goods worth £2.10s.6d.

Again on the 10th of December the same year, the said William Davis had taken from him, for not appearing in arms, by Cornelius Campion and William Neale, serjeants, with a warrant under the hand of Capt. Joseph Jennings, twelve yards of speckled linen, at 1s.10d. per yard, and seven handkerchiefs at 1s.3 1/2d. each, the whole amounting to £1.11s.1/2d. But this, though their demand was but 20s., did not satisfy them, but they came again, and took three more handkerchiefs worth 3s.9d. . . .

ANNO 1687. George Parsons . . . , for refusing to send his servant in arms, had taken from him by John Daly and John Tilcock, serjeants of Colonel John Borden's company, for 4s. demanded, four yards of strip'd ticken worth 5s.

John Pike, of Port-Royal, joiner, for not bearing arms, and for refusing to contribute towards the charge of their feasts used on their field-days, for a demand of 10s. had taken from him by Daniel Burton and one Ellison, serjeants to Capt. Henry Ward, four frying-pans worth 18s.9d. of which they returned him only 1s.3d.

Thomas Gun, of Port-Royal, cooper, for refusing to bear arms, had taken from him for 10s. demanded, by Richard Pye, serjeant to Captain Ward, one iron-bound cask worth 15s. . . .

Peter Dashwood, for refusing to bear arms, was summoned to a court-martial, and sentenced to ride the wooden-horse, with a musket at each leg, for one hour. This punishment was twice inflicted on him, and the latter time, (*viz.* on the 12th of the sixth month 1687) the horse's legs being struck away, he received a dangerous fall, by means of which he was lame for some time after. . . .

ANNO 1690. . . . Thomas Norris had taken from him by order from Capt. Reynard Wilson, for a demand of 18s. for not appearing in arms, a gun which cost £3.

He had also taken from him at another time, for 10s. demanded for the same cause, one pair of hand-screws, three hand-saws, one silver spoon, and four candlesticks.

ANNO 1691. Thomas Norris aforesaid, for his son's not appearing in arms, had taken from him for a fine of 10s. by serjeant Thomas Parr, by order from Josiah Heathcoat, lieutenant of the company, three leather chairs of the value of 10s.

7

Alternative Service
and the Quakers of Antigua

The Society [of Friends] in Antigua, during its last days, passed through one crisis which developed out of the perennial difficulty in reconciling the claims of the State with the Quaker interpretation of the teachings of Christianity. The appearance of the French fleet in 1705 had evidently frightened the authorities of the island into active preparations for defence, but they honestly tried to respect the scruples of Friends by assigning them not to direct service in the militia, but to subsidiary work. Hereupon there arose a division of opinion in the Society. The older Friends, remembering bygone days of persecution, advised the acceptance of this compromise, while some young men declared that the work was inconsistent with their principles. . . . [The] dispute was so sharp that in 1708 two Epistles to London crossed the Atlantic, one signed by the Clerk of the Meeting, Jonas Langford, and the other by the dissentient young men Friends.

The official document sets forth that the alternative service offered to Friends, in view of bearing arms or building forts, was "the public service of the island, that is to say, building of watch-houses, clearing common roads, making bridges, digging ponds. . . . Also they are willing to accept of us without arms only appearing at their training place, and also that we should go messages from place to place in the island, in case of danger by an enemy. These things they require of us, and we have performed them, for which we have been excused from bearing arms." But now these young Friends say that such work is "all one" with actual military service. The same kind of scruple had arisen a generation before, when Friends hesitated about

From Margaret E. Hirst, *The Quakers in Peace and War: An Account of Their Peace Principles and Practice* (London, 1923), 322–26.

"planting potatoes for them that watched and builded the forts," and the matter was referred to "George Fox and the Meeting in London for advice . . . and their advice was they were innocent things and might be safely done." It was on this occasion that Fox sent his letter to . . . Friends [on the island of Nevis], to which Langford and his party [now] referred for guidance. In any case (they conclude . . .) they would welcome a ruling from London, as these scruples have produced more strife and contention in the Meeting than has been known in the past forty years.

The Epistle from the younger Friends, which follows, is a remarkable and interesting declaration. They, too, they explain, would welcome a decision on these points, which to them are matters of conscience. They then state very clearly the actual nature of the "public service" imposed on them.

"Whereas it is often ordered by the Government that fortifications are to be built, for the accomplishments whereof ponds for holding water (for the use of these persons who defend these places and inhabit them) are also to be dug, now [our older] Friends do think that if the government will excuse them from carrying of great guns to these places, and digging of trenches, building of bulwarks, and such warlike things, and instead thereof employ them in digging these ponds, building of bridges, repairing of highways, building of guard-houses, and such things, they can freely do them, yet we do think that in such a case to dig ponds or the like to be excused from carrying of guns, etc., is not bearing a faithful testimony against such things, but below the nobility of that holy principle whereof we make profession, and (at best) but doing a lawful thing upon an unlawful account and bottom. Yet we are very willing to dig ponds, repair highways, and build bridges, or such convenient things when they are done for the general service of the island and other people at work therein equal with us, and not to balance those things which for conscience' sake we cannot do."

On the question of appearing unarmed at the Militia muster, one Monthly Meeting has agreed with them that the practice is inconsistent with Friends' principles. "And as concerning alarms or invasion of an enemy, we are free to give notice to the magistrate of any approaching danger or be serviceable as far as we can at such times, in going to see what vessels may be off or giving them information in such things, though as to carrying of permits for vessels of war 'quietly to pass' such and such forts, when we are sensible their commissions are to kill, sink, burn, and destroy the enemy, we are scrupulous and not free in that case. And as concerning watching, we are free to do it in our own way," that is, unarmed, as Fox had recommended to the Friends of Nevis. The signatures to the letter are "John Brennan, John Darlow, junior, Henry Hodge, William Haige [*sic*], John Butler, John Fallowfield."

The answer returned by the Meeting for Sufferings in 1709 is instinct with that spirit of timidity and caution, combined with a genuine loyalty to the tolerant English Government, which marked Quaker leadership in the first half of the eighteenth century. The writer (possibly John Askew, who is the first name among the signatures) barely mentions the receipt of the young Friends' letter, while he speaks warmly of "our ancient worthy Friend Jonas Langford." A wish that "condescension in the spirit of love" may reconcile the disputants, is followed by approval of "the intentions of love and favour granted by the magistrates" of Antigua. In its view of what military works are possible for the Quaker conscience the Epistle goes beyond the concessions of the elder Antiguan Friends. "As for digging ditches and trenches and making walls, they are of like use with doors, locks, bolts, and pales, to keep out bloody wicked and destructive men and beasts; and to give warning and to awake our neighbours by messengers or otherwise to prevent their being destroyed, robbed, or burnt, doubtless is as we would desire should in the like nature be done and performed to us."

The most serious feature of the Epistle is its general inaccuracy of reference. It gives in inverted commas, as if a direct quotation, a summary of Fox's Nevis letter, which, whether intentionally or not, almost stiffens it into an argument for military defence against attack. . . . It should be Friends' aim to show themselves to Governors and magistrates, not as "a self-willed and stubborn people," but ready to do the will of the authorities in anything "that is not an evil in its own nature, but service and benefit to our neighbours." . . .

How the advice was received in Antigua cannot be known, for intercourse seems to have been broken off for some reason, and the next letter from the island is dated 1718. In it John Brennan wrote sadly of "a poor handful of people dispersed in a dark and barren island." Smallpox and the great drought had driven Friends away, among them Henry Hodge and his family to Pennsylvania, and William Hague and his family to Carolina. Ten years later the few remaining Friends "are inclinable to leave this island on account of the sickliness of the place," and after 1728 London hears no more from Antigua. If the Quaker records of the island had been preserved, we might have known whether the conscientious objectors agreed to work on "trenches and bulwarks," or whether it was a recurrence of the old difficulty that drove Henry Hodge and William Hague from their homes.

NOTES

Text

1. At that date Quakers, though they believed in treating slaves humanely, had not yet launched out as antislavery advocates. Their first protest against slavery came in 1688 when Germantown Friends issued a forthright declaration on the issue. "Have not these negroes," it asked ironically, "not as much right to fight for their freedom, as you have to keep them slaves?" But it then took over a century of hard work to eradicate slaveholding from Quaker ranks.

2. Joseph Besse, *A Collection of the Sufferings of the People called Quakers, for the Testimony of a Good Conscience* (London, 1753), 2:278. Cf. Besse's similar comment on Jamaica, ibid., p. 388.

Documents

1. Besse prints details of 110 cases between 1670 and 1678.
2. Note that women, either singly or together with their husbands, might be liable to military obligation if such liability depended on ownership of land. This practice prevailed on the American mainland as well as in England.

BACKGROUND READING

Brock, Peter. *The Quaker Peace Testimony 1660 to 1914*, 62–74. York, England, 1990.

Hirst, Margaret E. *The Quakers in Peace and War: An Account of Their Peace Principles and Practice*, 307–26. London, 1923.

III

R E V O L U T I O N A R Y

A M E R I C A

For the peace sects of colonial America the outbreak of the War of the Revolution in 1775 brought a time of troubles such as they had not hitherto experienced. Yet the penalties they had to pay to uphold their pacifist convictions proved perhaps not so extreme as one might have expected in a period when partisan passions rose on each side and rival armies marched through the land.

The peace sects tried to remain neutral. But they refused, while the fighting continued, to renounce their allegiance to the king. On the other hand, they resisted any attempt to win their active—or passive—support for the British side in the struggle against the "Patriots" who upheld the new revolutionary regime. As New England Quakers declared in an epistle they drew up in July 1776: "We have enlisted ourselves as soldiers under the Prince of Peace, [and] must [therefore] wear his uniform and march according to his step."[1] True, there were some Friends, as well as some Mennonites and German Baptist Brethren, who abandoned their hereditary peace witness and fought for—or otherwise actively supported—the Patriots.[2] But they remained a fairly small minority. Collectively, these groups maintained their testimony against war intact throughout the Revolution.

Conscientious objection during wartime covered a wide spectrum of resistance. For a peace sectary of military age the requirement to bear arms remained, of course, the major problem. After Pennsylvania for the first time imposed a compulsory draft in March 1777,[3] there was no area under Patriot rule where the militia draft was not enforced. As usual, exemption could easily be gained either by hiring a man to take one's place in the ranks or by paying a small fine—provided, in this case, that one had the money to do so. Quakers, as unconditionalists, refused either alternative and suffered the consequences (Document 8). The property then seized by the authorities from the delinquent to pay for a substitute often exceeded, as earlier, the amount required to do this. Protests were rarely effective, though frequently made since Quakers believed in standing up for their rights as citizens. We read of Quakers being severely ill-treated on account of their draft resistance, and a number of their draftees found themselves in jail for a matter of days or even months.

Members of the German peace sects, however, only rarely suffered this fate since their principles did not forbid them, as they would have put it, to render Caesar his due provided that Caesar did not require them to disobey what they considered their duty to God. In Pennsylvania Lancaster County tailor John Miller articulated their position admirably when he told the authorities that, as a conscientious objector to bearing arms, he was "at the same time . . . willing to render his services in any other way for the protection of his country that may be looked upon [as] equitable and just in lieu of his [military] service" (Document 10). Here, in a nutshell, we have the alternativist position stated: a contrast with the Quakers' unconditionalism maintained into the twentieth century. Concerning the permissibility of hiring a substitute, Mennonites continued to hesitate, though the consensus went against it. The small community of German Baptist Brethren wrestled, too, with this issue. The Brethren in 1781 were finally to approve this practice in guarded terms while still seeming to feel it might really be wrong (Document 11).

Military service did not exhaust the demands made by the revolutionary authorities in connection with the war effort. Compulsion to perform various kinds of paramilitary duties often created dilemmas of conscience among peace sectaries subject to them. Perhaps the ones that aroused the most heart searching, especially among the more sensitive members of the Society of Friends (Document 9), concerned payment of a war tax[4] and the handling of Continental paper currency (the latter "professedly for the special purpose of promoting . . . war"). Work on constructing fortifications, earthworks, and trenches clearly constituted a form of military service. Quaker meetings, therefore, disowned members who complied with such requisitions whereas Mennonites and Brethren usually felt such labor was Caesar's due. They likewise, unlike Quaker farmers, performed wagon service with a good conscience. In fact, Mennonite teamsters often profited from such service since they were usually paid handsomely for it: obviously that added an additional complication, even if we may presume most conscripted teamsters acted in good faith and not in the hope of material gain.

Among Mennonite craftsmen there were some extremely skilled gunsmiths. In time of peace they turned out hunting guns; but in wartime their products could be used for killing men. How should they react now if they knew the weapons they made were bought explicitly for the latter purpose? Each Mennonite gunsmith answered this question for himself; no church ruling seems to have been framed to guide them. Among a number of other wartime demands we may mention the loyalty oath or "test," which comprised a renunciation of allegiance to the monarch and a declaration of allegiance to the revolutionary regime. All the peace sects rejected the test, partly on political and partly on pacifist grounds. As the Quakers put it, their peace testimony required that they "keep clear from any party engaged in disputes that are to be determined by military forces."[5]

So far we have been dealing with the three best-known peace sects. There were others of course, like the Schwenkfelders, for instance, who, in May 1777 had issued a forthright declaration on the military question,[6] or the emergent Brethren in Christ,[7] or the Amish (though these really formed part of the Mennonite community). We also know of a few isolated war resisters. Though these men based their refusal to fight on their religion, they did not belong to a denomination that recognized conscientious objection as an acceptable alternative to combatancy. The most interesting of these cases that have so far come to light is, I think, that of Jesse Lee (1758–1816), a Virginia farm boy who, along with his parents, had been converted in a Methodist revival at the age of sixteen. With little formal schooling, he was naturally gifted as a speaker so that, despite his comparative youth, he became a local preacher for his church and was much sought after in this capacity. In July 1780, at age 22, he was drafted into the state militia, which had been put on a war footing. But without hesitation he decided that he would not consent to become a combatant. "As a Christian and as a preacher of the gospel," he declared, "I could not reconcile it to myself . . . to kill one of my fellow creatures" (Document 12). Lee was ordained to the Methodist ministry in 1790 by the famous Bishop Francis Asbury. In 1809 he became a chaplain of the U.S. House of Representatives and in 1814 chaplain of the U.S. Senate.[8]

In conclusion, I should mention what I have described elsewhere as the ambiguous noncombatancy of the eighteenth-century Moravian Brethren.[9] Their conscientious objection to arms-bearing combined aversion to shedding human blood with an even more powerful reluctance to mix with an unregenerate world. The founder of the Moravian Church was a German aristocrat, Count Nicolaus Ludwig von Zinzendorf (1700–1760), who succeeded in settling some of his followers in the New World, chiefly in Pennsylvania and North Carolina. As in England, Moravians obtained exemption from the colonial militia, too. During the Revolutionary War it became clear that there was a division within the brotherhood between the pacifists, led by John Ettwein at Bethlehem, Pennsylvania, who inclined, like the other German peace sects, toward passive loyalism (Document 13A), and those church leaders whose support for continued noncombatancy derived from a desire to remain aloof from a secular world rather than from unconditional pacifism (Document 13B). But there were also some Brethren, especially among the younger generation, who supported the revolutionary cause and believed that Brethren should defend it by arms if called upon to do so.[10] As a Moravian elder at Nazareth, Pennsylvania, exclaimed in alarm about the young men of his congregation: "They are talking about freedom (*Sie reden über Freiheit*)".[11]

In the new republic the Moravian Church continued officially to uphold a noncombatant stance—but with rapidly waning enthusiasm and contrary to the obvious wishes of the younger generation. This position was finally abandoned during the early decades of the nineteenth century.

⚘ 8 ⚘

Quaker Militia Penalties

1778.—In the beginning of the year 1777, the new Assembly passed an act entitled, 'An Act to Regulate the Militia of the Commonwealth of Pennsylvania;' directing that all the men between the ages of eighteen and fifty-three, should be enrolled as soldiers, and go out to war by turns, two months at a time; and if any one should refuse to go or send a man in his stead, it was enacted that certain officers should hire a substitute in his room, and seize upon his effects to pay said substitute; on which account was taken from Friends as follows, viz.:—

James Dunn, and several men with him, took—

From Joshua Baily, a colt, worth	£20	0s.	0d.
" Thomas Passmore, a colt, worth	20	0	0
" Isaac Baily, a colt, worth	20	0	0
" Aaron Baker, horse, "	15	0	0

—McClelland and others, took—

From John Passmore, mare, bridle, &c.,	31	1	0

From Ezra Michener, ed., *A Retrospect of Early Quakerism; being Extracts from the Records of Philadelphia Yearly Meeting and the Meetings Composing It* (Philadelphia, 1860), 376–78.

Thomas Irwin took—

From Ellis Pusey, colt and two heifers,	26	0	0

Henry McClelland, and others, took—

From George Harlan, two mares and blanket,	30	16	0

Samuel McClelland, George Copeland, James McCarlin,
and others, with muskets and other arms, took—

From Joseph Pyle, a horse, bridle, &c.,	19	5	0
" Thomas Jackson, mare and blanket,	31	5	0
" Caleb Jackson, two cows, ten sheep, &c.,	19	0	0
" Caleb Hurford, horse and bridle,	30	0	0
" Caleb Johnson, mare and blanket,	28	15	0
" John Jackson, Jr., yoke of oxen, two cows, &c.,	24	12	0
" Caleb Swayne, young mare,	30	0	0
" Jonathan Chalfant, watch and blanket,	9	0	0
" " " for a balance, bull,	5	0	0
" Edward Hoin, mare and bridle,	30	4	0

1778.—Robert McGomery, by orders from
Thomas Strawbridge, took—

From James Way, a horse and mare,	37	0	0
" Thomas Millhouse,[1] colt and bridle,	20	0	0
" Thomas Wood, a mare,	16	0	0
" Jacob Wood, a horse,	22	0	0
" John Wickersham, a mare,	20	0	0
" George Passmore, a mare,	23	0	0
" Lewis Pusey, a horse,	28	0	0
" John Pusey, a mare,	30	0	0
" Joshua Pusey, a mare,	24	0	0
" Francis Lamborn, a horse,	12	0	0
" Thomas Lamborn, a mare,	25	0	0
" Josiah Lamborn, horse and 20 bus[hels] corn,	12	0	0
" Joseph Richardson, mare,	15	0	0
" Stephen Cook, mare and colt,	18	0	0
" Samuel Jackson, two horses, gear, &c.,	36	5	0
" Francis Wilkinson, mare,	20	0	0
" Samuel Sharp, yoke of oxen,	28	0	0
" Richard Flower, horse, wagon, &c.,	32	0	0
" Rumford Dawes, mare,	20	0	0
" William Allen, 40 bushels wheat, 6s.,	12	0	0
" Jacob Halliday, mare,	15	0	0

By an order from Andrew Boyd, John Sharp took—

From Joshua Edwards, a horse and bridle,	15	5	0

And by orders from said Boyd, James Dunn took—

From Joel Baily, mare and cow,	32	0	0
" David Windle, mare,	28	0	0

" Samuel Swayne, horse and three cattle,	29	0	0
" Caleb Pennock, horse,	25	0	0
" William Windle, two cows and three cattle,	18	0	0
" Caleb Johnson (a balance), two cows,	15	0	0
" Isaac Pyle, one heifer and eight sheep,	11	0	0
" William Baily, twenty-one yards linen,	2	12	6
" Elisha Baily, cart, and watch,	11	0	0
And by an order from said Boyd, was taken by Francis Ruth—			
From Isaac Woodraw, mare and bridle,	28	0	0
" Caleb Pusey, young mare,	26	0	0
And for a fine for Moses Windle, six young cattle,	22	0	0
From Aaron Baker, Jr., feather-bed,	6	0	0
" Joseph Pyle, three cows,	19	10	0
" Jeremiah Barnard, one fat steer, being for a fine charged on his nephew of the same name,	9	11	0
	£1130	8s.	6d.

❋ 9 ❋

Dilemmas of a Quaker Tax and Paper Currency Objector

The rulers of America having made a paper currency professedly for the special purpose of promoting or maintaining said war; and it being expected that Friends would be tried by requisitions for taxes, principally for the support of war, I was greatly exercised in spirit, both on the account of taking and passing said money, and in regard to the payment of [war] taxes, neither of which felt easy to my mind. I believed a time would come when christians would not so far contribute to the encouragement and support of war and fightings as voluntarily to pay taxes that were mainly, or even in considerable proportion, for defraying the expences thereof; and it was

From the *Journal of the Life, Travels, and Gospel Labours of That Faithful Servant and Minister of Christ, Job Scott* (New York, 1797), 53–55, 64, 65.

also impressed upon my mind, that if I took and passed money that I knew was made on purpose to uphold war, I should not bear a testimony against war that for me, as an individual, would be a faithful one. I knew the people's minds were in a rage against such as, from any motive whatever, said or acted any thing tending to discountenance the war. I was sensible that refusing to pay the taxes, or to take the currency, would immediately be construed as a pointed opposition to the present war in particular, as even our refusing to bear arms was, notwithstanding our long and wellknown testimony against it. I had abundant reason to expect great censure and some suffering in consequence of my faithfulness, if I should stand faithful in these things, though I knew that my scruples were unconnected with any party considerations, and uninfluenced by any motives but such as respect the propriety of a truly christian conduct in regard to war at large. I had no desire to promote the opposition to Great-Britain; neither had I any desire on the other hand to promote the measures or success of Great-Britain. I believed it my business not to meddle with any thing from such views; but to let the potsherds of the earth alone in their smiting one against another: but I wished to be clear in the sight of God, and to do all that he might require of me towards the more full introduction and coming of his peaceable kingdom and government on earth. I found many well concerned brethren, who seemed to have little or nothing of these scruples and some others who were like-minded with me herein. . . .

About the latter end of the 6th month this year [1776], an old acquaintance of mine, being now collector of rates, came and demanded one of me. I asked him what it was for? He said, to sink the paper money. I told him, as that money was made expressly for the purpose of carrying on war, I had refused to take it; and for the same reason could not pay a tax to sink it, believing it my duty to bear testimony against war and fighting. I informed him that for divers years past, even divers years before the war began, and when I had no expectation of ever being tried in this way, it had been a settled belief with me that it was not right to pay such taxes; at least not right for me, nor, in my apprehension, right in itself; though many sincere brethren may not at present see its repugnancy to the pure and peaceable spirit of the gospel. I let him know I did not wish to put him to any trouble, but would be glad to pay it if I could consistently with my persuasion. He appeared moderate, thoughtful and rather tender; and after a time of free and pretty full conversation upon the subject, went away in a pleasant disposition of mind, I being truly glad to see him so. Divers such demands were made of me in those troublesom times for divers years: I ever found it best to be very calm and candid; and to open, as I was from time to time enabled, the genuine grounds of my refusal; and that if possible, so far as to reach the understandings of those who made the demand.

✲ 10 ✲

The German Peace Sects of Pennsylvania and the Draft

[December 3, 1777][2]

John Miller . . .

Says that he makes matter of conscience of bearing arms, but at the same time is willing to render his services in any other way, for the protection of his country that may be looked upon [as] equitable and just in lieu of his service, *Tailor.*

Judg[men]t—to serve his two months in making clothes for the continent[al army] or pay twenty pounds fine.

David Merkey . . .

Says that he has a bad rupture, and is also lame in his arms by times. Conscientious. *Plantation.*

Judg[men]t—to do two months garrison duty or pay thirty pounds.

Jacob Risaire . . .

Says that he is not sick. But alleges he is not able to pay his fine. Has a plantation from his father paying him the third bushel as rent. Conscientious.

Judg[men]t—to perform two months' tour of duty or pay the sum of thirty five pounds.

Jacob Blickenderfor . . .

Hearty and in good health but is scrupulous of bearing arms from religious principles. Has a small family, and not able to pay the fine. *Labourer.*

Judg[men]t—to perform two months' duty or pay fifteen pounds.

Leonard Shartzer . . .

Says that when he gets cold he is subject to the colic but appears well. Scrupulous [about] bearing arms. Complains of poverty. Has a small plantation from his father, rented.

Judg[men]t—to do two months' duty in garrison or pay twenty pounds—Dec. 4, 1777 appeals.

Christian Blickensderfer . . .

Appealed for by his father, who says that he has got his leg cut with an ax, that he can't walk. Is poor and not able. Conscientious.

From Richard K. MacMaster et al., eds., *Conscience in Crisis: Mennonites and Other Peace Churches in America, 1739–1789—Interpretation and Documents* (Scottdale, Penn., 1979), 325, 326.

Judg[men]t—to find a substitute for two months' duty or pay fifteen pounds.

John Henry Baugh . . .

Says his principles will not admit his bearing arms. Has made considerable improvements and yet is in debt. Thinks the battalion fine beyond his ability, but willing to pay as adjudged. *Auger-Maker.*[3]

David Tannenberger[4] . . .

His principles forbid his bearing of arms. An organmaker [by] trade, no business done in that way, thinks he would not be able to pay but willing to pay as adjudged . . .

Judg[men]t—to find a substitute for two months' duty or pay thirty pounds.

Daniel Kristt . . .

Principles as above. A poor man and is not able to earn any more than what maintains his family, but willing to pay according to his ability.

Judg[men]t—to serve two months' garrison duty—by substitute, or pay fifteen pounds.

John Shank . . .

Principled as above. Says he is a single man, has nothing but what he earns by his trade. Willing to pay as adjudged. *Nailer.*

Judg[men]t—to do two months' duty by substitute or pay twenty pounds.

❧ 11 ❧

A Peace Sect Wrestles with the Problem of Hiring a Substitute

Annual Meeting of 1781

"A troublesome matter was faced by the Conferences of 1780 and 1781 held at Conestoga, Pennsylvania. Was a brother justified in hiring a substitute to do military duty in place of himself or a son? The ambivalence of the answer reveals that there was not a complete unity of mind on the matter. A

From Donald F. Durnbaugh, ed., *The Brethren in Colonial America: A Source Book on the Transplantation and Development of the Church of the Brethren in the Eighteenth Century* (Elgin, Ill., 1967), 353, 354.

further statement on the tax indicates that there were those who refused even to pay taxes to support the war, although most of the Brethren evidently did not go this far. Many Quakers took the position that they could not pay taxes levied directly for war purposes. They and those Brethren taking the same position underwent forcible seizure of property and sale at public auction to satisfy the demands of the rebel government" (Donald F. Durnbaugh).

Article 1. Inasmuch as at the great meeting at Conestoga last year, it was unanimously concluded that we should not pay the substitute money; but inasmuch as it has been overlooked here and there and some have not regarded it, therefore we, the assembled brethren, exhort in union all brethren everywhere to hold themselves guiltless and take no part in war or bloodshedding, which might take place if we would pay voluntarily for hiring men; or yet more if we become agents to collect such money. And inasmuch as some brethren have received written orders to tell their people and afterwards to collect (such money), accompanied by the threat of a heavy fine, we fervently exhort not to be afraid to do that which is right. Still, we exhort also that if a brother is fined, there should be provision made for such brethren, and assistance rendered as far as money is concerned. In case a brother or his son [is] drafted that he or his son should go to war, and he could buy himself or his son from it, such would not be deemed so sinful, yet it should not be given voluntarily without compulsion. But where this has been overlooked, and the substitute money has been voluntary, and (the brother) acknowledges his mistake from the heart and repents it, the church shall be satisfied with him.

If a brother bears his testimony that he cannot give his money on account of his conscience and would say to the collector: "If you must take it, then use your authority, I shall not be in your way"—with such a brother we should also be satisfied. But concerning the tax, it is considered that on account of the troublesome times and in order to avoid offense, we might follow the example of Christ (Matt. 17:24–27). Yet, if one does not see it so and thinks perhaps, he for his conscience sake could not pay it, but bear with others who pay in patience, we would willingly go along inasmuch as we deem the overruling of the conscience to be wrong.

✳ 12 ✳

The Conscientious Objection of a Methodist Preacher

Mr. Lee, who heretofore had been quietly engaged in the pleasing task of cultivating the soil, and of improving his spare moments in striving to aid in the reformation of his fellow men, now is suddenly interrupted in his career by an imperious summons given by his country, to exchange the implements of agriculture for the weapons of war; [f]or it must be recollected that at this juncture, America was engaged in a struggle for her national rights and liberties. . . . An invading foe was marching through the country. . . . On all hands was heard the sound of the martial trumpet, calling the friends of liberty to the banners of their country; but few who had arrived at the proper age were exempt from taking an active part in the conflict. The militia were drafted, and it fell to Mr. Lee's lot to go. How illy it accorded with his religious views and feelings, may be seen in the following extracts [from his *Journal*]:

"I weighed the matter over and over again, but my mind was settled; as a Christian and as a preacher of the gospel I could not fight. I could not reconcile it to myself to bear arms, or to kill one of my fellow creatures; however I determined to go, and to trust in the Lord; and accordingly prepared for my journey.

Monday July 17th, 1780, I left home and set out for the army, and travelled about 25 miles to Mr. Green Hill's, where . . . I tarried . . . all night.

Wednesday 19th, I set off early in the morning and travelled about 16 miles to Mr. Hines'. In the afternoon we had much conversation on spiritual matters, and in the evening, felt my heart more engaged with God in prayer than usual. I felt my dependence upon God, and though I believed that great difficulties lay before me, yet I resigned myself into the hands of God, and felt assured that he would protect and take care of me.

I did not join the army till the 29th. On the evening of that day I came in sight of the camp, and was soon called on parade, and orders were given for all the soldiers to be furnished with guns. I then lifted up my heart to God and besought him to take my cause in his hands, and support me in the hour of trial.

From Minton Thrift, *Memoir of the Rev. Jesse Lee, with Extracts from His Journals* (New York, 1823), 25–34.

The sergeant soon came round with the guns, and offered one to me, but I would not take it. Then the lieutenant brought me one, but I refused to take it. He said I should go under guard. He then went to the colonel, and coming back, brought a gun and set it down against me. I told him he had as well take it away or it would fall. He then took me with him and delivered me to the guard.

After a while the colonel came, and taking me out a little way from the guard, he began to converse with me, and to assign many reasons why I should bear arms; but his reasons were not sufficiently cogent to make any alteration in my mind. He then told the guard to take care of me, and so left me.

Many of the people came and talked with me and pitied me, and would leave me with tears in their eyes. We lay encamped at a tavern a few miles from the site of what was afterwards the seat of government for North Carolina. After dark, I told the guard we must pray before we slept; and, having a Baptist under guard, I asked him to pray, which he did. I then told the people if they would come out early in the morning, I would pray with them. I felt remarkably happy in God under all my trouble, and did not doubt but that I should be delivered in due time. Some of the soldiers brought me some straw to lay upon, and offered me their blankets and great coats for covering. I slept pretty well that night, which was the first, and the last night I was ever under guard.

Sunday 30th.—As soon as it was light, I was up and began to sing, and some hundreds of people soon assembled and joined with me, and we made the plantation ring with the songs of Zion. We then kneeled down and prayed; and while I was praying, my soul was happy in God, and I wept much and prayed loud, and many of the poor soldiers also wept. I do not think that I ever felt more willing to suffer for the sake of religion than what I did at that time.

A little after we were done prayer, Mr. Thomas, the tavern keeper, came out and talked with me, and told me he was in bed when he heard my praying, that he could not refrain from tears, and he had called to see me, and know if I would be willing to preach to them that day, it being sabbath? I told him I would preach provided he would procure a block, or something for me to stand upon; which he readily promised to do. I told him, withal, I wished him to go to the colonel, for we had no higher officer amongst us, and obtain leave for me to preach; which he did, and liberty was granted. It is but just to state, that Colonel Bru*** was a man of great humanity, although a profane swearer. When he heard that I was about to preach, it affected him very much, so he came and took me out to talk with me on the subject of bearing arms. I told him I could not kill a man with a good conscience, but I was a friend to my country, and was willing to do any thing that I could, while I continued in the army, except that of fighting. He then asked me if I would be willing to drive their baggage wagon? I told him I would, though I had never drove a wagon before; he said their main cook was a Methodist, and could drive the wagon when we were on a march, and I might lodge and eat with him; to which I agreed. He then released me from guard, and said when I was ready to begin meeting I might stand on a bench by his tent. When the hour arrived, I began under the trees, and took my text in Luke xiii. 5. *Except ye repent, ye shall all likewise perish.* . . . I was enabled to speak plainly, and without fear; and I wept while endeavouring to declare my message. Many of the people, officers as well as men, were bathed in tears before I was done. That meeting afforded me an ample reward for all my trouble. At the close of the meeting, some of the gentlemen went about with their hats to make a collection of money for me, at which I was very uneasy, and ran in among the people and begged them to desist. I could not at that time feel willing to receive any compensation for preaching. I thought if the people could afford to sit and hear me, I could well afford to stand and preach to them. I felt my heart humbled before God, and was truly thankful to him for the grace communicated to my soul at that time. I had no doubt but that all things would work for my good.

On Monday I took charge of the wagon, and felt much resigned to the will of God." . . .

From Thomas' tavern, near the present town of Raleigh, the army moved on towards the South . . . and the next day entered the state of South Carolina; and then to the banks of the Pedee River, where they encamped. During the week they made forced marches, and the soldiers could obtain but half rations of meal. . . .

[Again] we shall lay before the reader a few extracts from his journal.

"Sunday 13th of August, we lay by and did not march; about 3 o'clock in the afternoon, I preached to a large number of soldiers, from Isa. iii. 10, 11. *Say ye to the righteous, &c.* Many of the hearers were very solemn, and some of them wept freely under the preaching of the word. I was happy in God, and thankful to him for that privilege of warning the wicked once more. . . . For some weeks I hardly ever prayed in public, or preached, or reproved a sinner, without seeing some good effects produced by my labours.

Thursday 17th, about 10 o'clock in the morning, we received the unexpected news of general Gates' defeat, near Campden, which took place the day before; the news spread through the camp, and all were called out on parade. All appeared solemn; not an oath was heard for several hours. The mouths of the most profane swearers were shut. We then commenced a retreat back to North Carolina.

Monday 28th, we marched down to Romney's Mills, on Deep River. On the 29th, I was taken very sick. . . . I was brought to examine my heart closely concerning my hope of heaven; and was comforted to find that I had no doubt of my salvation; for I believed that should the Lord see fit to remove me from this world, I should be called to join the armies of Heaven.

Tuesday the 5th of September, the army marched from Deep River, and I [went with] them though quite unwell.

On the following morning the Colonel told me, inasmuch as I was not willing to bear arms, I must join the pioneers. I was afterward appointed sergeant of the pioneers, which was a safe and easy berth; there were but few in that company, and I had to direct them in their labours, which was not hard. The soldiers suffered much for the want of provision, for the greater part of the week. We crossed Harraway River, and came through Randolph County; we were frequently alarmed at night, so that I was much fatigued by severe marches by day, and sleeping little at night. But the best of all was, my soul was kept in peace, and at times, I felt great fellowship with the Father and with the Son! . . .

Sunday the 24th, Mr. Green Hill preached in the camp; his text was 1 Thes. v. 19. 'Quench not the Spirit.' The next morning before day we had orders to prepare and leave the ground in ten minutes, for the British were expected to be on us in a short time. We left the ground before day, and the wagons came on towards Salisbury about 16 miles, and then had orders to turn back to the Cross-Roads, which was about 9 miles; we retreated about 7 miles, and halted to get something to eat; we then had orders to march immediately. The enemy came to Charlotte, and had an engagement with our people, and several men were killed. Some who overtook us, who were with the baggage, were wounded and bleeding. We marched about 18 miles that day, and made it quite late in the night before we came to a halt. We stayed two or three hours, and cooked something, and eat a little; and then marched immediately, without taking time to sleep. We marched again sometime before day, and the roads were thronged with people, men, women and children, with their property, flying from the face of the enemy. The colonel rode up and said to me, 'Well, Lee! don't you think you could fight now!' I told him I could fight with switches, but I could not kill a man. We came to Salisbury and encamped in town that night, expecting the enemy would be after us every hour. The night was very cold. . . .

Tuesday the 10th [of October], general Butler came into camp with a number of men, and took command of the whole army.

At night the news arrived in camp that on Saturday last the Americans had a skirmish with the British and tories in Kings' Mountain, where our men gained a complete victory, and killed many of the enemy, and took the rest prisoners. We were all glad to hear the news; but some rejoiced with horrid oaths, and others determined to get drunk for joy. For my part, I felt thankful to God, and humbled before him, knowing that the battle is not to the strong.

October 13th, colonel Morgan joined us with a part of his regiment—some of our soldiers were very sick—I went among them where they lay in barns, at the point of death, and talked to them about their souls; and begged them to prepare to meet their God. When convenient, I attended the funeral of those who died, and prayed at the grave.

Wednesday the 18th, we had a sharp frost, which was a great advantage to those who were sick. In the evening Col. [William] Washington, with his troop of horse joined us. The next day we crossed the Yadkin River to the South, and the day following, marched a small distance above Salisbury, and took up late at night. On Saturday we were up before day, and after some consultation among the officers, we were informed that we were not to march that day. We were in constant expectation of an attack from the enemy. I felt my mind calm and stayed on God; but having my rest so much broken of late, I felt quite dull and heavy. . . .

Sunday Oct. 29th—On this morning I obtained my discharge. The general said as there were two sergeants of the pioneers, and one was sufficient, it would be best for me to resign, and as I was the oldest in office, I might have the privilege if I chose it. I accepted the offer—took my discharge—settled some business—took leave of many of my old acquaintances, and left the army."

ᘒ 13 ᘒ

The Moravian Brethren and War

A. The Pacifism of John Ettwein

Dearly beloved Brother Matthew [Hehl][5]

I have duly received your welcome [letter] of the 26th of May, and I thank you very much for having thus communicated your ideas concerning the course of action, which this attack upon our freedom of conscience in the matter of bearing arms makes desirable for us. While I was in [Herrnhut] in 1744, it also occurred that we had to furnish 2 recruits and were placed in a very distressing position. 2 Brethren volunteered to help the congregation out of its distressing position; but the following day 2 outsiders

From Kenneth Gardiner Hamilton, *John Ettwein and the Moravian Church during the Revolutionary Period* (Bethlehem, Penn., 1940), 239–42.

offered to serve for the sake of the money. From that time on, I have been firmly opposed to the bearing of arms. . . .

I consider the exemptions granted the Brethren in our day to be a great reward for the small degree of faithfulness shown by the Brethren from the beginning in this matter. I am not the only one who emphatically considers going to war in person or providing a substitute to be one and the same wrong (n.b. I refer to Brethren), only, in the one case, one's own life and ease are better safe-guarded than in the other. But I, also, make an essential distinction between the action of the lord of some manor or the proprietor of an estate, in paying for some recruits on behalf of that community or estate, and an individual Brother who is summoned either to serve in person or to provide a substitute; I do not consider the former action to be contrary to freedom of conscience. You write: "There are enough of those who count their life cheap and who do not deserve any better, to last for the present war." My scruples are not caused by the fact that I might bring about their misfortune and death, should I by my money encourage them to fight, but by the fact that I am to reward someone, whether by my wish or contrary to my wish, to destroy people or to do them other violence and wrong in my name and in my stead. And in the case before us there is this additional consideration: "Shall I defend myself per proxy by force of arms against the King and Parliament who have granted me one of the most glorious exemptions?" For a Brother that would be the greatest ingratitude and an infamy.

Your distinction between a soldier and a murderer is right and just; the Bible and the laws of England also distinguish between murder and manslaughter. In my opinion a soldier and a manslaughterer are one and the same; though some soldiers never actually kill a person, another may perhaps kill many. It is not in a soldier's own power to avoid shedding human blood. He who hates his brother is also a manslaughterer; yet I will gladly yield as regards this phrase, too, and allow soldiers to be classed with executioners. . . .

As [you have said], we are entangled [in the present state of affairs], at least the poor are, and we cannot evade suffering. Let a man pay his 70/- for refusing to drill and 5/- or 7/6 for each future occasion of mustering, he will have to permit himself to be robbed of his possessions and go to prison, unless he be willing to fight in the militia or provide a substitute. They are trying to make the latter alternative altogether impossible. In Bucks-County the officers immediately put the pay at £15 for 2 months, and in Cushehopen they have paid £25. How can a poor Brother pay such sums, even if he felt free in his conscience to hire such a ———? Why should one first corrupt the Brethren and spare oneself more than other peaceful, well-intentioned people do in this land? The consequences of our maintaining our position or giving ground and yielding are too important; and I hold we should try to stiffen the weak Brethren and encourage them not to fear the struggle. I would rather permit myself to be hacked to pieces than go to war, butcher people, rob people of their property or burn it down, swear that I owe no obedience to K. G. [King George], that I desire to help maintain the independence of Pennsylvania, until and before time and circumstances make it clear and incontestable that God has severed America from England.

For nothing can happen to me contrary to the will of my Father in heaven, and surely one can answer even a tyrant in the words of our Saviour: "Thou wouldest have no power against me, except it were given thee from above!" [John 19:11]. [It was in Litiz that the first Brethren determined not to meddle in any war;[6] God forbid that the Brethren in Litiz of today should stray from that course.[7]] The conditions which prevail in the country at present have made the wisdom and the importance of this particular article of the Brethren's Church so significant and invaluable, that I cannot describe the matter. Surely it is worth suffering somewhat for it. I only regret that one might answer me: "It is easy for you to say this; you are exempted from this temptation as a result of your position and age."

Dear Brother, bear with me in my having delivered myself thus and do not interpret it ill, that I have become so discursive.

B. Moravians and the Draft: An Ambiguous Witness

Extract from Salem Minute Books, 1775

Aug. 9, [1775.] The small amount of powder which we are reserving for our own defense (should that be necessary) shall be hidden by two Brethren, so that we do not get into trouble because of it. The guns which are in town should also not hang in sight, since we have conscientious scruples against bearing arms. The Brethren who have guns in their houses shall be asked to keep them hidden.[8] . . .

From "Memoir of Brother Bachhof," Friedberg, 1776

March 24, [1776.] Sunday. . . . A corporal arrived, and ordered our men to meet at a given muster place tomorrow. They resolved that tomorrow Adam Spach and John Müller should go thither, and in the name of all present the certificate given by Capt. Macay.

March 25. This was done, but the certificate was not accepted. . . .

From Adelaide L. Fries, ed., *Records of the Moravians in North Carolina* (Raleigh, N.C.), 2 (1925): 898; 3 (1926): 1112, 1113, 1117, 1118.

April 5. Good Friday. During the first service Michael Müller, a corporal, came to notify our Rowan County Brethren to attend muster next Monday, on penalty of 40 sh. fine for non-attendance. They decided to go, but to explain that they could not take part in the drill. . . .

April 8. In the evening Adam Spach, who with others had attended the muster at the designated place, told me what had happened. The three captains present had at first been very harsh, and had forced them to sign an affirmation that they would remain neutral; but later the captains had said that they were not authorized to excuse them from muster, and had advised them to take a petition to the Committee in Salisbury on May 23rd.

April 15. Adam Spach visited me. I asked him what he thought about the muster? He answered: "I will not attend muster, and will bear whatever that may bring upon me. I wish," said he, "that they all thought as I do, then one day in each week we would meet in the school-house, and unitedly lay the difficult circumstances upon the heart of the Saviour, instead of going to muster once a month." . . .

May 7. Our Rowan County Brethren went to muster, having been ordered to attend or pay £10: fine. Br. Tesch told Capt. Ekels that Col. Joseph Williams, who had been to Congress, had told him yesterday that no soldiers would be called from Rowan or Surry at this time, but he would not listen to him, nor to Billy Doughted, who brought the same as a verbal order from the Committee in Salisbury. Instead he first called for volunteers; then two impartial men were elected, with whom the captain conferred for an hour, giving them instructions, and then certain men and youths were drawn, some of them being present and some not, and their names were enrolled, and they were ordered to appear next Thursday, ready to march, on penalty of £10: or £25. Among these were the single men Adam Tesch, Johann Hartmann, Adam Spach and Jacob Volz. This gave their parents the greatest concern, and they absolutely forbade their sons to go, and Adam Spach and George Hartmann resolved to set out that night for Salisbury and do their utmost to persuade the Committee to exempt their sons. In this they failed, but they did secure a written order to Capt. Ekels not to take them on the expedition set for the 9th. . . .

June 27. We visited Adam Spach and George Hartmann, to learn what was done at the last muster. Practically all except Friedrich Müller and Adam Hartmann had signed the declaration that they accepted Congress as their ruler, and would obey its orders. Spach, George Hartmann and Walk had not attended. A committee is to be selected from among those who signed.

July 14. The married members of the Society . . . agreed that none of them would go out to fight, but would endure whatever this course might bring upon them. As they were starting home a lieutenant came to the door, and ordered the first and second classes of our Rowan enrolled Brethren and their sons to appear before Capt. Ekel next Tuesday, ready to march against the Indians. He at once received the answer: "We are not going to fight." Our Brethren who live in Surry were expected to appear in Bethabara to receive their orders, but they did not go. Meanwhile the young men, who were particularly called, retired into the woods.

July 15. A scouting party, sent for the purpose, looked for them at home and in the woods, but did not find them. In the evening Br. Pfaff and Martin Ebert came to me in great distress, and asked for a signed statement from me concerning their sons, to be given to the captain, to whom Lieutenant Binkel had given their names. And as they assured me that Br. Graff had advised this method I wrote one for each, in the following words: "I, the undersigned, testify herewith, that N—— N—— from childhood on has belonged to the Unity of Brethren, and is now a member of the Brethren's Society of Friedberg." . . .

July 16. The fathers took these certificates to Bethabara, but could not wait for the captain, so gave them to Br. Johann Schaub, who . . . was to give them to him. They rode home without learning the captain's decision, and knew no more than when they started.

July 17. We visited George and Christian Frey. The former had to go to Salisbury today, to see whether the colonel would excuse him from attending muster, and from going to war, as Capt. Ekels did fourteen days ago. Christian Frey is all to pieces over conditions, and often talks much and thoughtlessly.

July 18. Martin Ebert's wife is in great fright and distress over her son, who is still in the woods, and on account of the scouting parties she cannot call him in. She advised sending to Bethabara to find out from Schaub what the captain did about the certificates.

July 19. The captain refused to accept the certificates, saying they came too late, but adding that they might be taken to Col. Armstrong if they liked. I told them that if they wanted to try it could do no harm, but if they were going the sooner the better.

July 20. They decided to go to Col. Armstrong, taking the certificates, which I translated into English for them. . . .

July 21. Martin Ebert brought me the news that he and Br. Pfaff had been well received by Col. Armstrong, who had promised them that for his part, and unless he received contrary orders from the General or from Congress, he would not force children of Brethren to go into the war.

July 28. The Brn. Pfaff and Martin Ebert told me that today they and their sons had again been warned to come to the place of muster and march to Holston River. In answer to their query as to what they should do I said: "Better today than tomorrow go to the captain and see him about it."

July 30. We heard from [Br. Ebert's wife] that her husband and Br. Pfaff were well received by Capt. Schmidt, and he had said that unless he received further orders their sons might be free from muster and service.

Aug. 7. Most of the Rowan men attended muster, for which Christian

Frey had to furnish a barrel of cider. The men of the first and second classes, whose marching was recently countermanded, and also the men of the third class, were warned to hold themselves ready to march at any time.[9]

NOTES

Text

1. Quoted in Cecil B. Currey, "Eighteenth-Century Evangelical Opposition to the American Revolution: The Case of the Quakers," *Fides et Historia* 4, no. 1 (Fall 1971):28.
2. Fighting Quakers formed their own separate Society of Friends known as Free Quakers. But they numbered only a few hundred confined almost exclusively to Pennsylvania. After the war was over, they slowly dwindled, and they had disappeared altogether by the 1830s. A few Quakers fought for the British; these people eventually took refuge on British soil, mainly in Nova Scotia. But they failed to take root there. Among the German peace sects there were individual dissidents, but no splinter group arose on the pattern of the Free Quakers. The question of war taxation, however, did produce a schism among the Mennonites when one of their "bishops," Christian Funk, who urged payment, broke away to form a separate sect.
3. See Richard K. MacMaster et al., eds., *Conscience in Crisis: Mennonites and Other Peace Churches in America, 1739–1789—Interpretation and Documents* (Scottdale, Penn., 1979), 282–84. This volume contains a rich assortment of documentary materials and commentary dealing with the situation of the peace sects during the Revolutionary War.
4. "The most developed Quaker thought on war taxes in the period of the American Revolution came from the pen of Samuel Allinson, a young Friend from Burlington, New Jersey," write the editors of *Conscience in Crisis*. They print extracts from his "Reasons against War, and Paying Taxes for Its Support" (June 13, 1780) on pages 371–73. Allinson circulated his treatise among Friends, but it was never published. The Quaker collection at Haverford College has the manuscript of this work: 968 Box 11a.
5. See Dorothy Gilbert Thorne, "North Carolina Friends and the Revolution," *North Carolina Historical Review* 38, no. 3 (July 1961):331–33.
6. Printed in English translation in MacMaster, *Conscience in Crisis*, p. 312.
7. Also known as River Brethren and Tunkers (or "Dippers").
8. See the entry by Charles Yrigoyen, Jr., in the *American National Biography* (New York, 1999), 13:381, 382.
9. An archivally based study of this subject remains to be written. Meanwhile, for all its inadequacies, chapter 7 in my *Pacifism in the United States: From the Colonial Era to the First World War* (Princeton, N.J., 1968) is still the most detailed treatment available.
10. We should note that earlier, during the French and Indian War, there had been Moravian church leaders, like Augustus Gottlieb Spangenberg, who, at least privately, rejected the pacifist position categorically.

11. Quoted in James Henry, "Nazareth and the Revolution," *Transactions of the Moravian Historical Society* 2 (1886):41.

Documents

1. The Quaker roots of the late President Richard Millhouse Nixon came through the Pennsylvania Quaker Millhouse family.
2. From Appeal Docket for Lancaster County in the State Archives Division of the Pennsylvania Historical and Museum Commission.
3. "Tool for boring holes in wood" (*Concise Oxford Dictionary*).
4. A member of the Moravian community at Lititz. He "was one of the great American organmakers" (MacMaster, *Conscience in Crisis*, p. 352, n. 88). Like the Moravian Leader John Ettwein (see n. 5 below), Tannenberger, it would seem, adhered strictly to nonviolence—unlike some of his Brethren contemporaries.
5. Translation from the German of a letter to the Moravian Bishop Hehl, dated June 1 (probably 1777).
6. A reference to the establishment in 1457 of the Unity of Czech Brethren in Kunwald, a village situated on the estate of the Hussite nobleman and elected King of Bohemia, George of Poděbrady, at Litice. Ettwein was evidently aware that the Unity of Brethren had espoused pacifism during its early years, although it is doubtful if he knew that it abandoned this tenet of its faith during the 1490s. See my monograph *The Political and Social Doctrines of the Unity of Czech Brethren in the Fifteenth and Early Sixteenth Centuries* (The Hague, 1957). The Moravian Church claims descent from the Unity of Brethren (*Unitas Fratrum*)—on rather tenuous grounds.
7. Sentence later deleted by Ettwein.
8. From "Extracts from the Salem Minute Books, 1775" (Aufscher Collegium). Translated by A. L. Fries from the German.
9. From "Memoir of Brother Bachhof" (Friedberg, 1776). Translated by A. L. Fries from the German.

BACKGROUND READING

Brock, Peter. *Pacifism in the United States: From the Colonial Era to the First World War*, 183–329. Princeton, N.J., 1968.

MacMaster, Richard. *Land, Piety, Peoplehood: The Establishment of Mennonite Communities in America, 1683–1790*, 249–80. Scottdale, Penn., 1985.

———, et al., eds. *Conscience in Crisis: Mennonites and Other Peace Churches in America, 1739–1789—Interpretation and Documents*, 213–521. Scottdale, Penn., 1979.

Mekeel, Arthur J. *The Quakers and the American Revolution*. York, England, 1996.

IV

UPPER CANADA

The British province of Upper Canada came formally into existence in 1791. Because the province bordered on the south with the new American republic and possessed a thinly spread native Indian population, the home government, as well as the administrators it sent out to govern this remote area, considered the promotion of white settlement as one of their main priorities. It did not take long for Colonel Simcoe, the province's first lieutenant governor, to decide that among the most desirable settlers were the "plain" farming folk in New York, New Jersey, and Pennsylvania. These people, while they were opposed on principle to bearing arms, were skilled agriculturalists, hardworking and honest.

Though beginning to accommodate themselves to the new republican regime now firmly established in the former British colonies to the south, many Quakers, Mennonites, and Tunkers (Brethren in Christ) welcomed the opportunity, now offered by Lieutenant-Governor Simcoe, to resettle under the Crown, which offered them plenty of cheap arable land. Their families tended to be large; the movement westward was already in full swing and peace people formed part of it alongside their neighbors.

Governor Simcoe, moreover, showed himself quite ready to grant the exemption from bearing arms that these settlers considered essential. The governor wrote home to Whitehall on August 20, 1792: "I have not hesitated to promise to the Quakers and other sects the similar exemption from militia duties which they have met with under the British government."[1] Subsequent legislation, passed by the provincial assembly, confirmed Simcoe's promise and brought assurance to the new settlers that they would not be seriously troubled on this score (Document 14). When, in 1810, the legislators admitted the as yet unbaptized members of the Mennonite and Tunker brotherhoods (both of which practised adult baptism) to the blanket exemption from bearing arms previously granted only to baptized members of the two sects, their chief grievance was remedied. Henceforward, all that a draftee belonging to these two communities would need for militia exemption was to produce a certificate confirming that his father was a Mennonite or Tunker and that he had been "brought up and educated in the principles" of one of these sects.[2]

Quakers, because of their rejection of any alternative to unconditional exemption from the draft, did not fare quite so well. They suffered, as they still continued to do to the south, from distraints—and occasional brief bouts of imprisonment—for refusing to pay the fine that the law required for exemption from military training. And the familiar pattern continued of disowning any Friend who succumbed to pressure on this score and showed himself unwilling to suffer for the Truth (Document 15).

The War of 1812 brought increased requisitioning on the part of the British military, which weighed heavily on Yonge Street Quakers in particular since they were settled along a strategically vital line of communication (Document 16). For instance, serving as teamsters for the armed forces, which often involved hauling cannon or military stores, led to disciplinary action by the offender's meeting and ended inevitably in disownment if the man did not express contrition for his offense.

For Mennonites and Tunkers, on the other hand, such activity was not frowned on, still less penalized, even though the men concerned may often have entered upon such duties with reluctance. "Just how many Mennonites had their teams and equipment impressed is not known," writes the Mennonite historian Frank Epp, "but when it was all over at least 22 [Mennonite] farmers claimed loss or damage for two horses, 14 wagons, 17 harnesses, one coat, five blankets, 54 bags, 13 chains, two yokes, and four singletrees. . . . The heaviest loss was encountered by Henry Wanner, who claimed $500 for horses, wagon, harness, and bags."[3]

At this time the Quakers, Mennonites, and Tunkers continued to have close contacts with their coreligionists in the United States, both organizationally and doctrinally. In a way they were still Americans—or rather, they remained British North Americans. The shaping of a Canadian national identity was still indeed a matter for the future.

In Britain the last occasion on which compulsory militia service was enforced had come in 1831. In Canada the militia draft continued for over a decade longer, a result undoubtedly of the threat of invasion and annexation by the republic to the south. The rebellions of William Lyon Mackenzie in

Upper Canada (today Ontario) and of Louis Papineau in Lower Canada (today Quebec) toward the end of the 1830s served inter alia to exacerbate the tension between British Canada and the United States. As late as 1840, therefore, young Quakers in Upper Canada might still find themselves in jail for failing to attend one of the militia's periodic days of training (Document 17). But soon in Canada, as in England or in the United States, militia compulsion would become a thing of the past.

ᴟ 14 ᴟ

Legislative Exemption for Peace Sects

And be it further enacted, that the persons called Quakers, Menonists and Tunkers, who from certain scruples of conscience, decline bearing arms, shall not be compelled to serve in the said militia, but every person professing that he is one of the people called Quakers, Menonists or Tunkers, and producing a certificate of his being a Quaker, Menonist or Tunker, signed by any three or more of the people (who are or shall be by them authorized to grant certificates for this or any other purpose of which a pastor, minister or preacher shall be one) shall be excused and exempted from serving in the said militia, and instead of such service, all and every such person or persons, that shall or may be of the people called Quakers, Menonists or Tunkers, shall pay to the lieutenant of the county or riding, or in his absence to the deputy lieutenant, the sum of twenty shillings per annum in time of peace, and five pounds per annum in time of actual invasion or insurrection, upon producing such certificate, and being thereby exempted from such service as aforesaid, and if any such person or persons being of the people called Quakers, Menonists or Tunkers, and producing a certificate as aforesaid, shall omit or refuse to pay the sum of twenty shillings per annum in time of peace, and five pounds per annum in time of actual invasion or insurrection, instead of such service, it shall and may be lawful, upon the oath of any one credible witness of such omission or refusal before any justice of the peace, for such justice to issue his warrant to levy the same by distress and sale of the offender or offenders' goods and chattels, returning so much of the said distress as shall exceed the said sum of twenty

From *Statutes of Upper Canada*, 33 George 3, c. 1, sect. 22 (1793).

shillings per annum in time of peace, and five pounds per annum in time of actual invasion or insurrection, after deducting the expences of levying the same, to the person or persons upon whom such distress shall be made. And if any measures shall be used in making such distress which may by such person or persons be thought oppressive, he or they may complain to the lieutenant or deputy lieutenant at the next meeting, who shall hear and finally determine the same.

ꙮ 15 ꙮ

Quakers and Military Requisitions,
1810–1817

Friends had not been settled very long in the Province of Upper Canada when they found themselves in the midst of military preparations. The government was by 1808 making preparations to defend British North America against an anticipated invasion from the United States.

Friends were instructed by their Meetings not to pay military taxes or levies, and not to aid the army in any other way. The minutes of the Yonge Street Preparative and Monthly Meeting tell of the sufferings of Friends who maintained their testimony against war.

18th Day of the 1st Month 1810:

> The Committee appointed on the case of sufferings reported that upon careful inspection they find that the property of 48 Friends from the 1st of 2nd Month 1808 to the 1st of 1st Mo. 1810 amounts to £243-11-6½ New York currency, for military demand. And that 8 Friends have suffered each 1 month's imprisonment on the same account . . .

17th Day of 1st Mo. 1811:

> The Com. on Sufferings cases produced an account of 69½ dollars taken from 7 members in lieu of military demands of $4 each since last year.

From "Quakers Opposed War Preparations in Upper Canada," *Canadian Friend* 69, no. 1 (February/March 1973):10, 11.

17th of 1st Mo. 1812:

> Value of property taken from 7 Friends last year in lieu of military requisitions amounts to 69.65 dollars.

Later entries in the minute book record the seizure of property by the Government. One entry dated 1st Mo. 1816 reads, "$67 (in the form of property) taken from Yonge Street Monthly Meeting in lieu of Military Requisitions." The last record of difficulty with the authorities was in 1817, almost 9 years after the first entry, and records "value of property taken from 3 Friends 6th Mo. 1817—$58.50."

The Yonge Street Meeting dealt with Friends who violated their instructions against involvement in war. An example of the type of forbidden activity is recorded in the minutes.

13th-IV-1813:

> Reported from Yonge Street Preparative Meeting that Isaac Lundy has been employed hauling cannon for the use of the Army. Wm. Lundy and James Varney and James Kinsey and John Haight are appointed to visit him on the occasion and report.

No further report appears in the minute book. Enrollment in the militia was a serious offense and in one instance resulted in disownment. The case is recorded as follows:

12th of 5th Mo. 1808:

> Peter Hunter has attended at a military training and answered to his name in order to save his fine. Thomas Linville and Samuel Hughes are appointed to visit him and report their sense in his case.

16th of 6th Mo. 1808:

> The Friends appointed to visit Peter Hunter informed that they have had an opportunity with him. And he still appears disposed to continue in the practice of training. After solid consideration they ask Lewis Powell to visit him and if they have not course to forebear, to prepare a testimony against him for the approbation of next meeting.

By the 8th Month of that year a committee of Friends had "found no cause to forebear", had delivered a testimony against Peter Hunter, and had reported to the Meeting that their task has been completed.

Canadian Quakers have a testimony against war and support of war preparations that goes back to the time they first moved to British North America. The refusal to pay military taxes, to fulfill requisitions for goods, or to submit to military training is illustrated in the early minute book of Yonge Street Preparative and Monthly Meetings.[1]

✤ 16 ✤

A Quaker Family in the War of 1812

Father was exempt by age, but brothers William and John, were both drafted in the Militia. William, neither willing to fight nor to go to jail, took refuge, with some others, in the woods. There were often parties in search of him, but never caught him. The officers took Thomas[2] prisoner, and took him before Colonel Graham, who sent him to jail, where he lay for about six weeks, and by father interceding for him with Col. Graham, he at length gave an order for his release, and, I think was not troubled any more. . . .

In the year 1814 my brother-in-law Peter Wisner, having his team pressed[, went] to Fort George with Government stores. He chose to go himself, rather than to trust his horses to strangers. He was about two weeks, in winter, the roads bad and poor accommodations. He came home sick and died in about a week, leaving my sister a widow (Phebe) with one child to mourn her loss. While Thomas lay in jail, a young man, a Friend, Joseph Roberts died there, rather than violate his conscience.

✤ 17 ✤

Quaker Conscientious Objectors
in Rural Upper Canada, 1840

A few days before the close of the 8th month (August) [1840] we set off with a large company of Friends, in a train of three capacious open wagons, on a pilgrimage of 120 miles, to Yonge street, north of Toronto, where the

From "Recollections of an Immigrant: Clayton Webb 1799–1883," *Newmarket Historical Society Occasional Papers* 1, no. 2 (1987):14. A copy of this rare item is available in the Metropolitan Toronto Public Reference Library. The passages I have cited here have also been printed by Albert Schrauwers, *Awaiting the Millennium: The Children of Peace and the Village of Hope, 1812–1889* (Toronto, 1993), 44, 45.

From Joseph John Gurney, *A Journey to North America, Described in Familiar Letters to Amelia Opie* (Norwich, England, 1841), 336–41. The volume was "printed for private circulation."

half-year's meeting of Friends of Upper Canada was about to assemble. . . . After [arriving in Toronto], four of our company waited on Sir George Arthur, the Lieutenant-Governor, with whom we conversed with great freedom respecting the moral and political character of the people. We were glad to assure him that some persons of a seditious character who went by the name of Quakers, had little or no connection with our society; and that the body of Friends in Canada wished for nothing better than to pursue their peaceable avocations under the Queen's government.[3] The lieutenant-governor is a gentleman of kind demeanour, much benevolence, and I believe decided piety. He listened with great kindness to the appeal which we ventured to make to him on the subject of capital punishment—this having been enforced on several occasions after the late rebellion. . . .

The roads through the settled districts of this country are called "streets." Yonge-street begins at Toronto, and goes on thirty miles in a perfectly straight line to the north, until it reaches the settlement of Friends, which we were now about to visit. The country on the whole route is well settled; good brick houses on fertile and fairly cultivated land, are to be seen on either side of the street. It is evidently a very productive country, and pleasant in its appearance—far superior to the notions that I had previously formed of it. At Yonge-street settlement we found a convenient abode among hospitable Friends, ready for our reception; and were met by numerous members of the society, many of whom had arrived from a great distance both from the east and west. They were come to attend the half year's meeting, which is here held in lieu of the Quarterly meetings usual in other parts of America.

This part of the country as well as the neighbourhood of Norwich, was much agitated during the late rebellion. It was near this place that the people took up arms under the persuasion and command of the restless Mackenzie.[4] . . .

The half year's meeting was held in a large rustic meeting-house; it occupied parts of three successive days, and was an occasion of much interest. The sincere and simple-hearted, though generally unpolished people of whom it was composed, excited both our regard and our sympathy. They had been exposed to many troubles during the late political excitement. An earnest desire prevailed in the meeting, that the members of our society, in all parts of the province, should keep clear of all the jarring and tumults of political parties—that they might "study to be quiet and do their own business." This indeed was already their general habit, and not much fault could be found, in reference to the subject even with the young; yet every one felt that it was a day of temptation and difficulty. In the mean time, however loyal the Friends might be, they could neither serve themselves in the militia, nor pay any tax in lieu of such service. On this ground they were exposed, by the laws of Upper Canada, either to the distraint of their goods, or the imprisonment of their persons. Two of our young men had actually been thrown into jail at Hamilton for sixteen days. The subject was re-

spectfully urged on the attention of Sir George Arthur; as it had been previously on that of Lord Durham;[5] but it so happens that I have never heard
the result of either application.

NOTES

Text

1. *The Simcoe Papers*, vol. 1, 1789–1793 (Toronto: Ontario Historical Society, 1923),
   198, 199.
2. "An Act for the relief of Minors of the Societies of Menonists and Tunkers," passed
   on March 12, 1810; *Statutes of Upper Canada*, 50 George 3, c. 11.
3. Frank H. Epp, *Mennonites in Canada, 1876–1920: The History of a Separate People* (Toronto, 1974), 104.

Documents

1. Extracts from the Minute Book of Yonge Street Preparative and Monthly Meeting
   of the Society of Friends, 1804–1818, made by Elma Starr.
2. Presumably a third brother of Clayton Webb.
3. Some young Quakers had taken an active part in the unsuccessful rebellion of
   1837–38, led by the radical William Lyon Mackenzie.
4. Reference to William Lyon Mackenzie.
5. The first Earl of Durham, who died earlier that year, had been Governor-General
   and High Commissioner to British North America. A liberal, he composed the famous *Report on the Affairs of British North America* (1839), which inter alia ad-
   vocated extensive Canadian self-government.

BACKGROUND READING

Brock, Peter. "Accounting for Difference: The Problem of Pacifism in Early Upper
   Canada." *Ontario History* 90, no. 1 (Spring 1998):19–30.
Dorland, Arthur Garratt. *The Quakers in Canada, A History*, 313–24. Toronto,
   1968.
Epp, Frank H. *Mennonites in Canada, 1786–1920: The History of a Separate Peo-
   ple*, 99–107. Toronto, 1963.
Sider, E. Morris. "Nonresistance in the Early Brethren in Christ Church in Ontario."
   Mennonite Quarterly Review 31, no. 4 (October 1957):278–86.

V

THE NEW REPUBLIC

TO ANTEBELLUM

AMERICA

Over three-quarters of a century elapsed between the end of the Revolution and the outbreak of the Civil War. At first pacifism and conscientious objection continued to be confined to the peace sects, whose members had soon accommodated themselves to the new republican regime, even though for a time a certain suspicion lingered on each side. But from 1815 onward a new impetus was given to the promotion of peace with the founding of a series of nonsectarian peace societies. Partly because not all supporters of the new peace movement were absolute pacifists, some peace sectaries (including, rather surprisingly, many American Quakers) regarded these societies with suspicion, fearing cooperation with them would adulterate the purity of their own otherworldly peace witness.

Throughout the period under consideration the militia draft in theory continued in force in most states, although as before draftees, if they so wished, could escape attendance at compulsory mustering by paying a small fine. The Mexican War of 1846–1848 did not lead to a more rigid enforcement of the system, and in the course of the final antebellum years that system became increasingly obsolescent.

At the end of the 1780s, under the inspiration of the Jeffersonian republican James Madison, a proposal arose to enact a far-reaching constitutional guarantee of conscientious objection as part of the Bill of Rights. As it stated: "A well regulated militia, composed of the body of the people, being the best security of a free state, the right of the people to keep and bear arms shall not be infringed; but no person religiously scrupulous shall be compelled to bear arms." But this proposal failed to gain much support either in the Senate or the House of Representatives. A similar proposal (but one that required payment of a fine in lieu of bearing arms) reemerged in Congress during 1790 but again lapsed, despite warm support from Madison.[1] However, even if it had been accepted, an exemption of that kind would certainly have failed to satisfy the Quakers, who still stood for unconditional exemption from an activity they regarded as wrong.

Indeed Quaker scrupulosity prompted more sensitive members of the Society of Friends not only to suffer repeated distraint on their property for refusing to pay militia fines but also to examine their conduct in other areas so as to discover if they were giving support to war, even if unwittingly (Document 18). It might, for instance, be a case of an ordinary tax in which, however, a component destined for military use was concealed, or of an excise duty, which a Quaker shopkeeper was required to pay on goods he sold to his customers. Response by officials varied. Sometimes the latter reacted harshly; more often they showed understanding of these rather peculiar neighbors, who otherwise behaved as good citizens. True, Quakers' outspoken antislavery sentiments made matters increasingly difficult for them in North Carolina and Virginia, where they had long been settled. But this factor did not play a role in the case of Quakers living in the north and west.

In 1810 Quakers in Virginia had drawn up a petition asking the state legislature for unconditional exemption from the militia for their young male members (Document 19). At the core of the Quaker argument, as presented in the document, lay an appeal to "the fundamental principles, upon which the civil and political institutions of this country are established."[2] This position indeed had long been implicit in Quaker pleas for exemption, though it had rarely been stated so clearly as here.

Mennonites and Brethren encountered few difficulties over the militia question during this period. They paid their fines and were not further troubled by the authorities; and they were content in this way to render Caesar his due while at the same time preserving the purity of their conscience. But several small pacifist sects took the Quaker position and refused on principle to contribute money in lieu of militia service, regarding compliance with this requirement as inconsistent with religious freedom and their civil rights. Such was the case, for instance, with the Rogerenes, whose origins went back to the late seventeenth century. Their members, all of them farmers or craftsmen, were settled exclusively in Connecticut.[3] As Jonathan Whipple, a Rogerene carpenter from Connecticut's seaport of Mystic, declared: "I [will] never do military duty, or pay any fines; of course they [can] imprison me, or do what they [will]. But they [cannot] make me do what I [think] wrong and wicked" (Document 20).

Equally outspoken in defense of what they considered to be their rights as citizens were the members of the communitarian—and celibate—United Society of Believers, commonly known as the Shakers, who had come into existence during the Revolution under the inspiration of the charismatic "Mother" Ann Lee (1736–1784). From small beginnings the Shakers, by the second quarter of the nineteenth century, numbered about 6,000 members in eighteen societies scattered throughout the states of Maine, New Hampshire, Massachusetts, Connecticut, Ohio, and Kentucky. Their peace testimony, as it finally crystallized around 1815, resembled that of the Quakers in its uncompromising character. Shaker pleas for militia exemption addressed to the legislatures of the states in which they resided, a number of which survive in printed pamphlet form, incorporated a New Testament–based nonresistance together with an assertion of the natural rights of man and the constitutional rights of the American citizen.[4] We must, however, wait until the Civil War before we find a document reflecting the personal experiences of a Shaker conscientious objector.

Even though the nonsectarian peace movement that emerged in 1815 at the conclusion of the Napoleonic wars included both nonpacifist peace advocates and absolute pacifists, the two wings of the peace movement eventually came under one umbrella—that of the American Peace Society, formed in 1828 as a result of the fusion of the Massachusetts Peace Society and the New York Peace Society, which had pioneered the movement since 1815. But in 1838 a split occurred, with radical peace advocates hiving off to form the New England Non-Resistance Society under the leadership of abolitionist William Lloyd Garrison (1805–1879). For these nonresistants all governments, as at present constituted, were evil; and Christians, if they were to live up to the pacific principles of the founder of their religion, were required to boycott politics. "A bullet is in every ballot" became their slogan. Moderate pacifists, however, like the "learned blacksmith" Elihu Burritt, could not follow as far as this, nor could most Quakers.

Conscientious objection was not really a major concern of the antebellum peace movement. But we do learn of some of its younger members having to confront the militia draft (as had Garrison himself in 1829 [Document 22]). Moreover, both moderates and radicals sought to extend legal provision for conscientious objection so as to include not only members of one of the recognized peace sects but sincere objectors unaffiliated with any of them. (The idea of a non-Christian pacifist or a selective objection did not enter the picture at that date.) Thus, both the conservative Massachusetts Peace Society (Document 21A) and the "ultra beyond ultra" Garrisonian nonresistants (Document 21B)[5] came out publicly in support of this proposal.

The question whether "pacific exempts" should pay militia fines was warmly debated during the second half of the 1830s, when the whole peace movement was in a state of turmoil over the nonresistance issue. In 1836 a leading exponent of moderate pacifism, Thomas C. Upham (1799–1872), a professor of mental and moral philosophy at Bowdoin College—then an important New England cultural center—discussed the matter in his textbook *Manual of Peace* (Document 23). In the previous year the students at the college had formed a Peace Society "on the most thorough principles," the members of which were "resolved to carry out their principles, in their intercourse with their fellow-men, so far as to decline all military service, or the payment of military fines." In Boston a Bowdoin Street Young Men's Peace Society was also set up on the principles established by the Bowdoin College boys and their mentor.[6]

Some of these young men, on further reflection, must finally have decided to comply with the law and pay the small fine, which was all that was required to be excused from attending a muster if called upon to do so. (After all, even as staunch a "no-government" man as William Lloyd Garrison saw nothing wrong in doing this, though some of his followers disagreed with their respected leader on this point.) On the other hand, we learn from the press of several militia objectors suffering repeated terms of—brief—imprisonment for their conscientious delinquency (Document 24B). Thus, in the ingenuous dialogue between two boys, Frank and William, which the Garrisonian nonresistant Charles Whipple composed in 1838, when Frank, incredulous, asks William, "But do men ever go to prison rather than train?" William is able to reply with a definite "Yes" (Document 24A).

To return in conclusion to the Quakers, by the 1830s their church leaders were finding it difficult to maintain a consistent witness with respect to not paying militia fines. (This had never been very easy.) Certainly there were some who did not hesitate to pay the penalty of refusal (Document 25B), but there were others who, perhaps quite sincerely, saw no point in offering resistance to an institution whose futility was now obvious to so many of their fellow citizens. The elders might regard such Friends as "weak" in "complying" with an "unrighteous" law, but many in the Society seemed to share the latter's view (Document 25A).

"An ineffective militia system involved a large portion of the male population for one or two days per year. This was hardly enough to build a strong military organization but was a persistent irritant to pacifist groups such as the Quakers and Shakers." Until the end of the 1850s the minutes of Quaker meetings continued to record militia fines as well as failures to uphold the Society's peace testimony in refusing to "pay tax in lieu of military service."[7] But, seemingly, disciplinary action was no longer taken against these delinquents. And as for the New England Non-Resistance Society, this body, once so ardently pacifist, had virtually ceased to function by the end of the 1840s as increasing numbers of its former members came to support the use of force to end slavery.

The coming of civil war in April 1861 radically changed the situation of America's conscientious objectors.

❦ 18 ❦

Continuing Quaker Witness against War,
1801–1824

From the Journal of Rufus Hall, April 10, 1801

10th, was our preparative meeting, in which life arose and light shone triumphant over all, to the encouraging of some of our minds. It being the time of answering the Queries, some things were closely searched into; particularly that of paying a tax, which many Friends thought was principally for the support of warlike purposes; such as building fortifications, ships of war, &c. But this tax being so blended with other taxes and duties, made it difficult: some Friends not being free to pay it, as believing it inconsistent with their religious principles and testimony against war; while others had paid it. A concern was felt that Friends might be preserved, so as to act with consistency therein. It was understood by some that Friends in New York generally paid it; and it was alleged that formerly while we were under the king of England, we had to answer a query in relation to not defrauding the king of his dues; and they could see no difference in this respect between king and congress; and that therefore we might pay those taxes now as well as formerly. On the other hand, it was stated that the ground on which we were raised to be a separate people or society, was that of tender scruples of conscience; and it was on this ground, or principle of Divine light, that the reformation had always stood, and must still stand, if it is carried on; and therefore that Friends would not do well to look to New York or London, nor even to former customs, for direction; seeing we had to go forward and not backward, nor yet to stand still with the work of reformation. As to defrauding any of their dues, there was no such thing in the case; for *to defraud* was wilfully, obstinately, or craftily to detain a thing from the right owner. But in this case there was neither will, obstinacy, nor craft; but purely a tender scruple of mind or conscience; and therefore it ought to be attended to, and Friends should not desert the ground (now in a day of ease) on which their predecessors stood, and nobly maintained it in the times of hot persecution.

On the whole, it appeared to me that the weighty concern of the meet-

From *A Journal of the Life, Religious Exercises, and Travels in the Work of the Ministry, of Rufus Hall, late of Northampton, Montgomery County, in the State of New York* (Byberry, Penn., 1840), 112, 113.

ing was against paying the tax; but as the subject was new to some, and others were not altogether clear, by reason of long custom, so as to see the inconsistency of paying it,—it was thought best to let every Friend act according to their freedom therein. I was truly thankful that Friends were preserved in such unity and harmony, that I did not discover any hardness towards one another; but all spoke with coolness of mind, and none showed any symptoms of heated zeal; which is too often the case in such matters.

From the Journal of Isaac Martin, 1813

Soon after, a weighty concern attended my mind on account of a tax on shop keepers, who dealt in foreign articles, to be appropriated towards carrying on the war against England. I felt much scrupulous in my mind, respecting the consistency thereof with our peaceable principles. For about ten years I had kept an apothecary shop; which business suited my inclination and capacity; being from my youth circumscribed, both in shop-keeping and my trade of a hatter, on account of the prevailing fashions. After much seeking to the Lord for counsel and direction, I believed my peace of mind would be affected, if I paid the said tax. So I resigned myself to the Lord's will, let the event be as it may. But scarcely a day passed, that I had not to turn customers away, who applied for articles which I had on hand, but could not sell, on account of the heavy penalty. But I am well satisfied, feeling the testimony against war to be very precious, and worth suffering for, if thereby the peaceable government of the Messiah may be promoted.

How shocking the carnage and miseries of war! I am informed that within about two years and a half, near fifty thousand lives have been lost in the present wars between this country and England. How awful the reflection, that so many precious souls should be thus hurried into an endless eternity, to meet the Judge of quick and dead! Where shall we find the least spark of Christian love, in the spirit of war? Nay a diabolical spirit is the author and promoter thereof; and it tends mightily to strengthen the kingdom of darkness, and to lay waste every Christian virtue, every spark of redeeming grace and love in the souls of those who are instrumental in promoting, or carrying it on. Yet, Oh how lamentable! that those who assume the title of Christ's ministers should aid in person, and by what is called preaching! Some of whom, if not all, I believe know better than they practise; but the fear of man, or perhaps the loss of their yearly salary, turns the scale of true judgement in their hearts. Thus, the leaders of the people cause them to err, and the blessed cause of truth and righteousness in the earth is frustrated by them.

From A Journal of the Life, Travels, Labours, and Religious Exercises of Isaac Martin, late of Rahway, in East Jersey, Deceased (Philadelphia, 1834), 113–15.

From the Journal of William Evans

Second month 24th, 1814. I was compelled to appear before a court-martial sitting in this city, to answer a charge of disobedience of the orders of the President of the United States, in refusing to march as a militiaman last spring. I stated to the court-martial, that I was conscientiously bound to decline all warlike measures, and could not by any means comply with such requisitions. That I was a member of the Society of Friends, and although we cannot actively comply with laws that would violate our consciences, yet we do not rise against the Government; we passively suffer the penalty which they inflict—at the same time we think it right to plead for liberty of conscience, to maintain our rights in a peaceable manner, and not tacitly suffer distraint or imprisonment without law. They heard me patiently and respectfully, making but little exception to what I advanced. I understood they decide the question by vote, whether the fine shall be exacted: what was their course in my case I never heard, but they never attempted to collect any fine of me, and I suppose they voted me free.

It is very important at all times to bear a clear and faithful testimony to the coming and kingdom of the Prince of peace; and when the noise and spirit of war are over the land, and wicked men are ready to make a prey of those who cannot join in their measures, the times call for increased watchfulness that we may not be caught with that spirit, and the desire of success on the arms of either belligerent party, or in any manner let the testimony against war and bloodshed fall to the ground.

From the Autobiography of Benjamin Hallowell

GOODS SEIZED FOR MILITIA FINES

A little over a year after we commenced housekeeping in Alexandria, D.C., in 1824, the captain of the militia of the district presented to me a bill of fifteen dollars for muster fines for the past year, five musters in the year, and a fine of three dollars for absence from each. I told the captain the discipline of the religious society to which I belonged required that its members should be in no way active in anything connected with military affairs, but suffer peaceably whatever penalty the law imposed. He said he would then have to distrain my property for the amount of the fine, and requested me to designate what goods I could best spare. I told him I could say nothing upon the subject, but left it all to him to do what the law required. He then

From the *Journal of the Life and Religious Services of William Evans, a Minister of the Gospel in the Society of Friends* (Philadelphia, 1870), 32, 33.

From the *Autobiography of Benjamin Hallowell* (Philadelphia, 1883), 210–12—"written at the request of his daughter . . . for his children and grandchildren, in the seventy-sixth year of his age."

levied on our parlor furniture, taking a large looking-glass, my portable writing-desk, brass andirons, shovel and tongs, and several other things; goods selling so low at *such* sales, which no respectable people attended, it took more than we could replace for fifty dollars to pay a fine of fifteen. But I cheerfully made the sacrifice to the Society, for the many privileges I enjoyed from it, although our parlor did look very much stripped, and I thought such a stripping every year, which was the prospect before me, would be a severe tax.[1] . . .

I have a testimony against military training as a preparation for war. But I have a high respect and regard for law. I am at heart a law-abiding citizen, never to be active in opposition to law, but ready and willing to comply with the law or suffer the penalty which it imposes for non-compliance.

As a member of civil society, I think it would be right for *me* to pay the penalty which the law imposes for non-compliance in this respect, believing the general effect would be far better than the present mode prescribed by Friends' Discipline, of having the penalty collected by distraint. But estimating very highly the privileges my birth-right of membership in the Society of Friends has given me, and yet gives me, I will not pay such fines while the Discipline of the Society requires its members not to do so. Is this the right course? Do we not blame the Pope and the Roman Catholic Church for a similar thing—for placing the obligations of the citizen to a religious society above his obligations to his country?

⚜ 19 ⚜

A Quaker Petition against Militia Conscription, 1810

TO THE LEGISLATURE OF VIRGINIA,
THE MEMORIAL AND PETITION OF THE
RELIGIOUS SOCIETY OF FRIENDS,
COMMONLY CALLED QUAKERS

From *A Memorial of the Religious Society of Friends to the Legislature of Virginia, on the Militia Laws, with a Letter from Benjamin Bates, (Bearer of the Memorial) to a Member of the Legislature* (New Bedford, Mass., 1813), 3–9, 15–18.

. . . your Memorialists, estimating the high regard with which the Legislature will be disposed to consider every subject affecting the great principles of civil or religious liberty, beg leave to solicit your attention to the militia laws of this commonwealth, and to the incompatibility which sometimes results between the requisitions of the law, and the obligations of religious duty.

In this enlightened age and country, and before this Legislature, your Memorialists conceive it unnecessary to urge the unalienable rights of conscience, or to adduce any arguments to shew that the relations between man and his Creator, neither can, nor ought to be prescribed or controlled by any human authority. It is unnecessary, because the proposition is self evident, and especially because it is one of the fundamental principles, upon which the civil and political institutions of this country are established. This principle is recognized in the bill of rights; it is confirmed by the law of 1785, passed in the enlightened and liberal spirit of that instrument; and the *state itself*, by its convention which ratified the federal constitution, expressly declared, that "the liberty of conscience cannot be cancelled, abridged, restrained, or modified by any authority of the United States." The free exercise of religion, therefore, is not merely tolerated; it is declared in the most solemn form, it is confirmed in the most explicit manner.

But the liberty of conscience, your Memorialists conceive, cannot be restricted to the mere liberty of thinking, or to the silent and unseen modifications of religious opinion. Religion has duties to be performed, and it points out offences to be avoided; its free exercise must therefore consist in an active compliance with its dictates, enforced by no legal compulsion, restrained by no legal impediment.

Your Memorialists, in common with every virtuous citizen, would disclaim any exemption, under the colour of religious liberty, from the universal obligations of moral duty. But the law of 1785, in making "overt acts" of an injurious nature the limit of the privilege, and the criterion of the abuse, removes all danger to the community. Any encroachment on the rights of others, or violation of the moral law, under pretence of liberty of conscience, would immediately betray its own guilt and hypocrisy, and afford a legitimate cause for the interposition of the civil authority.

These considerations are suggested, as applicable to the case which is now submitted to the wisdom and justice of the legislature.

Your Memorialists are Christians; and impressed with the firm conviction that war is forbidden under the gospel, they cannot bear arms. To require it under legal penalties, is to reduce them to the alternative of refusing a compliance with the laws of their country, or of violating what they most solemnly believe is *to them* a law of God, clothed with the same most awful sanctions.

Your Memorialists plead no new doctrines, they set up no novel pretensions. They ask *permission* only to practice the precepts of Jesus Christ—to adhere to the principles which prevailed through the first centuries of the Christian dispensation, which pious men through every subsequent age have maintained; and which their predecessors from the time they have been known as a religious society, under various forms of government, and through sufferings imposed by rigorous and persecuting laws, have uniformly supported.

It is true that in the lapse of time the spirit of persecution has faded before the lights of truth. Our own country as already stated, has been particularly distinguished for maintaining the principles of civil and religious liberty, and for rejecting those of coercive law and religious intolerance. The very grievance to which we now solicit your attention, has been acknowledged and redressed. A legislature, composed of enlightened statesmen and sages, who had assisted in establishing the chartered rights of America, who had seen the principles which your Memorialists maintain, tested through the revolutionary war, convinced, it is believed, of their sincerity and the justice of their claim, exempted them from the obligation to bear arms, and from certain fines and penalties which had been imposed on their non-compliance with military requisitions. But the laws are changed. They now require that your Memorialists, notwithstanding the insuperable objection of their religious scruples, should be trained to arms. Their refusal subjects them to fines, which, within certain limitations, are fixed at the discretion of the courts martial, and become in numerous instances extremely oppressive. Nor is this all: Your Memorialists conceive that the voluntary payment of a fine imposed on them for adherence to their religious duty, or the receiving of surplus money arising from the sale of their property seized for the satisfying of these demands, would be to acknowledge a delinquency which they cannot admit, and to become parties in a traffic or commutation of their principles. Hence also considerable loss is sustained. And notwithstanding your Memorialists may acknowledge that many officers of the government, in these cases manifest great reluctance, and execute their trust with scrupulous regard to the sufferers; yet there are other instances, in which wanton depredations are made on the property of individuals.

Your Memorialists are aware that it may be said that the law does not discriminate between them and others, and that they ought equally to support the public burdens, and yield their services to the exigencies of the State. This objection supposes that a general law cannot have a partial or unequal operation. It supposes too that what may be deemed a national concern, may supercede the chartered rights and privileges of the people. But your Memoralists cannot suppose that these principles, which indeed are no other than maxims of tyranny, will ever be deliberately adopted or acted upon by this Legislature. If one member of the community believe it is his duty to fight and slay the enemies of his country, and if any believe that he is prohibited by divine command from planning the destruction or shedding the blood of his fellow creatures; the question as relates to the present subject is not which or whether either is wrong, but whether the law commanding *both* to take arms would not operate *unequally*, and violate the rights of conscience? It would operate unequally because it does not discriminate — because to the conscience of the one it would enjoin the performance of a duty; to that of the other the commission of a crime. It would violate the liberty of conscience, because it would compel under pains and penalties the performance of an act, which is believed offensive to the Divine Being. Human authority cannot, like the Great Searcher of hearts, try the spirits of men respecting truth and error; it cannot remit the penalties of sin, or control the convictions of the heart; and therefore in this country at least, the liberty of conscience is wisely placed beyond the sphere of legislation, and protected from the encroachment of any power in the government.

It may be recollected too, that in every nation of the civilized world where this society is found, they profess and maintain the same principles. That no hope of reward, no dread of punishment, nor confiscations, imprisonments, or death would induce them to bear arms against this country, or in any other cause whatever, and that every attempt to coerce them would result on the one side, in the triumph of principle, however severely tested, and in unavailing persecution on the other.

While it is therefore evident that the ostensible object of the law, or training them to arms cannot be effected, and it is presumed from the general notoriety of their principles, that it is not even expected to be attained — while your Memorialists believe that the principles they hold can in no sense prove injurious to the community, and are persuaded that this legislature would disclaim the idea of raising revenue by laws inflicting fines on the free exercise of concience — they trust that a privilege conferred by the Supreme Being, and by the highest authority in this country declared sacred and inviolable, may be safely expected from its justice and liberality. They therefore respectfully petition: that the laws imposing military requisitions and penalties for non-compliance, may be considered as they respect your petitioners, and such relief afforded as to the wisdom of the legislature shall seem just and necessary.

Signed by order and on behalf of a meeting of the representatives of the aforesaid society, held in Dinwiddie county, the 17th of the 11th month, 1810. By

BENJAMIN BATES,
Clerk at the time.

[*The following Letter was addressed by* BENJAMIN BATES, *(bearer of the foregoing Memorial) to a Member of the Legislature.*]

The friendly manner in which we discussed together the principles of our Memorial, (now before the Legislature) induces me to hope, that a few additional observations, will receive a candid and impartial consideration. . . .

Admitting that the liberty of conscience is both a natural and constitutional right, and that it is physically impossible to control the free agency of the mind, still it is contended, an expedient may be found which shall protect those rights from violation, and at the same time satisfy the law, which would otherwise infringe them.

Thus, if the legislature enjoin the performance of certain duties on which it is supposed the very existence of government depends, and those duties happen to interfere with the constitutional rights of any individual, let that individual pay an equivalent and be excused. If it be a military service for instance, and his religious principles forbid him to fight, let him pay a tax for the support of schools, and make the tax equal to the military service.— The argument fairly stated stands thus:—The legislature shall not restrain the free exercise of conscience, but they may *levy a fine upon the advantages derived from the exemption.*

Have I any objection to the support of schools? Far from it—I should rejoice to see knowledge and virtue diffused among the lower classes of society. I would cheerfully pay an equal tax for the purpose, and might be disposed to encourage it by a voluntary contribution. But *when I pay a partial tax—a fine*, I am neither discharging the common duties of a citizen, nor doing an act of benevolence; I am paying what is considered by the government as a debt; and for what consideration? plainly for being allowed the liberty of conscience. But I do not desire the liberty of conscience from the government; I hold it by a tenure antecedent to the institutions of civil society—it was secured to me in the social compact, and was never submitted to the legislature at all; they have therefore no privilege to grant or withhold at their pleasure, and certainly no pretence of right or *authority to sell it for a price.* It appears then, that this exclusive tax for the support of schools is a groundless and oppressive demand. It is a muster fine in disguise, and violates the very principle it seemed to respect. But is it not unreasonable, it is asked, that our fellow citizens who believe war to be allowable and necessary, should be subjected to the hardships and privations incident to the training and service, while we, under the protection of our religious privileges enjoy complete exemption?

We answer no. If those citizens do believe that war is necessary for their defence, if they conceive it to be their duty and their interest to fight—if it accords with their religious principles to repel aggressions by the sword—if in the full exercise of their privileges, they give to the government authority to command them in these services, this is their own act, and they cannot complain of the consequences.

But a man is not the judge of his neighbour's conscience, and if the powers they surrender for themselves, involve constitutional privileges, they are binding only on those who have consented to them. . . .

The power to whom we are indebted for all our enjoyments, and whose divine providence is their best protection, has not committed to us the right to destroy our fellow creatures, or to seek the redress of our wrongs by the shedding of human blood. But we know that he has communicated to man a principle capable of silencing war and violence. There is, my friend, in the religion taught by Jesus Christ, a power able to reconcile us to God and to one another. It can divest the heart that receives it of its propensities to wrongs and violence; and implant in their place the disposition to suffer wrongs and violence for its sake. Thousands of living witnesses bear testimony to this divine principle—thousands who would suffer any privation or punishment, rather than impede by their example its influence and increase. And ought it not to console the friend of his country, and of his species, to see its growth, and to be assured by indubitable evidence, that it is possible in its support, to return good for evil, to love even our very enemies, and for Man, in all situations, to be the friend of Man?

ꙮ 20 ꙮ

A Small-Sect Militia Objector

When I became 18 yrs of age, I was called in question by governmental laws to learn the warrior's art. But I refused and gave my reasons. Which was, "I profess to be a Christian. I can kill no one, even my enemy; and I don't wish to learn the trade." But giving my reasons did not prevent their continued call. And some threats were given out, but that altered not my views, nor caused me to comply with that which I *knew* to be wrong. From childhood I knew it to be wicked to kill human beings; I had been taught that by my parents. And after I became of suitable age to read, and understand what I read, I found that the New Testament Scriptures taught the same . . . While I was quite young and prompted by my quick irritable disposition, if I was . . . what I considered insulted, all that kept me in check was my Christian parents. I *knew* that, if I undertook to retaliate . . . I, at once, should be called to an account, and an acknowledgement demanded by them. And I should have to go and make a humble confession to the child I had quarreled with. There was no excuse for me to make. That the child

From "Diary of Jonathan Whipple (1794–1875)," 32, 33, 66–69, microfilm, Friends Historical Library of Swarthmore College. This MS appears to be a copy of Whipple's original manuscript.

commenced upon me. The demand of my parents to me was, or would be, "Jonathan, you are told not to quarrel. It matters not what the boy has done to you, you must never quarrel. Now, if you choose to go alone, and confess to the boy, very well; and if not, you must go with me."

* * *

Such was the training I had while young. And it had such an effect upon me, that, as irritable as my disposition was, I never had one quarrel with any person after I was 14 years old. I still had my disposition, but through teaching and experience, I had found a better way than to resort to violence — at an early age. After making a profession of religion, I took an interest in reading the Scriptures, both old and new testaments, and in reading them, I found that the new superceded the old, as Christ himself forbade that which was allowed, and even commanded under the Mosaic dispensation, in the first sermon he ever preached, which commences at the 5th Chap. of Matthew. In that sermon we find, killing, slavery, sueing at law, swearing, lying, stealing etc. all emphatically forbidden, and this was what I had been taught by my parents. They had taught that Christ was a peacemaker and had pronounced blessings upon peacemakers. Well, time passed on; I was well, healthy, and labored on in trying to do well, and be a Christian. . . . At [this] time they were enlisting soldiers to carry on the war with our mother country. . . . For two years previous, they had had my name enrolled in their training department. And now required me and others, whose views were similar to mine, to come before their officers and excuse ourselves for not doing military duty as the law "directs." But I and others, who were in my condition, had fathers who felt a great interest in the cause, accompanied us, and spoke in our behalf. The officers had made up their minds that they would bear our nonappearance to do military duty no longer, [and they] sent for us. The place appointed was some seven miles off. And the day happened to be very rainy. But we all attended to the call. For that we could do with a good conscience. After making our appearance before the authority, we found many there upon the same business — to make their excuses. Yet theirs were not the same [as] ours, for none of theirs were for "conscience sake." We waited and waited, hoping that they would get through, but one case after another came up, and finally we told them that, as we lived quite a distance, we should be glad if they would have the goodness to hear us, as soon as convenient. Said they, "We will hear you anon." And they gave us the opportunity next.

There were three of our fathers present. One of them arose and stated that "As all of these young men's excuses are the same, I shall include all under one head." And then [he] stated that our excuse was "That they all believed in the teachings of Jesus Christ, who came into the world the Prince of Peace. And as he has left his doctrine for his followers to order their lives and conversations by, and as he has emphatically forbidden his followers doing anything by way of retaliating by violence, to even enemies, and much more in being active in helping kill them, or in making any preparation by way of learning the art or trade, which was the trainer's business to do, therefore their only excuse is (in order that they may have a conscience void of offence before God and Jesus Christ) they have to wholly refuse to take any part in the man killing business. Let the consequence be whatever it may." They, the fathers, stated that, "if our sons have to endure suffering in consequence, it will be no more than we have to do." Then two of the fathers stated that, because they were not at liberty to do what "you require of our sons to do, we had to suffer the loss of property etc." After hearing our excuse, said the authority: "Friends, your excuse is quite different from any we have heard today. We will take it into consideration. You are dismissed for the present." We left for that time.

*   *   *

Not long after I saw a [near] neighbor—a Major who was not present to hear our excuse. And he told me what he had told the higher officers. "I advise you to let them Quakers[2] alone, you can do nothing with them, but make trouble for yourselves, and for them. They never will do *military* duty. They are friendly good people. Let them alone." The Major told me this. While this set of officers had command, we were let alone, we were struck off the Roll. After a while another set came up who knew us not. And they were full of authority and threats, and soon commenced telling what they were going to do. That there was no mistake, we should be made to do military duty, pay our fines, or be carried to jail and there stay until we were dead and rotten . . . And our names were all enrolled again. And I was warned, but I heeded it not. Soon after I was notified that I was fined. I gave no heed to that. Soon after I was notified that there was an execution out against me, and if I wanted to save expense I had better attend it.[3] But I paid no attention to that either. (This was after I had a family.) But the execution of the law seemed to be delayed. I at the time was at work where the son of the officer whose hands the execution was in and to be put in force by [also worked]. The son appeared very friendly in stating to me all the particulars, and then said, "Now Mr. Whipple, there will be no getting rid of this, short of doing military duty, paying your fine, or going to jail." And [he] then told what the Captain had told his father. I told the young man that I should never do military duty, or pay any fines; of course they could imprison me, or do what they would. But they could not make me do what I thought to be wrong, and wicked. As I and the young man continued to work at the same place and each went home every Saturday night, I to my family and he to his father's, he brought me news every week from his father, and of course told his father news from me. But the execution was never prosecuted. And I never had anything taken from me wrongfully during my sojourn here.

✺ 21 ✺

Pleas for Exemption of
Nonsectarian Militia Objectors

A. From the Massachusetts Peace Society, 1818

DIALOGUE

Telemachus. My object, Sir, in this visit, is to converse with you on the subject of the petitions that have been preferred to our Legislature [i.e., Massachusetts], in which individuals have requested an exemption from military duty, on the plea that their consciences forbid them to bear arms as soldiers. I have been not a little disgusted, that men, who do not even pretend to be Quakers, should prefer such petitions to disturb the public mind and to excite suspicions of the equity of our excellent laws. The petitioners have hitherto failed in their attempts, but they will probably renew their petitions unless something can be done to give a check to such fanaticism and impertinence.

   Mentor. I am happy in an opportunity to converse with you on the subject proposed. It is one of great importance; one which should be carefully examined and patiently discussed, aside from the influence of prejudice and party passions. I have a favorable opinion of the legislators of this state, and have no doubt of their disposition to allow their constituents those rights to which they are entitled by the Constitutions of our country. But on questions which have the whole weight of tradition and the opinion of a vast majority on one side, and on the other, little else than arguments which have seldom been impartially examined, we are not to expect an immediate decision in favour of a few individuals, however reasonable may be their request. In the case before us, whether the request be reasonable, or not, is certainly a question of magnitude, one in which the welfare of the state is deeply concerned. It ought therefore not to be dismissed with disdain, nor rashly decided.

   In regard to the justice of the petition, I do not see much force in the remark, that the petitioners do not even pretend to be Quakers. Had they been Quakers they would have had no occasion to petition, because the ex-

From *A Dialogue between Telemachus and Mentor on the Rights of Conscience and Military Requisitions* (Boston, 1818), 2–4, 8, 14–16. The Massachusetts Peace Society seems to have been responsible for the publication of this pamphlet.

emption for which they plead, is already granted to that denomination; and though I respect the Quakers, I am of the opinion that other Christians may have *consciences and rights* as well as they; and that the consciences and rights of other Christians should be equally respected by the Legislature, and by every individual of the community. Men may agree with the Quakers on some points, while they disagree on others. Whether the opinion in which the petitioners agree with the Friends be correct or erroneous is not the main question. It is an opinion which many good and peaceable citizens conscientiously entertain; and if the opinion were universal, neither you nor any intelligent man would think it necessary to devote much time for learning the *art of Manslaughter.*

T. That may be true. But the opinion is *not* universal. Hence it becomes necessary for every nation to be always prepared for war; and it seems reasonable that every citizen should share in such necessary expenses, by devoting a part of his time to learn the use of arms.

M. Of what advantage can it possibly be to the community, for a man to learn an art which his conscience forbids him to reduce to practice. If a man verily believes that God has required him to love his enemies, and in no case to indulge the spirit of revenge by rendering evil for evil, can it be any advantage to compel such a man to spend his time in learning to handle the weapons of death? Will he not be far more useful to the community, as well as to his family, in some other employment?

T. Well—let him pay his fine, then, and say no more about it.

M. Pay his *fine!* for what? Is a man to be punished as a *criminal* for being of such a benevolent and pacific character that he does not wish to learn the art of killing his brethren? I should think that a man of such a conscience and such a disposition ought at least to be *tolerated*; and that there would be more propriety in fining men for a war spirit, than for imitating him who was meek and forgiving. . . . You profess to be a friend to *liberty*; I would ask whether you mean to include *religious liberty?* . . .

T. Do you suppose that the exemption for which you plead, properly falls under the denomination of *religious liberty?*

M. Verily I do, in the most strict and proper sense of the terms. For it is a religious principle which is in question, as truly so as any possible sentiment which relates to the worship or service of Jehovah. . . .

T. What do you think the great Washington would have said of a law for exempting men from military services on account of their religious opinions?

M. I can tell you what M. Brissot [de Warville, the Girondin Leader] has stated of the opinions of General Washington respecting the Quakers. "He declared to me, says Brissot, that in the course of the war he had an ill opinion of this society; he knew little of them, as at that time there were but few of that sect in Virginia: and he had attributed to their political sentiments the effect of their religious opinions. He told me that having since known them better, he acquired an esteem for them; and that, considering the simplicity of their manner, the purity of their morals, their exemplary economy, and their attachment to the Constitution, he considered this society as one of the best supports of the new government, which requires moderation, and a total banishment of luxury."

T. It would seem from this account that Washington did not regard their pacific principles as endangering the government.

M. True; and perhaps on due reflection you will be of the same mind. It is not from the principles and spirit of peace, but from the principles and spirit of war that the greater danger is to be apprehended.

T. I have not much fondness for war; I am aware that its evils are great; and if it will not endanger our liberties, I am willing that every man should be exempted from military duty, who can honestly make the plea of conscience.

M. If a man should urge the plea of conscience in favor of liberty for burning his neighbor's house, or murdering his family, or promoting sedition, insurrection and havoc in society, there would be no reason for a law to tolerate such outrages; but if a man conscientiously desires to be exempted from every species of war, and from every requisition which in his opinion is inconsistent with following the Prince of Peace, I think he ought to be not only tolerated but respected. Such men will never blow the coals of strife, nor seek the overthrow of our government. They are not the materials to be wrought upon either by foreign or domestic incendiaries or demagogues who may wish to rise by creating a fire or a hurricane in our republic. Those who cordially adopt the principle, that "it is better to suffer wrong, than do wrong," are not the men by whom our government will be demolished, or the public tranquillity endangered. Those who may be disposed to despise, oppress or abuse such men, on account of their pacific principles, are themselves far more dangerous members of society, notwithstanding all their boasted patriotism and their readiness to fight for liberty. Their love of country, their love of liberty, or at least their consistency, may justly be suspected, while they are disposed to trample on the rights of conscience in the case of peaceable and inoffensive brethren.

T. I am aware that much of the spirit of war in any community endangers the liberty and the rights of individuals. But what would be our fate if a majority of our citizens should adopt the principles of the petitioners?

M. Our rulers would then learn to settle their controversies with other nations on the principles of peace, which would occasion a vast saving of property and blood. The more there are in any community of a peaceable character, the less is the danger both of war and insurrection; and the more there are of an opposite character, the greater is the danger, both to the community and to individuals. Instead, therefore, of oppressing and harassing men of peace, it should be the aim of rulers to encourage them, and to increase their number. How happy it would be for our race if they should all adopt and exemplify pacific principles! And shall a Christian Legislature discountenance principles, which if they should become universal, would fill the world with brotherly kindness, and exclude from the abodes of men the horrid crimes and ravages of war, violence and murder? This, I think, will never be done by such enlightened men as now compose the Legislature of Massachusetts.

B. From the New England Nonresistance Society, 1838

Report of a Committee

Appointed by the PEACE CONVENTION, to take into consideration the case of those citizens of this Commonwealth, who are conscientiously scrupulous of bearing arms, but who are required by the existing laws to do military duty.

The subject which has been entrusted to your committee, is one which they regard as of the deepest interest to all the friends of peace, as citizens and as Christians. As citizens, they feel that they do not stand upon the same platform of equal rights with the rest of their fellow-citizens; as Christians, they find themselves called upon by the law of the land to do that which they conscientiously believe to be morally wrong. They find themselves placed in a position where they are obliged to elect which of the two they will serve, God or man; and though they cannot for a moment hesitate which alternative to choose, they cannot but feel it a wrong and a hardship that they should be placed in so painful a predicament by the operation of human law. They feel themselves called upon, by every motive of prudence and of conscience, to do all that in them lies to extricate themselves from this unpleasant dilemma.

Before suggesting any measures or course of conduct proper to be pursued under these circumstances, let us briefly consider the situation in which the friends of peace are placed in this regard. The great principle which distinguishes those who have assumed the cross of this reform is, that it is a sin to take the life of man in personal or national defence—or, in other words, that the taking of the life of man, by man, under any circumstances, is a sin against God. Full of this faith, they regard the most famous fields of battle as but so many scenes of foul and unnatural murder. The very multitude of the victims and of the assassins, far from diminishing the horror of the deed, to their minds and hearts, does but make it the more harrowing and hideous. The false and delusive veil which conceals the grim and blood-

From *Report on the Injustice and Inequality of the Militia Law of Massachusetts, with Regard to the Rights of Conscience* (Boston, 1838), 3–12.

stained features of the war-demon from the gaze of his worshippers, has been torn aside for them, and to their eyes he stands revealed in all his native deformity. Their allegiance to the true God forbids them to bow down before this bloody idol and serve him. The religion to which they cling as their support in life and their solace in death, teaches them to love their enemies. To love them as well when they approach them with hostile purpose and mortal weapons, as when they sue for mercy and help, clad in the weeds of peace. They do not so read the teachings and the life of their Master, as to think that they can maim and destroy the image of God in their brother, and yet have their hearts overflowing with love and brotherly kindness towards him. They do not believe that they comply with the command of the great Lawgiver when they love those only who love them, and do good to those only from whom they can expect a return. They perceive no permission, either express or tacit, on the part of the Prince of Peace to his followers, to fight and destroy one another—in cases where they deem it expedient or necessary. They hold that his positive command forbids his disciples from using the sword in their defence. These being their views on the question of personal or national defence, they can regard every preparation for the destruction of human life in such defence, only as the deliberate preparation for the commission of a high crime against God and man. They hold that no just distinction can be made between the men who are marshalled in glittering lines, their death-dealing weapons glancing in the sun, and their hearts filled with the pride of glorious war and a thirst for blood, for the purpose of accomplishing themselves in the art of destroying the life of their brother, and the banditti who in their lurking places rehearse their trade of death. In their eyes, he that killeth his brother is a murderer, whether he wear the uniform of a field marshal or the sordid garb of a common stabber; and they hold that he that arms and disciplines himself for the business and with the deliberate purpose of man-killing, is already a murderer in his heart.

* * *

These are the opinions held by most of those who are commonly designated as peace men, briefly and perhaps strongly expressed. These opinions are their religious opinions. They are the conclusions which their reason deduces from the revealed will of God. The sacredness of human life, and physical non-resistance to evil, they believe to be laws of God; and they believe that it was to bring these laws to light that the Son of God came into the world. Now, these opinions which they entertain, may be right or wrong—the holding of these doctrines may be the indication of a high degree of Christian perfection, or it may be the sign of the most hopeless fanaticism—but still, such being their conscientious belief, it is no less a hardship and a wrong in our laws, in either case, to compel them to do that from which their souls revolt as from a most flagrant violation of God's laws. Liberty of conscience is but very imperfectly understood and secured, if men are to be required by human enactments to do that which they conscientiously believe to be a violation of a divine command. It is but of little moment to us that we are permitted by the laws of our country to enjoy and express without interruption, our peculiar speculative views of theology, if we are to be forbidden to apply our religious belief to the business of life. Our liberty to interpret the word of God for ourselves is of but little value to us, if we are not permitted to obey the divine commandments which we find there promulgated. The spirit of persecution is the same, whether the laws in which it is breathed forth compel us by penalties to hold our peace with regard to points of faith which we deem of vital importance, or oblige us to perform acts which we conscientiously believe to be a gross breach of the divine law.

But it may be said, the penalty is but a little one, and it is not worth the time and trouble which it would take to procure a repeal of the laws exacting it. To this it may be briefly answered, to a rightly judging mind, that no sum is small which is fixed as the alternative of a crime. He who regards the bearing of arms as a sinful act, cannot consider the sum which he pays as an equivalent for its performance, as a trifling one—especially as it goes to swell the treasury of the man-killing system. But the principle involved is one of the greatest importance to the whole religious world—and the duty of endeavoring to establish it is in no wise affected by the smallness or the magnitude of the penalty incurred by maintaining it. He who believes that it is contrary to natural right and christian liberty, for men to be compelled by human laws to do what they believe to be morally wrong or to be punished for refusing obedience, is recreant to his duty if he do not all that in him lies to procure the repeal of such laws. And his duty is made neither less nor more imperative by the magnitude of the penalty incurred—whether it be the sacrifice of life, or a farthing's fine.

Such being the importance which in the opinion of your committee attaches to this matter, they would recommend to the consideration of the Convention the following measures, as those which must sooner or later (probably very soon) bring about the change in existing laws which is desired.

In the first place, they would recommend an earnest and persevering application by petitions and memorials to the legislatures of our several States, setting forth the grievance under which they labor, and praying for relief. Your committee believe that many persons, who would not concur in the speculative opinions of such petitioners, but who are yet jealous of the rights of conscience, would join them in their petitions. Your committee believe that the legislatures of the several States would soon be brought to see the injustice of the present laws, and their inadequacy to accomplish the end they propose. The object of these laws is to compel every citizen to be in readiness to resist forcibly the foreign or domestic enemies of the country; but in the case of those who would apply for relief in this matter, they must be wholly inoperative, whether they remain in force or not, so long as they retain and abide by their pacific principles. The laws may remain in force, and their penalties may be indefinitely increased, but they can never inspire a martial spirit into the hearts which are full of love and good will to all mankind; and they can never array the men who have such hearts in their bosoms in deadly opposition to their brethren.

It will, no doubt, be alleged, that the exemption of those who are conscientiously scrupulous of bearing arms from military duty, would afford an opportunity to unprincipled and unscrupulous persons to evade a burden which annoys them, but who are molested by no conscientious scruples on the subject. To this it may be answered, that it is no reason for withholding a right from one class of the community which is entitled to it, because certain others, who are not, may by false pretences lay claim to it. Besides, it is not probable, that the profession of peace principles will be for some time to come so popular, that many worldly-minded persons will be willing to incur the odium of being of that sect every where spoken against, for the sake of saving a few dollars.

In our case, moreover, we approach our legislatures with this advantage, that the principle for which we contend has already been recognized by existing laws in most if not all the N.E. States. The Society of Friends have enjoyed an exemption from military duty for many years in England and in most of our own States. The grounds on which we rest our application for relief, are precisely those upon which the privilege enjoyed by the members of that society are based. It is not to be supposed that there was any thing in the peculiar doctrines or habits of that class of christians which entitled them to the especial favor of the lawmakers. The Society of Friends were exempted from military duty, from the feeling that it was a violation of natural right to compel men to perform what they conscientiously believed to be a sinful act. And it is difficult to conceive of any objection to the extension of the same immunity to christians of other denominations who are possessed of the same scruples, which would not apply with equal force to the exemption of the Friends. The legislature, too, of this State at least, recognized the principle for which we contend in another particular, by the extension of the privilege of affirmation, formerly confined to the Society of Friends, to all persons conscientiously scrupulous of taking oaths.

Your committee are therefore confident, that an earnest appeal to the feeling of natural justice and the common sense of the representatives of a christian people, seconded by numerously signed petitions in aid of such application, would be crowned with a successful issue.

In the second place, your committee would recommend to all the sincere friends of peace, firmly, though meekly, to refuse to comply with the requisitions of the military laws. He who believes that any countenance given to a military system, is a consent to the principles upon which all such systems rest, and to the consequences which are their unfailing concomitants, can hardly reconcile the least compliance with their requisitions, with a true sense of duty. All the elements of bloodshed, fraud, violence, rapine and contempt of the rights of others, all the base and brutal passions, the hatred, malice, revenge, all the irreligion, immorality and vice of which war is the unhallowed source, are wrapped up in the system which at set times fills our streets with mimic warriors, as truly as in any of the great military establishments of the old world. The spirit is there, though it be dormant. Whenever it is aroused, it will spread the devastation over God's moral and material world which has ever attended its awakening, and its deadly progress. He who is not against the system of which this is the spirit, of which these are the fruits, is for it. No man can serve two masters. If it be impossible for a man to serve God and mammon,—

> Mammon, the least erected spirit that fell
> From Heaven,—

still less can he obey the commands of the Prince of Peace—the Captain of our salvation, while he yields the faintest shadow of allegiance to the sanguinary, merciless moloch of war. The true lover of peace should regard the man-killing system, in all its shapes and modifications, as the accursed thing—"touch not, taste not, handle not," should be his amulet of protection from its baneful intoxications and deadly enchantments.

*　*　*

Some of the most consistent and honored of the friends of peace, are of opinion that they do not give their due testimony against the military system by simply refusing to obey its laws and paying the penalty of disobedience, but believe that their duty requires them to refuse to pay the penalty until it is exacted by process of law or satisfied by imprisonment. Such devotion to duty is worthy of the highest honor and reverence. While your committee believe that the strict claims of duty may be satisfied by refusing to obey the law and submitting to the penalty; they still are of opinion that the triumph of their great principles may yet require of the lovers of peace to take up the testimony to their faith in them, which has already been so nobly borne by some of their brethren. When this line of conduct is plainly indicated by duty, your committee feel assured that the friends of peace will not shrink from adopting it. The inconvenience or loss to which a steady adherence to his principles in such case may subject the consistent advocate of peace, will surely be endured with joy by one who believes that he is bearing a testimony to the truths he regards as the most important to the interest of the individual and the race, the force of which will be widely felt and the sincerity of which can scarcely be doubted. The example of his fidelity to truth, of his unflinching devotion to the right, of his unwavering obedience to the dictates of duty and conscience, would preach a more effectual lesson to all within the sphere of his influence, than could be embodied in a thousand homilies. Every reform which has gladdened the face of this breathing world, has called upon all those who have devoted themselves to its advancement for sacrifices of personal ease, comfort and quiet—upon many for the sacrifice of friendships, natural ties and worldly success—upon some for the testimony of their lives. Can we expect that this latest, and yet first of reforms, should be accomplished at a less expense? They who are unwilling to give this least proof of their attachment to the cause of peace on earth and good will towards men, may be assured that they want that armor of heavenly temper which will enable them to hold fast the faith that is in them in the conflict which will beset them during the progress and before the final triumph of this reform. A great and golden image, of a ruthless and bloody demon, has been set up in the midst of our land, and all the inhabitants thereof are called upon to bow down and worship it. While multitudes prostrate themselves with fond and willing adoration, before the glittering and specious idol, yet a small remnant is left which will never bend the knee to the false God. Let all such resolve to bear no part in his impious ceremonials nor to swell with their voice his unholy liturgy. Whatever may be the doom to which his worshippers may devote those who refuse to do him homage, let those who disown his godhead submit cheerfully to its penalties rather than stain their souls with guilt. With regard to this requisition of their earthly lawgivers, let them address them in the language of the three holy children of old. "We are not careful to answer you in this matter. If it be so, our God whom we serve is able to deliver us from the burning fiery furnace, and He will deliver us out of your hands. But if not, be it known unto you that we will not serve your God, nor worship the golden image you have set up."

All which is respectfully submitted.
EDMUND QUINCY,
For the Committee.

22

William Lloyd Garrison as a Militia Objector, 1829

I had been residing eight months in the State of Vermont—inhabiting the invigorating air of the Green Mountains, and accumulating new treasures for the storehouse of memory—at the close of which period I made a temporary visit to my friends in Boston. It was a few days before the annual [militia] inspection in May. Immediately I received a "warning", as it is called (and a very ominous warning it proved in the sequel), to appear on a particular day, and at a particular spot, "armed and equipped, as the law directs"—namely, with a murderous weapon in the shape of a gun, knapsack, cartridges, etc. etc. As there was nothing supernatural in this *admonition*, it excited no apprehensions; and as I was a stranger in the city, I did not add to the "pomp and circumstance" of the muster.

In a short time, I was waited upon by the clerk of the company (a saucy, smutty-faced son of Vulcan,[4] as well as an ambitious follower of Mars) for the payment of a fine of four dollars for non-appearance. In defence, I pleaded near-sightedness and non-residence, and consequently refused to meet the extortion. Then came a summons from the Municipal Court to appear and shew cause, etc.; for which I had to pay two dollars and seventeen cents, in addition to the original fine.

I am not professedly a Quaker, but I heartily, entirely and practically embrace the doctrine of non-resistance, and am conscientiously opposed to all military exhibitions. I now solemnly declare that I will never obey any order to bear arms, but rather cheerfully suffer imprisonment and persecution.

What is the design of militia musters? *To make men skilful murderers.* I cannot consent to become a pupil in this sanguinary school.

From *Genius of Universal Emancipation* (Baltimore), n.s., 4, no. 2 (September 16, 1829):14. From an article by Garrison entitled "A Noble Example"—a reference to the recent "total abolishment of the militia system" by the state legislature of Delaware.

❧ 23 ❧

Should "Pacific Exempts" Pay Militia Fines?

It is possible, that some will make the inquiry here, whether, taking as we do the ground of refusing to perform military duty, we ought to pay military fines? Certainly not, if the fines, as is generally the case, are exacted and are applied for military purposes. As far as principle is concerned, you might as well fight yourself, as pay others for fighting. But if the legislature, taking the constitutional course of exempting from military duty and all military taxation those, who are conscientiously opposed to war, should at the same time impose on the Pacific Exempts, in consideration of their exemption, a tax, which should be expended for roads, schools, the poor, civil officers, hospitals and the like, it might be a question, whether it would not be a duty to pay it. But every one should be well persuaded in his own mind; he must feel well satisfied, that such a payment is not made to contribute, in any way whatever, to the purposes of war. If he can be fully persuaded of this, we are not prepared to say, that there would not be a benefit in such a tax. It would probably tend to satisfy public feeling, and to hush complaints; it would be an evidence of our sincerity; and would discourage those, (for undoubtedly some such would be found,) who might for the sake of saving their time and money, hypocritically pretend conscientious scruples in regard to war. We do not, however, express ourselves on this point with entire confidence; but would merely take the liberty to suggest this view of the subject, as worthy of deliberate consideration.—Whether such a tax could be imposed, consistently with some of the principles of the state and national constitutions may, indeed, well be questioned. But that is an inquiry, which time and the examinations of men learned in the laws will ultimately determine. All we ask now is, that we may have nothing to do with war, either directly or indirectly; and we ask it on the ground of our *religion*. We do not ask it, because we wish to save our time and save our money, although this would be a reason of some weight, since we believe that time and money expended upon war are worse than thrown away; but because we conscientiously believe wars to be forbidden. We wish to show ourselves good citizens in every possible way; but we ask to be exempted from compulsory disobedience to that great Lawgiver, whose commands should always take the precedence of those of every earthly legislator. If our legislatures choose to increase our burdens in consequence of our religion, whether they can do it consistently with our principles of government or not, we shall consider it of but com-

From Thomas C. Upham, *The Manual of Peace* (New York, 1836), 167–69.

paratively little consequence, *provided our religious rights are not violated.* But this is the point of difficulty. If by paying any tax whatever, on the principle of commutation, (that is to say, on the principle of *purchasing* an exemption from military duty,) we find that we are promoting, even in the least degree, the cause of war, we cannot rightfully do it. And if we are forced to pay such a tax, then there is a violation of religious right. Going on Gospel principles, no military service is to be performed; no military fine is to be paid; nor is there to be a payment of any commutation tax, imposed for exemption from military services, so long as such payment is in any degree subservient to the purposes of war. But whether this is, or is not the case in any given instance, it is desirable, that each one should examine for himself, and, as we have already said, should be persuaded in his own mind.

༺ 24 ༻

Nonsectarian Militia
Objectors in Jail

A. "But do men ever go to prison rather than train?"

[In this dialogue William explains to Frank that it is not only unchristian to fight but it is also wrong to train to fight. The discussion goes on as follows:]

Frank. . . But I thought they could compel you to train, whether you wanted to or not.

William. That would be a difficult matter. How would they go to work to compel me to buy a gun and cartridge box tomorrow morning, and to go to the common, instead of going to my store as usual?

F. I thought they could prosecute you if you did not go.

W. Very well. Then according to your own account, I can choose which I please, either to train or to be prosecuted. I prefer the latter.

F. But they will put you in prison.

W. Very well. Still I have the choice of training or going to prison, just

From [Charles K. Whipple], *Dialogues between Frank and William, illustrating the Principles of Peace* (Boston, 1838), 41–43.

which I like best. This is not compulsion; and I had much rather go to prison than train.

F. Oh, William! Go to prison?

W. Certainly, Frank. And I hope *you* would go to prison, if necessary, rather than deliberately do something you knew to be wrong. I see you are shocked at the idea of a prison, because you think that none but bad men are put there. But men have sometimes been sent to prison for being good, and when that is the case, it is no shame, but rather an honor.

F. But do men ever go to prison rather than train?

W. Yes. A friend of mine was put in Leverett Street jail last year for that very reason. I went to see him there two or three times. He was confined in the prison about a week.

F. Was he not very dull and miserable?

W. On the contrary, he was remarkably cheerful. He carried his books and papers there, and occupied himself pleasantly in reading and writing. And above all, he carried with him a good conscience, which can make even a jail pleasant.

F. But is everybody put in jail that refuses to train?

W. No. Many people escape by paying a fine.

F. Why then should you not pay the fine?

W. I do not think it would be right. These fines are paid to the [militia] companies, and go to support the military system. I must not escape doing a wicked thing by paying other people to do it for me. . . .

[Then Frank inquires if it is not true that Quakers are granted exemption from militia duties. Yes, William replies, and goes on to explain that they had won this right only after having long and patiently borne persecution on account of their refusal to bear arms.]

F. But if you have the same scruples, why should not you be excused too?

W. There is no good reason why I and all who think thus should not have the same exemption.

B. From Boston's Leverett Street Jail, 1839 and 1840

Leverett St. Jail, Cell No. 21.
Boston, Sept. 4, 1839.

Brother Editors:

You see from whence I hail. My cell is in full view of the monument erected upon the site of the celebrated Bunker Hill insurrection. This is the third time

From *The Non-Resistant* (Boston) 1, no. 18 (September 21, 1839):[2,3]; 2, no. 5 (March 11, 1840):19.

I have felt, in a similar manner, the wrath of his grim majesty, the god of war, because I was not "ready, at what time ye hear the sound of the cornet, flute, harp, sackbut, psaltery, and dulcimer, and all kinds of music" to "fall down and worship the image" which he "has set up" in Massachusetts;—only the third time, I say, which his wrath has visited me in the form of imprisonment; notwithstanding for fifteen years I have refused at the "sound of all kinds of music" to worship his splendid military image, set up at so great an expense. I have found Christ to be altogether the best "Captain," and shall therefore adhere to his interests and kingdom "during the war." . . .

But, although there are many things farcical about this military business, yet the great point is a serious affair. Many whom I love as Christian brethren, and professed "ambassadors of peace," have overlooked the iniquity of the thing altogether, through a fallacious mode of reasoning. For instance, I was present at a religious meeting last Sabbath evening, where this subject was introduced, not by way of discussion, but as a matter of fact alluding to my own case, it having been determined that I should go to prison during the week. It was there said by a clergyman, who "is not slow" in matters of principle and duty, that to go to prison, rather than pay an equivalent in money for neglect of military training, was not required of a christian! and that for any one to do thus, (alluding to my case,) it would be "manufacturing a cross"!! and no virtue in "taking it up." I do not speak of this, because there was a personal allusion to me—I have no feelings on that point. The remarks came from one whom I love and esteem, and in so good nature that any one, more sensitive than myself, would not have complained. But I introduce it, in this connection, to give emphasis to the enquiry—"If these things are done in the green tree what shall be done in the dry?"

In support of the argument, that a christian should not "train," but avoid a "manufactured cross" by paying an equivalent in money, the speaker introduced the passage in Matt. 22: 16–21, relating to the lawfulness of paying tribute to Caesar. The labored point was, that tribute paid to Caesar went into the general treasury, and the Roman, being a military government, therefore this tribute money went to support war. The natural inference from this argument is, that Christ's disciples were authorized by their master to become Roman soldiers, or pay an equivalent in money. The same argument would apply to pagan worship with equal force. Paganism was as inseparable a part of the Roman government as war. Every christian martyr, from the reign of Nero to Diocletian, might have escaped, had this doctrine prevailed in the early christian church. . . .

But I will pursue this subject no farther at present. When I took up my pen, it was mainly to inform your readers, that I was happily situated here for six days, and add my testimony to the excellence of the doctrine of "non-resistance."

Yours in the *bonds* of universal PEACE,
DAVID CAMBELL.[5]

Military Duty

The question of what christian consistency requires of persons, conscientiously scrupulous of doing military duty, as to the payment of a military fine, has been discussed in the *Liberator*, by Charles Stearns[6] of Hartford and William L. Garrison. Mr. Stearns, believing it wrong to pay the fine as well as to do the service, was committed to jail, where he lay until released by some unknown friends. While in durance, he wrote to Mr. Garrison asking his views of duty in these circumstances, stating the reasons which induced him to refuse payment. The reply to his request took a different view of duty—placing a military fine on the same footing with any other enforced tribute, which might be innocently paid. Mr. Stearns was not satisfied with this position—conceiving that a distinction should be made between a tax and a penalty. . . . This is a nice question, and one that demands serious consideration. . . . We confess that we are undecided in our own mind on the point, and wish for light. It is of course a point of the practical application of our principles, which each must be left to settle for himself, but it is all-important that the truth should be ascertained, that we may all, if possible, bear a consistent testimony. The devotion to duty of our brother Charles Stearns, however, is worthy of our warmest love and respect. The testimony he has borne cannot fail of its effects on the world, and, at all events, must be of a blessed influence on his own soul. We trust that he will continue to set us all an example of fidelity to the commands of duty at all hazards, and at whatever cost.

E. Q.[7]

❧ 25 ❧

Dilemmas of Quaker Conscientious Objectors in Antebellum America

A. Militia Fines

War—Militia Fines

From a knowledge of the character of the present collector of militia fines in the city of Philadelphia, and the unusual efforts recently made to collect them, taken in connection with the very small number of cases sent up to our late quarterly meeting, I have been led to fear that our Christian testimony against war has not been maintained as it should have been. Perhaps there are not *many* (are there not *some?*) who deliberately pay the demand, and openly violate the testimony of the Society; yet it may reasonably be feared, that under our name are to be found individuals who *connive* at its payment by others, and secretly rejoice that they can thus avoid suffering, without putting the Christian principle of peace to open shame. Such are not only injuring themselves, but bringing reproach upon truth. "Have you no friend to pay it for you?" is the enquiry of the collector; "Friend so-and-so always *has his paid.*" "Mr. S——is a Friend, and he pays me his fine; so does Mr. T——; they never make a disturbance about it."

The secret payment of this fine in lieu of military service or training, or the connivance at its payment by others, is a direct encouragement of the onerous militia system. If Friends were faithful to maintain their testimony against war in all respects, even keeping in subjection a warlike spirit in relation to this very oppression, and no one through mistaken kindness being induced to pay the fine for them, in a very little time the system would be exploded. Were nothing to be gained but the incarceration of peaceable citizens in prison for conscience sake—no reward but the accusations of a troubled spirit—no honour but the plaudits of militia officers, and the averted looks of the considerate of all classes, it would require stout hands and unfeeling hearts long to support the system. Yes! let it be impressed upon the weak and complying among us, that they are supporting this oppressive system—that it is to *them*, mainly, that the militia system, as far as

From *The Friend* (Philadelphia) 8, no. 19 (February 14, 1835):151.

it regards Friends, is prolonged—that *they* are binding their fellow professors with this chain; and that if entire faithfulness was maintained on the part of *all* our members in refusing to pay these fines, or allowing others to do it, the spoiling of our goods and the imprisonment of our members for this precious cause—the cause of peace on earth—would soon be a narrative of times that are past.

Is not this a testimony worth suffering for? "Love your enemies, bless them that curse you, do good to them that hate you, and pray for them which despitefully use you and persecute you,"—especially when the consolatory reason is given, *"that ye may be the children of your Father which is in heaven!"*

One weakness begets another—the laying waste of one part of the enclosure of the Society, enfeebles and makes way for the prostration of another portion of the hedge. When called upon to pay militia fines, some of our members who have already departed from plainness of dress and address, are *ashamed*—yea, *ashamed*—to acknowledge the motive which should induce them to refuse compliance with these demands, from a consciousness *that they do not look like Quakers*, that if they are sheep, they are not in their clothing, and, through weakness begotten of this very cause, they fancy themselves compelled to act in accordance with their appearance.

It is very much to be desired that the testimony to the peaceable nature of Christ's kingdom on earth may not be lowered in our Society, at a time too when the views so long *peculiar* to Friends in this respect, are spreading with others; but that *all*, more especially those who can no longer be ranked among the youth, the middle aged, may be aroused to the importance of having clean hands in this respect. It is not a mere matter of business between you and the collector; you are not to solace yourselves with the belief that no harm will come of it; every fine paid in this manner goes to encourage and sustain the system, to weaken your own hands, to bind fetters upon your brethren, to lay waste the testimonies of the Society, and to prepare for yourselves moments of bitter reflection when the unflattering witness comes to commune with you in the cool of the day.

Many of the younger class of our Society, it is encouraging to believe, have a proper view of the unlawfulness of war for Christians, and are endeavouring to walk worthy in this respect of their vocation, and while these may be encouraged to continued faithfulness, it is desired that some who are a few years their seniors may profit by their example.

PACIFICUS.

B. Imprisonment of Four New York Quakers, Spring 1839

[My father, Nathan Swift,][8] was plowing out in our north field when a constable came to inform him he must go and train for military service or else go to jail. He knew he could not conscientiously do the former so he unhitched his horse leaving the plow in furrow and went home and hurriedly packed what few things he thought he would need while his mother put up some provisions and bedding. The constable proceeded to notify Cousin William Swift, Barclay Haviland and Humphrey Howland who all had similar scruples against training and in a short time he had them all loaded up and they started for Poughkeepsie, stopping at Eghmie's Hotel at Washington Hollow. The constable got old Daniel Emugh [sic] to come out and try to persuade them to pay a little money and he thought they would be let off. He said "He always thought the easiest way was the best and the payment of a little money would be easier for them, easier for the constable and better all around."

But they told him they would not feel it right to do that. Anymore than they felt it not right to train for military service. So the constable climbed in and they drove on to [the] old hotel at the end of Market Street where the constable left them for quite a while, giving them ample time to escape if they had been at all inclined, and on his return he said "Well, all here yet, eh! Well, if you won't train and won't pay a fine, I suppose I must take you to jail." So they all went over to the Poughkeepsie jail. Father and Cousin William were put in one cell and Barclay Haviland and Humphrey Howland in another. The provisions and bedding from home contributing much to their comfort. They were permitted to come out in the hall for exercise and general conversation during the day and so they got along very comfortably.

While they were confined, there was a terrific storm and a great freshet doing considerable damage throughout the county. Their sentence was for 21 days [and] soon after they were taken to prison. Uncle Beriah Swift went to Albany to intercede with Governor William Seward on their behalf, and Governor Seward signed a paper ordering their release. And Uncle Beriah brought that to the officers in Poughkeepsie and the boys all came home after only a week's confinement and Father found the plow in the furrow just as he left it for it had rained so they could not have done anything at home and everything turned out for the best and they bore their testimony.

From Alson Van Wagner, "Dutchess Quakers Maintain Their Testimony against Military Participation," *Dutchess County Historical Society Year Book* (Poughkeepsie, N.Y.), 70 (1985):50.

NOTES

Text

1. See Richard Wilson Renner, "Conscientious Objection and the Federal Government," *Military Affairs* 38, no. 4 (December 1974):142–45.
2. Lillian Schlissel in her anthology *Conscience in America: A Documentary History of Conscientious Objection in America, 1757–1967* (New York, 1968), p. 63, prints a short extract from this document. She gives 1813 as the date of its composition instead of the correct date, 1810, and thus mistakenly connects its composition with "Quaker . . . anxieties . . . about possible changes in the militia laws as the War of 1812 went on." But it is quite likely, of course, that wartime anxieties led to Friends' undertaking its first publication in 1813.
3. Schlissel, *Conscience in America*, pp. 60–62, prints a "Petition to My Fellow Countrymen" (1810) written—"for my rights and privileges"—by an eighty-three-year-old Rogerene, Alexander Rogers, in connection with his "under age" son. "It is against my conscience to send him into the train-band," writes the anguished father. "For which cause, I have sustained the loss of my only cow that gave milk for my family; through the hands of William Stewart, who came and took her from me and the same day sold her at the post."
4. Schlissel, *Conscience in America*, pp. 73–79, reprints (slightly abridged) the text of one of these documents, addressed in this case to the Legislature of New Hampshire: "A Memorial of the Society of People commonly called Shakers, containing a brief statement of the principles and reasons on which their objections and conscientious aversion to bearing arms, hiring substitute, or paying an equivalent in lieu thereof, are founded, 1818."
5. This document was drawn up by a committee at, and then accepted by, the peace convention held in Marlboro Chapel in Boston in September 1838. The convention also approved the establishment of the radical pacifist New England Non-Resistance Society. Edmund Quincy (1808–1877), who presided over the committee that framed the *Report*, became editor of the new society's journal, *The Non-Resistant*.
6. Rufus P. Stebbins, *Address on the Subject of Peace, Delivered at the Odeon, on Sabbath Evening, February 7, 1836, on the Anniversary of the Bowdoin Street Young Men's Peace Society* (Boston, 1836), 28, 32. We may note the establishment also of a Bowdoin Street Ladies' Peace Society to work alongside the Young Men's Peace Society.
7. Alson Van Wagner, "Dutchess Quakers Maintain Their Testimony against Military Participation," *Dutchess County Historical Society Year Book* (Poughkeepsie, N.Y.), 70 (1985):56, 57.

Documents

1. As it turned out, Congress at its next session exempted teachers and students in "all the institutions of learning in the District of Columbia" from militia duty in peacetime. Hallowell, who was then employed by Georgetown College, was thus spared further troubles over this issue. "I immediately obtained a copy of the laws of that session, when they were printed," writes Hallowell, "and the next year, upon the collector's presenting his bill of fifteen dollars [for failure to muster], I showed him

the law, which he had not before seen. After examining it carefully, he said it exempted all persons connected with our establishment in time of peace, and he seemed to be gratified with it. The change was greatly in my favor."

2. The major obviously confused the Rogerenes, to which sect Whipple belonged, with the more widely known Quakers—understandably, since the two groups had much in conmmon.

3. I.e., the militia muster.

4. I.e., a blacksmith.

5. David Cambell was publisher of the *Graham Journal of Health and Longevity*, a health reform organ. For a number of years he underwent an annual six-day prison term for refusing to attend the compulsory mustering of the militia.

6. Charles Stearns was then a clerk in the Anti-Slavery Depository at Hartford where he was imprisoned for refusing to muster. Later, in the 1850s, as a result of his experiences as a journalist in "bleeding Kansas," he abandoned his pacifism. In a letter he wrote in December 1855 to the *Anti-Slavery Standard*, he declared: "When I live with men made in God's image, I will never shoot them; but these pro-slavery Missourians are demons from the bottomless pit, and may be shot with impunity."

7. Edmund Quincy, editor of the *Non-Resistant* (see text, note 5).

8. From a manuscript, written in 1900, by Nathan Swift's daughter-in-law, Mary. For further information concerning the four young Friends then arrested and the response of their Quaker meeting to their incarceration, see Van Wagner, "Dutchess Quakers," 51–53. Also see pages 53–57 for a valuable survey of "The Militia System in New York State, 1823–1860."

BACKGROUND READING

Bowman, Rufus D. *The Church of the Brethren and War, 1708–1941*, 101–13. Elgin, Ill., 1944.

Brock, Peter. *Pioneers of the Peaceable Kingdom*, 217–72. Princeton, N.J., 1970.

———. *Radical Pacifists in Antebellum America*. Princeton, N.J., 1968.

Curti, Merle Eugene. *The American Peace Crusade, 1815–1860*. Durham, N.C., 1929.

Mabee, Carleton. *Black Freedom: The Nonviolent Abolitionists from 1830 through the Civil War*. New York, 1970.

Schlabach, Theron F. *Peace, Faith, Nation: Mennonites and Amish in Nineteenth-Century America*, 141–54. Scottdale, Penn., 1988.

Ziegler, Valarie H. *The Advocates of Peace in Antebellum America*. Bloomington, Ind., 1992.

VI

⬥⬥⬥⬥⬥⬥

C I V I L W A R A M E R I C A

Civil War America presented pacifists, especially in the North, with an agonizing dilemma, for many of them had been in the forefront of the antislavery movement. How could they refrain from support of the Unionist war effort without betraying their antislavery past? On the other hand, how could they participate in war without abandoning their pacific principles and belief in nonviolence? During the early months of the war many young Quakers in the Northern states volunteered for combatant service. The recent study by Jacquelyn S. Nelson of Quakers in wartime Indiana has shown that, even in a rural state, the number of Northern Quakers who became combatants must exceed previous estimates. Sometimes these men were disciplined by their meetings; more often disciplinary action on the part of the meeting was postponed until the war was over, thus making reconciliation easier, or it never occurred at all. A broadly similar situation can be seen among Northern Mennonites and Brethren, though defection from traditional pacifism was not so widespread as among the Quakers.

In the Confederate States members of the peace sects were known to be antislavery people and opposed to secession. This certainly caused difficulties with the authorities. Nevertheless, there were prominent Confederate officials who respected these sects' nonbelligerent stance and strove to obtain legislation granting them exemption from military service on terms they could accept honorably. However, eighteen months elapsed before a

Confederate law was passed allowing their draftees at least the option of paying a commutation fee in lieu of serving in the Confederate army. During the intervening months the only way out was to hire a substitute, an option frowned on by these churches and often beyond the means of their members, many of them poor farmers or rural craftsmen.

On the Unionist side, provision for conscientious objection was more generous. Lincoln himself and his secretary of war, Edwin M. Stanton, both showed understanding of the pacifist viewpoint and proved sympathetic, on the whole, to the peace sects' plan for exemption of their members from army service. At first, though, the conscription law, while it permitted exemption on payment of a commutation fee of $300, did not distinguish between those who refused to serve on grounds of conscience and those who were unwilling to serve for some other, less conscientious reason. The Quakers, in particular, found this situation extremely unsatisfactory, even though some Friends were now prepared to waive their Society's previous prohibition of paying a "fine" in exchange for exemption. Mennonites and Brethren were also unhappy, in particular since many of their people could ill afford the sum required. The situation improved somewhat in 1864 when the government permitted genuine objectors, if they did not wish to pay a commutation fee, to choose hospital work or "the care of freedmen" as an alternative to being drafted into the army. However, if after all they opted for the first alternative, they were now assured that the money would no longer be used for directly military purposes but be assigned instead to help "sick and wounded soldiers." Obviously none of these options could satisfy a Quaker draftee who was unwilling to abandon the traditional unconditionalist stance of his society.

The documents presented here on the experiences of the Civil War conscientious objector (CO) begin with an almost absent witness: that of the organized peace movement. As soon as fighting began, both the American Peace Society and the overwhelming majority of former adherents of the extinct New England Non-Resistance Society had rallied to the support of the Unionist war effort, though a few elderly stalwarts of the antebellum peace movement remained loyal to their pacifism in face of the challenge of an armed struggle that would end in bringing freedom to the enslaved. Garrison himself, despite his urging on the government to war to the finish, retained a personal pacifism (Document 27). Among the women who had played such a significant role in the activities of the New England Non-Resistance Society during the 1840s, few besides the unorthodox Quaker Lucretia Mott and the ex-Quaker Elizabeth Buffum Chace (Document 26) withheld their support for the prosecution of the war, however much they might regret what they considered a harsh necessity. We know of only one or two Garrisonian nonresistants of military age who became COs,[1] though the nonviolent anarchist Ezra H. Heywood, not liable to the draft himself, publicly opposed the war on pacifist grounds.[2]

War fever even carried away a few members of Adin Ballou's Hopedale Community. But the overwhelming majority of community members, including Ballou himself, continued in their rejection of all war—a reflection perhaps of the dominating role of the community's founder and virtual director, who had participated actively in the New England Non-Resistance Society from its inception. From the early 1850s Ballou had been extremely critical of the mounting belligerency of his fellow—and uncloistered—workers in the nonresistance movement, even if he fully shared their detestation of slavery and desire to see it disappear at the earliest possible moment. Other communitarians, like the Shakers, for instance, continued to espouse pacifism even after the outbreak of hostilities. But both Hopedale and the Shakers had become communities of the middle-aged rather than of the young as they had been at the beginning. Few of their male members, therefore, were called up for service in the Unionist army. The two CO documents printed here from this source (Documents 28 and 29) concern boys raised in their respective communities. Though clearly these boys did not resent gentle pressure to conform to the group mores, indeed even conformed with enthusiasm and complete sincerity, the community nevertheless seems to have played the decisive role. And it was undoubtedly the support of his community that gave eighteen-year-old Shaker Horace Taber the strength to endure his "conscript troubles." At the same time, one cannot help being struck, in reading the touchingly naive letters that young "Orris" wrote from his army camp captivity, by the already mature spirit of this New England farm boy. For all his naivety he was obviously a bright and observant fellow.

We know most about the experiences of the Quaker COs of the Civil War—whether from official records or from autobiographical materials left by the men themselves. Understandably it is to them that Edward Needles Wright devotes the greater part of his exemplary monograph *Conscientious Objectors in the Civil War* (1931). As we know, consensus no longer existed among Friends as to how their draft-age members should respond to call-up. But despite the warm feelings that existed among some leading Quakers for the Lincoln administration, the CO position remained the official doctrine of the Society of Friends. As Lincoln himself wrote to the "weighty" Quakeress Eliza P. Gurney: "Your people, the Friends, have had and are having a great trial. On principle and faith opposed to both war and oppression, they can only practically oppose oppression. In this hard hard dilemma some have chosen one horn and some the other."[3]

One of those young Friends, who chose the path of the unconditional objector to army service, was twenty-four-year-old Cyrus Guernsey Pringle (1838–1911),[4] a largely self-educated Vermont farmer[5] (Document 30). Drafted on July 13, 1863, Pringle refused to pay the $300 fine that without more ado would have allowed him to return to his farm and family; he also prevented his uncle from contributing the money on his behalf. "Kindness and cruelty," writes Henry Cadbury, was the fate of Pringle and his Quaker fellow conscripts during the months they spent as unwilling soldiers. "Pringle's experience might have been much more severe," Cadbury adds, pointing to the fate of Quaker and other COs in the Confederate army. Noteworthy, too, is Lincoln's role in the affair. For, Pringle testifies, "the President was moved to sympathy in my behalf" after being informed of the circumstances by an influential Quaker.[6] Yet another example, surely, of a satisfactory resolution of the tension between power and conscience.

The treatment of Quaker COs in the Confederate South was much more severe than in the territories under Unionist control. Take the case of the eighteen-year-old apprentice potter Tilghman Vestal, whose unwilling soldiering—as a private in the 14th Tennessee regiment—overlapped in time with Cyrus Pringle's army experiences (Document 31). Like Pringle, Vestal refused to opt out of service by paying commutation money. Unlike Pringle's, Vestal's situation was complicated by the fact that only one of his parents, his mother, was a member of the Society of Friends, so that despite his mother having reared him in the Quaker faith, he was not covered by the CO exemption in the Confederate draft law of October 11, 1862. This had accounted at the outset for his induction into the army; it was, however, the boy's stubborn adherence to Quaker principles in rejecting exemption through commutation that led to his retention in the ranks of the Confederate army and the almost continuous ill-treatment he suffered there.[7]

In Document 32 we discover a quite different mindset from that of men like Pringle and Vestal. Jesse Macy (1842–1919) was a birthright Quaker from Iowa.[8] Torn between the pacific principles of his ancestral faith and his desire to make a worthwhile contribution to the Unionist cause, he had hesitated to volunteer for the army as many of his peers were doing. His parents indeed would have paid his $300 commutation willingly and have got him back from college to work on the family farm. But Macy, on being drafted, decided to report for service so that he would be able to do something positive to help the oppressed. He felt he could do this now that the administration would allow draftees of Quaker and like persuasion to undertake hospital duty or work with freedmen. As we see from the narrative he wrote later detailing his army experiences, events turned out rather differently from the way he had expected they would. Thus he emerged at the end a saddened and frustrated man. "At the close of the war," he wrote, "I felt a lasting regret that my peculiar position in the army had been a source of annoyance to military officers whose work I regarded with sympathy and approval. . . . I felt that I had done practically nothing. . . . [I] had passed through the momentous period in a troubled state of mind, uncertain what was the path of duty."

In contrast to the divided mind of young Macy, we may place the striking witness of the middle-aged Friend Joshua Maule, no longer liable to the draft but anxious, as an active member of his Society, to avoid any kind of support for war, even if only indirect (Document 33). Therefore, we find Maule, after the outbreak of war, consistently deducting from his tax bill the precise sum he calculated the government would have assigned to the prosecution of the war. He then waited patiently for the authorities to make distraint on his property to recover the money they considered that he owed them. Maule refused to be discouraged by the fact that only a few of his coreligionists followed him in this challenge to the warmaking state. On the other side, local treasury officials treated him with at least politeness while obviously regarding him as an amiable—though otherwise harmless—eccentric.

Mennonites and Brethren were not troubled by the problems that worried a Quaker like Maule. For they believed it was their religious duty to pay the taxes demanded by the powers that be. What was then done with the money they handed over was entirely Caesar's business. The period between the Revolution and the Civil War had proved fairly uneventful insofar as Mennonite and Brethren nonresistance was concerned. Their young men paid their militia fines and continued to work on the family farm. The authorities gave little thought to the traditional antiwar stand of the German-speaking peace sects. They were good citizens whose work in opening up the continent they could scarcely fail to acknowledge. The opening of hostilities changed this situation, at any rate in the South where Mennonites and Brethren were settled, particularly in Virginia. In the North, however, there were fewer problems.

On both sides of the battle lines, nevertheless, both Mennonites and Brethren had to grapple with the problem of how to obtain exemption for those among their boys who were not strictly eligible for this because they had not yet been baptized into full membership of their church. There was at first only one way out: hiring a substitute to take the draftee's place in the army where the man would almost certainly be required to kill—and be killed himself if luck went against him. Here indeed was a dilemma not easily resolved, for the churches' teaching condemned unreservedly the hiring of a substitute to shed blood, as it were, vicariously (Document 34).

In the South, until the passing of a Confederate draft act that allowed specified peace sects to opt out of service in the army, young Mennonites and Brethren remained in a precarious situation. There was confusion among the congregations when, early on, the Virginia state militia was called out for service with the Confederate army, since now in wartime payment of a small fine, which in time of peace had excused their draftees from attending muster, no longer existed as a possible option. In these circumstances the young men mostly entered the army silently resolving to maintain their church's peace witness by never using their weapons to kill. Their stand was confirmed in the memorable words of Confederate general "Stonewall" Jackson: "There lives a people in the Valley of Virginia, that are not hard to bring to the army. While there they are obedient to their officers. Nor is it difficult to have them take aim, but it is impossible to get them to take correct aim. I, therefore, think it better to leave them at their homes that they may produce supplies for the army."[9] And this was in fact what usually happened. Meanwhile, however, some potential draftees had gone into hiding, emerging only after legal exemption had become possible again, while several groups attempted to escape to the North. They were intercepted and interned until, through the lobbying of their church leaders, the Confederate authorities agreed to release them (Document 35). Among the officials involved, Sidney S. Baxter, from the War Department, was gratefully remembered by Mennonites and Brethren for the courtesy and understanding he showed them in their plight.

In the final phase of the war a shortage of manpower led the Confederate Congress to pass a more stringent conscription law that contained no provision for conscientious objection. If hostilities had not soon come to an end, the peace sectaries living under Confederate rule might possibly have had to face renewed persecution for their beliefs.

Conscientious objection during the Civil War was not confined to the historic peace sects with a long tradition of abstention from bearing arms. For the two adventist sects, which emerged out of the debacle of the Millerite movement in the mid-1840s when the coming of the millennium foretold by its leader, William Miller, failed to materialize, the arrival of war had presented a new problem. In the case of the Second Adventists, centered in New England, much heart searching took place among those liable to the draft (Document 36). Some of them, at any rate, resolved to refuse induction and take the consequences.

The military question soon became an important issue also with the recently formed Seventh-day Adventist church, whose adherents celebrated a Saturday sabbath. Under the charismatic leadership of Mrs. Ellen Gould White (1827–1915) the sabbatarian Adventists, centered at Battle Creek (Michigan), expanded rapidly across the continent and long before Mrs. White's death into Europe and other parts of the world, too. At first there was no unanimity as to the appropriate response for the brethren to adopt toward the draft. Then in 1863 Mrs. White, though strongly antislavery as were almost all her coreligionists, came out unambiguously against participation in the army. "God's people," she wrote, "who are His peculiar treasure, cannot engage in this perplexing war, for it is opposed to every principle of their faith." To shed human blood—or to work on Saturdays—were activities equally taboo to the faithful. Alarmed in case the government failed to recognize it as a pacifist denomination entitled to CO status for its members, the church now proceeded to mobilize its forces to gain exemption for its draftees, in which endeavor they proved indeed successful.[10] At the end of the war, in May 1865, the church reaffirmed its noncombatant stand: "While we . . . cheerfully render to Caesar the things which the Scriptures show to be his, we are compelled to decline all participation in acts of war and bloodshed as being inconsistent with the duties enjoined upon us by our divine Master toward our enemies and toward all mankind."[11]

Finally, let us look briefly at the two restorationist sects: the Disciples of Christ, founded by immigrant theologian Alexander Campbell (1788–1866) in the antebellum era, and the Christadelphians, whose founder, the expatriate Englishman Dr. John Thomas (1805–1871), had originally been Campbell's disciple. Campbell's creedless Biblicist faith spread rapidly as a religion of the frontier. Though ambivalent in his attitude toward slavery, Campbell remained staunchly antiwar; his pacifism, however, was not shared by the majority of the Disciples. In the Civil War, while on each side the overwhelming majority of church members (by 1860 the Disciples numbered around 200,000) bore arms when drafted, pacifist pockets emerged in both North and South and individual Disciples, some of them in responsible positions in the church, branded the war as a "fratricidal" conflict. In Middle Tennessee the church leaders had espoused unconditional pacifism, and they urged their young men to refuse to bear arms if drafted, even though they were not at first covered in law by any CO exemption.[12] I have not been able to discover any Disciple COs in the North. But there may well have been a few who took this stand—to offset the Unionist general James A. Garfield, Disciple of Christ and future U.S. President. At any rate, the Disciple journalist Benjamin Franklin came very near to conscientious objection during the Confederate action against Cincinnati where he was then living (Document 37). Clearly he would have become a noncombatant soldier should the ballot have fallen upon him to serve. The last document (38) illustrates Dr. Thomas's efforts in 1864 to gain exemption from the Unionist draft for his followers. Though the sect had only emerged as a distinct body on the eve of the war, his efforts were crowned with success; the Christadelphians' right to conscientiously object to bearing arms was now recognized alongside that of the established peace sects.

⚜ 26 ⚜

A Garrisonian Mother and Her
Draft-Age Sons

It was a long time before it became natural for Mrs. Chace[1] to feel as an Abolitionist that it might be her duty to let her son enter the army. . . . [Indeed] being what she was as an individual, she could not think that her young boys had a right to decide for themselves, in opposition to her principles, and take that allegiance oath. This scruple, however, must have passed later, but her peace principles remained unabated in force. It was wrong to fight even "to make men free." She never in the least modified this opinion.

That is all there is to be said about it; she did not want her sons to act according to opinions which were not her own. Still, I believe, had the war lasted longer, she would have yielded to the more adult conviction and desire of her son Sam. Yet there was also in her opposition some maternal impotence for self-sacrifice, which I think might be pardoned in a woman who had followed five of her children to the grave, and who now, as a mother, was touched in her most easily quivering fibre. It was Sam who wanted to go to the war, and her feeling was peculiar for him, the first of all her ten babies who had survived infancy. She could hardly bear to let him go out of her sight. "I know why thee wants to go home," said her husband to her when they were together on a summer excursion. "Thee wants to be with Sammie." How could she let that boy go into peril? How could she believe that he could take care of himself away from her, and his brother Arnold? Above all, how could she let Sam do anything of which she, herself, did not morally approve?

He tried several times to gain her consent, but lacked just the characteristics which would have made him act without her permission. Perhaps, to some extent, both were justified in their attitude, she in her opposition, he both in his desire and in his passive obedience. He was only seventeen when the war began; only a few months over twenty-one when the Rebellion staggered into the abyss.

Once she said to him, "I think the time will come in which thee will be very glad thee did not go into the army."

From Lillie Buffum Chace Wyman and Arthur Crawford Wyman, *Elizabeth Buffum Chace, 1806–1899: Her Life and Its Environment* (Boston, 1914), 1:217, 219, 220, 241–43.

I suppose she meant that in time he would be glad because he would have accepted her forbidding peace ethic. The boy answered:

"No, I shall never be glad that I did not help to save the Union." . . .

William Lloyd Garrison to Mrs. Chace

Boston, Aug. 7, 1862. I find your letter desiring to know what I intend doing, in case any of my sons are drafted for the war.

I have three sons of the requisite age—George, William and Wendell. Wendell is in principle opposed to all fighting with carnal weapons. So is William. In any case, they will not go to the tented field but will abide the consequences. George is inclined to think he shall go, if drafted, as he does not claim to be a non-resistant.

Your sons have not reached their majority, and consequently are still under recognized parental care. Whether opposed in principle or not to all war, like my own sons, they are liable to be drafted and if they refuse to go when called, I presume neither pleas of conscience nor the claims of filial obedience will avail aught with 'the powers that be.' What the penalties of refusal will be, I do not know; but, no doubt, they can be made pretty severe in the matter of fine and imprisonment, unless substitutes are hired; and one conscientiously opposed to all war could not employ another to do what he could not do himself. . . .

I do not object to my children suffering any hardships, or running any risks, in the cause of liberty and the support of great principles, if duty requires it; but I wish them to know themselves, to act from the highest and noblest motives, and to be true to their conscientious convictions.

I trust you and your husband will be spared the pain and anguish of seeing either of your sons drafted; and I am inclined to think the liability of a draft, unless a still larger requisition be made by the government, is growing less and less probable. You must give them the best advice in your power, but conjure them to act as duty may seem to require.

Have your sons returned from the White Mountains?

Wife unites with me in kindest regards to yourself and husband.

❧ 27 ❧

William Lloyd Garrison and His Son's Exemption from Military Drill at School

TO FRANCIS GARDNER
Boston, Jan. 13, 1864.

Francis Gardner, Esq.

Dear Sir—

My son Frank informs me that, henceforth, the boys connected with the first and second classes in the Latin school are to be subjected to military drill at Boylston Hall, from time to time, as a part of their educational training.[2] I trust the drill is not to be an arbitrary enforcement; but, doubtless, it will meet with general acceptance, and, therefore, exceptional cases may the more readily be allowed. In relation to my son, I very respectfully request and earnestly desire that he may be excused from participating in the drill aforesaid; and this I do on the ground of conscientious scruples on my part, as well as in accordance with his own wishes.[3]

Yours, with high esteem,
Wm. Lloyd Garrison.

❧ 28 ❧

Conscript Dilemmas at the Hopedale Community

In the summer of 1863 one of our faithful and worthy members, J. Lowell Heywood, was drafted into the military service of the United (?) States

From Walter M. Merrill, ed., *The Letters of William Lloyd Garrison*, vol. 5, *Let the Oppressed Go Free, 1861–1867* (Cambridge, Mass., 1979), no. 72, pp. 184, 185. From the Garrison Papers, Boston Public Library.

From Adin Ballou, *History of the Hopedale Community, from Its Inception to Its Virtual Submergence in the Hopedale Parish*, ed. William S. Heywood (Lowell, Mass., 1897), 317–20.

under the Conscription Act of March 3 in the same year. This was a sore trial and a cause of much anxiety to himself and family, and scarcely less so to all the rest of us. That he could not enter the army and serve as a soldier there, was a foregone conclusion. The only question was whether he should pay the prescribed $300.00 commutation money, as the law allowed him to do, or submit to such military penalties as might be pronounced against him, however severe they might be. Public opinion among us was divided upon that question. A strong feeling prevailed that absolute consistency required that he should suffer a heroic personal martyrdom, and thus bear the most effective testimony to his religious principles; but it was also thought that the commutation money might be paid by himself and friends in good conscience and without blame, if it were done under protest, thus saving him from indefinite incarceration in fortress or prison, or from possible death, should military infatuation or madness, as might be the case, carry the matter to such an extreme. My personal sympathies for his family in their distress overruled my sterner convictions, and I gave my adhesion to the latter view, drawing up a paper in remonstrance for presentation at martial headquarters, which, at the time, I persuaded myself met the moral demands of the case. This course was finally approved by a majority of our members and carried into effect. As a further token of our position at that great crisis of our national history, and of our adherence to our standard of faith under perplexing circumstances, the document is herewith submitted:

To the Governmental Authorities of the United States and their Constituents: The undersigned, John Lowell Heywood of Hopedale, in the town of Milford, in the eighth Congressional District of Massachusetts, respectfully maketh solemn declaration, remonstrance and protest as follows, to wit:

That he has been enrolled, drafted and notified to report himself as a soldier of the United States, pursuant to an Act of Congress, approved March 3, 1863, commonly called the Conscription Law:

That he holds in utter abhorrence the Rebellion which the said law was designed to aid in suppressing, and would devotedly fight unto death against it if he could conscientiously resort to the use of deadly weapons in any case whatsoever:

That he has been for nearly nine years a member in good and regular standing of a Christian Community whose religious confession of faith and practice pledges its adherents never to kill, injure or harm any human being under any pretext, even their worst enemy:

That, in accordance with his highest convictions of duty and his sacred pledge, as a member of said Community, he has scrupulously and uniformly abstained from participating in the state and national governments under which he has lived—not only foregoing the franchises, preferments, emoluments and advantages of a constituent co-governing citizen but also the privilege of righting his wrongs by commencing suits at law and of calling on the government for personal protection against threatened violence, in order thereby not to make himself morally responsible for their constitutional dernier resorts to war, capital punishment and other kindred acts, and also in order to commend to mankind by a consistent example those divine principles which prepare the way for a higher order of society and government on the earth:

That, nevertheless, it is one of his cardinal Christian principles to respect existing human government, however imperfect, as a natural outgrowth and necessity of society for the time being, subordinate to the providential overruling of the supreme divine government, and therefore to be an orderly, submissive, peaceable, tribute-paying subject thereof; to be no detriment or hindrance to any good thereby subserved; to countenance no rebellion, sedition, riot or other disorderly demonstration against its authorities; to oppose its greatest abuses and wrongs only by truthful testimony and firm moral remonstrance; and in the last resort, when obliged for conscience sake to non-comply with its requirements, to submit meekly to whatever penalties it may impose:

That, with such principles, scruples, and views of duty, he cannot conscientiously comply with the demands of this Conscription Law, either by serving as a soldier or by procuring a substitute. Nor can he pay the prescribed three hundred dollars commutation money, which the law declaratively appropriates to the hiring of a substitute, except under explicit *remonstrance* and *protest* that the same is virtually taken from him by compulsion for a purpose and use to which he could never voluntarily contribute it and for which he holds himself in no wise morally responsible:

And he hereby solemnly *protests*, not only for himself but also in behalf of his Christian associates and all other orderly, peaceable, tax-paying, nonjuring subjects of the government, of whatever denomination or class, that their conscientious scruples against war and human life-taking ought in justice and honor to be respected by the legislators and administrators of a professedly Republican government; and that, aside from general taxation for the support thereof, no person of harmless and exemplary life, who is conscientiously opposed to war and deadly force between human beings, and especially no person who for conscience sake foregoes the franchises, preferments, privileges and advantages of a constituent citizen ought ever to be conscripted as a soldier either in person or property.

Now, therefore, I, the said John Lowell Heywood, do pay the three hundred dollars commutation money to the government of the United States under military constraint and in respectful submission to the powers that be, but earnestly protesting against the exaction as an infraction of my natural and indefeasible rights as a conscientious, peaceable subject. And for the final vindication of my cause, motives and intentions, I appeal to the moral sense of all just men, and above all to the inerrible judgment of the Supreme Father and Ruler of the universe.

Subscribed with my hand at Hopedale, Milford, Mass., this eighteenth
day of August, 1863.

John Lowell Heywood

*   *   *

Upon more deliberate and dispassionate examination of this whole matter,
I had serious misgivings as to the rightfulness of the course that was pursued. The Protest, though inherently just and good, was too weak to meet
the moral exigency of the case and produce salutary results.

❧ *29* ❧

Draft Experiences of a Conscripted Shaker

The Conscription, Arrest & Sufferings of
Horace S. Taber

In accordance to the Proclamation of Abraham Lincoln President of the
United States of America a draft was taken at Concord, Mass. for thirty two
men, as the quota of Shirley, Mass. on the 11th day of July 1863.

Among the 32 men so drafted were three members of the United Society in said Shirley viz. Lorenzo D. Prouty, a member of the Church Family,
Nathan C. Prouty, Horace S. Taber, both members of the North Family or
gathering order.

John Whiteley.   Lucretia M. Godfrey
Betsy F. Maynard
being Elders at the time stated.

On Sabbath July 26th Edgarton, the Enrolling Officer for the town of
Shirley, came to notify the Brethren, giving to each a printed notice, of
which the following is a copy:—

Form 39.
Provost Marshal's Office—
7th District State of Massachusetts
July 24th 1863.

From "Letters & Documents respecting the Conscription, Arrest & Suffering of Horace S.
Taber, a Member of the United Society, Shirley Mass: Compiled by John Whiteley 1863," folios
1–9, 23–29, 37–39, 44–46, 49–54, 62, 66–77. From the Shaker MSS, Series 6–B, vol. 50,
Western Reserve Historical Society Library, Cleveland, Ohio.

To

Horace S. Taber—   Shirley—

Sir—

You are hereby notified that you were, on the 11th day of July 1863, legally drafted in the service of the United States for the period of three years or more—in accordance with the provisions of the Act of Congress "for Enrolling & calling out the National Forces—and for other purposes"—Approved March 3d 1863. You will accordingly report,—on the 18th of Aug. 1863—at the place of rendezvous in Concord or be deemed a deserter—and be subjected to the penalty prescribed therefor by the rules & articles of war.—

Transportation will be furnished you on presenting this notification at the Depot in Shirley on the Fitchburg R.R. or at the station nearest your place of residence. . . .

*   *   *

Accordingly on the 18th of August the three Brethren drafted, accompanied by John Whiteley, went to Concord—feeling but little concern that all three would be honorably acquitted on account of physical disabillities, Shortly after their arrival the roll was called—and the drafted men placed in an anteroom. The selected men were called for, also the Enrolling Officer and a few others were admitted to the examination room. Among them John Whiteley the writer, who would here observe that there *seemed* to be a good share of friendship and candor in the proceeding. In fact, the only objections that I could have made at all was to the fact of the Enrolling Officers sitting close to the Chairman of the Board, continually whispering in his ear, & also to the repeated whisperings to the Examining Physician by said Chairman of the Board. This might all be construed to mean something unfair—*perhaps* it was all right. Be that as it may, the two Brothers Lorenzo & Nathan Prouty had no difficulty in obtaining exemption on account of a loss of their teeth. Not so, however, in the case of Br. Horace, who although he had but one eye to see with—and is at times a great sufferer from bronchitis & neuralgic pains—was accepted & held to serve.

. . . Three days furlough was granted him to find a substitute—pay three hundred dollars ($300.00) or report himself for duty.

This, of course, brought him into a deep labor, and tribulation of spirit. But after some consideration he concluded to maintain his faith, trusting in God for deliverance.

This determination on his part awakened a deep concern for him. Frequent & fervent supplications were made. Assurances of love and sympathy given, & thus matters went on.

He paid no attention to the expiration of his furlough, but continued about his usual duties on the farm until the 28th day of September.

The writer's being on a visit to New Lebanon arrived home on the evening of that day, & was told that Deputy Sheriff Howe of Groton had that day been & arrested Horace as a "Deserter". It was said that Howe expressed regret at having so painful a duty to perform—and conducted himself in the performance of it in accordance with the assertion. Horace, who was helping at the wash house at the time, went and changed his clothes and returned to the office where Elder Grove Blanchard, Jonas Nutting & others of the Brethren & Sisters were talking with Howe. . . . At this point a very affecting scene was presented: surely it would take a more able pen than mine to describe it.

Horace sung while standing on the Office steps, with eyes closed & with an unfaltering voice, while all around were weeping in sympathy, these words—

> Farewell each dear gospel friend
> Farewell in love which hath no end.
> With you I'm bound heavenward
> To the holy City of my God.

> On his arrival at Concord, or soon after Horace
> wrote the following:—
> Concord, Mass, September 24th 1863.

Elder John:—

As I have been requested to write, I will try to do the best I can. I am in the "Guard House"—in Concord, among those whom I do not know, and do not wish to know. They are a hard set, I assure you. Such swearing I never heard before. It does not seem much like home to me. I feel very sorrowful, & I hope & pray that I shall find relief, for I do want to come home to my gospel relations. I am all the time praying to Mother [i.e., Ann Lee, founder of Shakerism] to protect me from harm—and I hope you will all remember me in your prayers, for I am poor & needy & I wish to keep my faith pure & undefiled. I told them that I could not bear arms & had rather be shot than to do it, and I *will* be before I will bear arms. They said, they thought I should not be required to do so; but I have to wear the uniform. I hope I shall not have to long. I sent some of my clothes home by express, but wish I had not, for I need a jacket to keep me warm. I have only one pair of trousers.

I do not know whether I shall go to camp tomorrow or not. I hope I shall not, for I want to see some of you. O do pray for me, for it seems like hell here. O how I want to come home. I do not know as I can say anything more at present. Give my best love to all my gospel friends. Excuse all blunders for my mind is unsettled. Love, love, love to all. Yours truly.

> Horace S. Taber.

Next day he writes from Boston as follows:—

Boston, Mass. September 29th 1863.

Dear Elder John:—

I am now in prison, locked up in a cell—a place which I never was in before. It makes me think of dear Mother Ann. I often pray to her for protection & deliverance from this awful place. I do not know but I have done wrong in putting on this uniform, if so I am very sorry.

Howe told me that they forced it on to a Quaker Friend the other day, and I thought if I put it on it would not make me any less a Shaker at heart. Do you think so? if you do not it must be that I have been led by a wrong spirit. I do not mean to be anything else, God knows, & I hope you will not forsake me, for I need help & strength to bear my sorrows and afflictions. O, do not forget to pray for me in this trying hour. I often think of you, and my dear home. Yes, it is dearer to me than anything else.

I do not know how long I shall have to suffer in this way. I am willing to as long as it is God's will.

I was taken this morning from the Guard House, and chained by the wrist to another person, and followed by two guards to Concord Depot & brought here where I am waiting to be taken to Long Island, Boston Harbor; where you, or any one else can find me who wishes to. I assure you it seems hard to me to be confined so that I cannot go out without having to be guarded. You can write to me any time. Direct to the Island. Please give my love to all my gospel relations, for I love them all. Yes I do.

Farewell at present.

Horace S. Taber.

Temple, N.H. Oct. 2nd, 1863.

This is to certify that I resided in Shirley Village during six years previous to April last. That during that period, I was principal medical attendant of the Shaker families in that Village and during the time was well acquainted with Horace Taber—being often called to attend him for sickness, especially for neuralgic affection of heart & chest & for bronchitis, to which he was uniformly subject on any exposure to cold & fatigue. I do not consider him an able bodied man.

Nathaniel Kingsbury, M.D.

Shirley Village, Mass, Oct. 2nd 1863.

To all whom it may concern—this may certify, that the subscriber has the management of the Farm belonging to the North family of the United Society in Shirley, and that Horace S. Taber, now a conscript under the name of "Orris Taber"—at Long Island, Boston Harbour, has for some time been employed on the said farm with me. But by reason of ill health has *frequently* been unable to do work for two or three days at a time.

In witness thereof I do hereby affirm the above to be true and place my signature.

Nathan C. Prouty.
Shirley Village, Oct. 2nd 1863.[4]

Long Island, Boston Harbor.
October 2nd 1863.

Dear Elder William:—

I received your letter of the 1st by Elder John and was very thankful to hear from you and my gospel friends. It seemed like food from heaven, to cheer my hungry soul in this time of trial.

I have seen hard times since I was taken from home. I was put in the Guard House at Concord, where I remained over night & could not go out without a guard.

Next morning I was chained by the wrist to another person & we were sent to Boston, where I was put into a cell & kept until four o'clock, when I was taken under guard to the steam-boat—for Long Island. On arriving there I was again put in the Guard House, where I had nothing but a cold floor to sleep on and truly was cold enough; for the window lights were broken out. Here I laid & suffered, & many tears did flow. I prayed to God & to Mother for deliverance from this awful place. I cannot tell half what I suffered.

There was a number of men in there beside myself, and an awful rough set they were, cursing, & swearing all the time. Before being put in there I was searched by the Provost Marshal, my money and all that I had being taken from me. He asked me why I did not report. I told him my conscience would not allow me to bear arms, & that I could not do it. He then told me I might have my choice, to bear arms or be shot. I told him my choice was to be shot. I told some of the men I wished they would shoot me, & put an end to my sufferings. *But I am not shot.* I was set free from the Guard House on Thursday, & am now in a tent with three others. I saw General Devens, and he told me that he would not ask me to bear arms while I remained on the Island. He also told me I might be examined again.

Elder Grove, and Elder John were down to see me, and I tell you it seemed to me as if the angels had been sent for my deliverance. But they could not get me released at present, but I doubt not will do the best they can.

I long to return to my gospel relations, for they are nearer & dearer to me than my life. O, could I see you all once more, it would give me joy beyond expression. When I think of the good meetings I have had with you, & the love & blessing I have received, it brings tears to my eyes, & a longing to be with you again, & I hope & trust it will be so if I am faithful to bear this trial of my faith.

Be so kind as to remember me in your prayers that I may be released; for

I am needed at home to help poor Nathan. Please give my love to him when you see him. And I want you should have my love. Give freely to the Brethren and Sisters. Please write again—Farewell in Love.
W. H. Wetherbee.   H. S. Taber.
Direct to me, 13th Mass. Detachment L. Island B.H.

Long Island, Boston Harbour—Mass.
October 4th 1863.

Dear Elder John:—

I am yet alive, & striving to do well & keep my faith, though I feel severely tried some times. I have all the tribulation I feel able to bear. This is a good place to try a Christian's faith, I tell you; but I hope I shall have patience to bear all that is for me. And I still hope I may be permitted to see my Brethren & Sisters at Shirley before long. I am tired of being among such swearing and gambling creatures. I am not used to such doings, & it seems hard for me to be placed here among them. And I pray to God & to Mother, for I know they are able to deliver me from this awful place.

I hope you will pray for me that I may not be shipped off South, for if I go there I am afraid I never shall see my good home again. I do not want to lie in a distant land. Nay, my interest is with my Brethren & Sisters in good old Shirley, among whom I have labored & toiled, and I do hope I shall once more see them.

I have taken cold lying on the ground in the tent, & my lungs are very sore, but I hope to be well again.

Coffee & bread morning & night, beef & beans at noon, makes a new style of living for me.

It rained very hard yesterday morning. Thunder and lightning were pretty plenty.

The Portland Maine boat brought a large Company here, & they had to put up their tents in the rain. At night the Boston boat *"Bellingham"* brought another large Company from New Hampshire, and a rough set they are too. Today is very fine & pleasant. The sea breeze is very soft and mild.

We have a meeting this forenoon at 11 o'clock but very short. They do not pay much regard to the Sabbath here. The band have been playing for them to drill their Company. Pretty good music, but not so good as Mother's children make at home.

I suppose Nathan feels lonesome without me. Tell him I wish I could help him, for I had rather work with him night & day without rest, than to be here in this place of wickedness & misery. Poor Nathan, give my best love & thanks to him for his good will to me; tell him I shall never forget him.

Give William my love for his kindness to me; also to Sister Mary, & to all the rest of my gospel relations. I have been thinking of you, and wishing

I could be to meeting with you. I asked the good spirits to convey my love
to you.

I want to ask one question. Have you sent on to Head Quarters about
me yet?

Please excuse all blunders. I will write as often as I can. Shall be glad to
hear from you soon.

Yours truly,
Horace S. Taber

John Whiteley.

Long Island, Boston Harbour.
October 6th 1863.

Dear Elder William:

I have some chance to write, so I think it right to improve it. I hardly
know what to say. But this much I can say, I have a very bad cold on my
lungs, which makes them very sore & painful. I do not know but I shall die
here, if they keep me much longer. I feel very uneasy, it is a hard life to live.
So much for "Camp Life".

How often my mind is with you, & wishing I were with you in body, laboring & toiling with Mother's children. It would be a comfort to me, and
not a burden; for the afflictions would be lighter for me, than to be in this
wicked place. Yes, what joy it would be to me, to see your place and faces
once more, & to enjoy the love and union of my Brethren & Sisters.

I do not know as it is best to mourn too much, only try to do the best I
can.

I know I should feel sorry if any other Brother was confined here. I hope
it will never be the case.

They say there is going to be another draft; but I hope not. It is
awful, awful to think of. I do not know but I have tried to do my duty
thus far.

The officers are having a great time today. There are a great many
Boston folks here. They are having a picnic. Some of our men had to go &
split wood for them to cook with. But as we do not share with them, we do
not feel any too well about it. We have a band of music which makes the
time pass a little pleasanter; but I had rather hear Mother's children sing the
good songs of Zion. This would cheer my drooping spirit and give life and
vigor to the soul.

We are entirely surrounded by water, so we have a pleasant view of
other islands & forts and vessels passing in & out. So I have plenty to look
at, but cannot see good old Shirley.

Don't know but I have said enough this time. I thank you for the love
sent in Elder John's letter by the Brethren & Sisters. Please receive my love
& give my gospel relations a goodly store. Give my love to little Gideon &
tell him he must be good.

I would like to hear from you again soon.

Farewell in love.

W. H. Wetherbee.   H. S. Taber.

P.S. I had written the above when yours of yesterday arrived. I can get any letters sent me if directed as it was.

I am doing some work, such as bringing water, washing dishes for the Lieut. & Officers, cleaning the street &c. My work is not hard, for they are now kind to me. If I can, I will try to find out respecting the New Hampshire Brethren. I am told there has been one here from Maine.* Elder William, I do not want to go South. I had rather die in Shirley if it is God's will.

I will let you know when there is any thing new. Excuse all blunders for it is getting dark,

So farewell in love, H. S. T.

Long Island, Boston Harbour, Oct 9th 1863

Dear Elder John:—

I am yet alive, but not well, & never shall be unless I can get home. I was examined on the 9th** but did not get any satisfactory answer with regard to being exempt. He asked some questions about my health. I told him how it was with me &c. Then he asked me where I belonged, to what detatchment &c, by which I understood he would call on me again before long, when I expect I shall find out whether I am to have a discharge or not. I hope God will befriend me in this case; for I am tired of staying in this sinful place, away from my friends and house. Sometimes I fear I shall never reach home again, which brings me into deep tribulation of soul. To think of being banished from my gospel kindred forever seems more than I can endure. Then something seems to cheer me up, & I still continue to hope for the best.

When I was in the Guard House I was told by some that they would take me away in the first boat. This made me feel bad, I tell you. So I prayed to God to protect me & not suffer them to take me any further from home. So when the time came for the boat to go the greater part of them were taken & poor Horace left behind.

Then if I did not feel thankful to God, I do not tell the truth. I felt sure my prayers were answered.

We have got a Lieutenant in command and he seems to be a very pleasant man. I have to take care of his tent & keep things all right.

I have found one person here I used to know in Shirley; it is Mark Powers. I am glad there is some one I can talk with. I am told there are two

*This must have been a Quaker Friend. J.W.

**By the surgeon on the island, not by the full Board. John.

Shakers here, or those who have made pretentions of being Shakers. It cannot be they are true Shakers. I have not seen them yet, & don't suppose I shall.

The Maine steamer brought 154 men this morning. They are putting up their tents close to us. They have to keep a guard stationed around them all the time.

One man ran the guard this morning & the guard threw his gun at him, but it missed the man. It is no use trying to run away here. There were two men shot for desertion in Fort Warren I am told.

I have got my money returned that was taken from me when I went to the Guard House. Be so kind as to receive my best love, & give freely to all the rest.

Do pray for me.

         Yours truly
         Horace S. Taber.

Elder John Whiteley.

         Long Island, B.H. Oct. 11th 1863.

Dear Elder William:—

I received yours of the 9th very gladly. My health is some better than it was. I am on the sick list yet & go to the doctor's every day, & get something for my lungs, which are very sore, but by being careful I think I shall yet recover.

I am thankful to Brother Alpheus for writing to me, & for the love & good will sent by him & Brother Calvin. It does my soul good to hear from my gospel relations. Yes, it gives me strength to endure the crosses & trials which I have to meet. I find this a very trying place; but if I am faithful to bear them well, I believe they will do me good.

There is a man named [John Wesley] Pratt who came here last night— and does not believe it right to fight, or to bear arms. He says he cannot do it. He says the officers put the uniform on him. They also placed a pen in his hand, & moved it along so to compel him to receipt for it.

He comes from Quincy, and was taken as a deserter the same as I was. He does not profess to be a Quaker Friend, but a believer in Christ's teachings. I bid him God speed in the right.

. . . I hear the Quaker Friends who were sent South would not bear arms, so they were sent to Washington to be court marshaled [sic].

The 13th Detachment is not expected to go this time, as there is not a full company of us. This is as I am told, though I do not believe the statement myself, for I feel sure they will.

I have been examined by another surgeon & feel sure of getting a discharge, although he did not say so. They say they keep very still about giving discharges till the papers are signed & approved in New York.

When I went to the doctor's this morning he asked me if I cooked. I then told him what I did. He then said, "You do not want to do duty." The other surgeon answered, "He is not fit to do duty." When he said that, it gave me assurance that I should be let off. This is the best answer I can give you at present.

I believe I have received all the letters sent me by you or Elder John. Will you ask Elder John to send me some more postage stamps for I cannot get them here. Be so kind as to sing for me, in your next meeting.

> O sweet Home, O sweet Home!
> How dear to my heart is my sweet Home.

I want my best, heartfelt love given to all in your family, & also my thanks for their kindness to me while here. I also thank good Br. Daniel for his love. My prayer is that I may so conduct myself that I may always have his love, & that of other good spirits.

Excuse all blunders, for I have written in haste.

So kindly farewell.   Horace S. Taber.

Long Island, B.H. Oct. 25th 1863.

Dear Elder John:—

I received yours of the 11th which was very interesting to me, I can assure you. Separated as I seem to be from my kind gospel relations & left to suffer in a cold world alone, though I do not know but there are others in the same condition, it would seem better to have some company of the same class with me in this trying hour.

It seems to me sometimes as though I had seen my gospel kindred for the last time in this world. And if I knew it were so, it would break my heart, for you cannot tell how much love I feel for you, & a longing to be with you, enjoying the peace and comfort that is within your borders.

It seems as though I was forsaken by all the good spirits & holy angels & every thing that is good. But I do not know but it is all right. I cannot find that which feeds my soul here, among this kind of people, & thus I have to suffer.

I often think of my good home, & wish, and wish again that I could be there with you taking comfort, for I do not like to be sent off South among strangers, for I do not know what will become of me, & it seems hard to think of it. I keep praying to God that it may not be so.

We have a man here [i.e., Pratt], who refuses to drill on account of his faith of the wickedness of war, so they have set him to digging a hole, & then he has to fill it up again. I told some here, before I would drill or take up arms I would dig too.

I have received yours & Eldress Lucretia's letter the day after you wrote them.

My health is not very good, I have not had a final examination yet, & do not know when I shall. It seems as though there was some underhanded game about it. I fear the surgeon on the Island is waiting for me to get well, & will then ship me off South. The folks here say he does not show much mercy. I do not know but I am wrong to think so. It is a hard life for me to live—no warm bed to sleep on—I sleep cold which is one reason why I do not get better, & it will surely take my life if I am not released.

Elder John, I need what I have not got & cannot get here, viz. a pair of good strong boots. If I do not go South I shall need them, for mine are thin. It is said we shall go South on the 20th perhaps before.

Do come & see me if you can, I want you to very much. I thank you for the good store of love you sent, it seems good. Do remember me in your prayers that I may be delivered from this sinful place.

I want to give my love to all my gospel friends and a good share to you. So kindly farewell.

H. S. Taber.

Elder John Whiteley.

Long Island B.H.
October 11th [sic] 1863.

Dear Elder John:—

I have had my *final* examination by Surgeon General Dale & the rest of the Board, and am to be discharged as soon as my papers can be got about, which may be in about a week. Then I shall return home to enjoy the comforts of the gospel.

There is another one in the same company who is to be discharged, & he feels very happy.

I went to the doctor to get something for my cold, and he told the sergeant to excuse me from duty entirely while I remained here.

I am now kindly treated by all, & for all this I thank kind heaven & all the good spirits who have watched over me. I do not know whether I shall need to send for my clothes or not, but will let you know before long if I do. Give my love to all my gospel relations when you have a chance to do so. Farewell in love

H. S. Taber.

Long Island, B.H. Oct. 24th 1863.

Dear Elder John:—

I received yours of the 21st & was glad to hear from you, & the rest of my gospel kindred.

My health is quite good at present, & I hope it will continue so as long as I remain here. I shall be happy when the time comes to bid this place a *long & lasting farewell*, for I am not contented to stay here much longer.

You say Elder Grove is coming down to me. I shall be very glad to see so good a man, & I wish I could come home with him; but I suppose it is of no use to wish.

There have been two more Companies brought from New Hampshire:— Yea, three. In fact, one landed this A.M. but I have seen no Shakers yet. . . .

One of our men forged a pass, & got off last night, & if they catch him, he will have to take what they have in store for him. When the roll was called this A.M., some one answered for him, & the sergeant says if he could find out who it was, he would have to suffer for it. It was not me, I assure you. I would not offend so kind a man as our sergeant is, or any one else let them be good or bad.

My box is in the Express Office & I shall get it this forenoon after it has been inspected. They are & have to be very strict on account of liquor.

I want you to give my love & thanks to all those who joined in sending the present, at the Church and at the North [Family]. I shall never forget the kindness that has been extended to me by my gospel relations while I have been here. I will strive to be more faithful, more thankful & more willing to suffer for Christ's sake. Give my love to Elder William. Tell him I will write him before long.

Friend Pratt wants I should tell you that he dug some new ideas out of that hole, he sends his best respects to you &c.

They are going to leave for the South next Tuesday—at least, so I am told. But what they will do with me is more than I can tell. It is getting [near] time for "Roll Call," so I shall have to stop. Give my kind love to John Henry, Nathan, William & all the rest Church & all, as well as yourself. Please sing, "From this vain world of sorrow I long to be free" &c.

Farewell in love.   H. S. Taber.

Long Island. B.H. October 25th 1863.

Dear Elder William:—

Though separated from you in body, I am with you in spirit, & thinking of the good meeting you are about to have, wishing I could be there too, to enjoy the love & union of my gospel kindred, sharing your griefs & sorrows, & your joys, though I have them here; but they are not like those of my gospel relations.

I know I am needed at home to share the burden of everyday life. I hope & trust it will not be long before I shall see my happy home. It may be a month or more, for great bodies move slow. It is a week since my papers left this place, & I have fears of being sent South, for "Uncle Sam" does strange things. I shall not feel safe until the boat is gone, which will be next Tuesday the 27th. Yet I must trust in God; for His arm is able to save.

I have received the box that was sent me, & all was safe. It seems like home to have such nice things. I have given some to my friends here; they were very thankful & liked them very much. Please give my love & thanks to those who sent me these nice things, or have had a hand in doing it, & I assure you, I shall not forget it. My love to Lorings for the box of nuts. I hope I shall see Elder Grove this week. I do not care how often I see good Believers. I should like to have you come down & see me if you can. I think it would do you good to get the sea breeze.

The man, who forged a pass, got to Boston, but was taken & brought back, & put in the Guard House. It will go hard with him I am thinking.

I have seen no Shaker conscripts yet. There was a Company came from N.H. last night, but I have seen none of our people among them. Perhaps they will be sent alone. I have a Quaker Friend who comes to see me when he has time. I like him very much. He is very friendly and kind. If they send him South, as I expect they will, he will have a hard time till they prove him, then he may be set free.

One man here stole a watch, & for doing so is to wear a ball & chain six months. The chain is six feet in length & is locked around his ankle. The ball weighs 32 pounds. Rather hard punishment I think. If there is any thing you wish to know that I have not written about, please inform me when you write again. Be so kind as to accept my love & thanks for your kindness, & give freely to all the rest of the family.—Yours truly—Horace.

Long Island, B.H. 27th October 1863.

Dear Elder John:—

The "Forest City" is here today to take a load of soldiers out South; and they have moved me up to the Invalid Camp on the hill, south of the Hotel. I expect there will be another load go today, and I don't know but they will take me off too, for they have taken some from here who have been discharged—or rather who were waiting for a discharge as I am. I do not know what it means. I cannot see what good it is going to do, to send me South because my papers do not come along. I am sure I do not want to go. I wish you would find out what it means. I do not like the place I am in. It is very cold, & I suffer very much. Last night I did not sleep more than two hours. I want to come home where it is more comfortable; where I can get round the stove & enjoy the society of my Brethren & Sisters; for it is very hard to be separated from them. It is more than I can bear, I do believe. O, I pray God to protect me, & to deliver me from this cruel war. I am not contented to be here. Is there no way out of this? Am I to be left alone in this trying hour? Am I passing through this scene of sufferings for nothing? It cannot be; for I believe some good will come out of it; if it is nothing more than to humble my proud haughty nature, it will do some good. But I hope & pray I shall see good old Shirley once more & if this favor is granted me, I will promise to be more faithful, more thankful than I ever was before,— more willing to bear the cross and set a good example before all.

I do not think of much more to say at present. But I should like to have you find out what I spoke of in the beginning of this letter, and please give my love to all my gospel relations, & keep a good store for yourself.—Yours truly—
Horace S. Taber.

On receipt of the above, Eldress Lucretia being at the Church visiting the Elders, I walked up there & we talked the matter over together with them. And finally concluded . . . that I had better go down next day & try once more what could be done.

Accordingly, Thursday 29th October, I take the first train & by being expeditious reach the wharf in season for the first boat for the Island. I go directly to the General's Office, find him absent; call on the acting Assistant, Adjutant General Hill . . . ask him if he can inform me respecting Horace's affairs . . .

[After a little] he . . . said—"Yes Sir, he can be released on giving his parole [of honor to appear when called upon]." "Well then, cannot he give his parole *now* as well as any time, and so go home with me on this boat," I said after enquiring if that was all that could be done at this time & having been told that it was.

He answered that it could be done now, as well as any time, but he could not administer the parole. I asked him, who could? He said he thought Capt. Goodhue could do it. And where is Capt. Goodhue? I enquired. Possibly at the boat, he answered. Well, then, will you be kind enough to call Horace & have him ready while I find the Captain. He said he would.

So I stepped into the Hall where I noticed a number of officers standing—asked for Capt. Goodhue of one, who pointed me to another close by, & said that is him. I accosted the captain and told him the conversation I had had with the Adjutant General. He stepped into the Office and . . . then ordered the Clerk to make out a furlough to the following effect:

Head Quarters Draft Rendezvous
Long Island, Boston Harbour, Mass.
Horace Taber has leave of absence for (30) thirty days.

. . . After this was attended to the Captain said Horace might leave his overcoat, or return it after he had got home, which, as it was rather chilly, Horace prefered to do the latter. The Captain went down to the boat with us, & conversed quite pleasantly. Horace then thought of a few things he was leaving behind, & the Captain told him to hurry back & get them. He did so, & almost as soon as he returned, the boat started for the city. We arrived there between 1 & 2 P.M. After dinner went to Charlestown & left for home, by the 4 o'clock P.M. train.

On arriving at Shirley Village we were met by Elder William & others and made what haste we could to get home, where we were warmly welcomed.

After seeing the folks at home, some of the Brethren walked up to the Church Office, where met quite a gathering of Brethren & Sisters, who all were delighted at Horace's return.

The evening was spent in asking & answering questions, & various expressions of sympathy, love & kind feelings. Among the rest the following little welcome was sung:—

Welcome home, dear gospel friend,
Joyfully we greet you.
Your Conscript troubles at an end,
How we rejoice to meet you.
We've prayed for you each night & day,
That you might be protected
And left to walk with us the way
That Mother has directed.

The week following the writer having occasion to go to the city in company of two Sisters, we took Horace's soldier overcoat & put it on board the steamer Bellingham, directed as we were ordered to by Capt. Goodhue. This was by the first boat on the 5th of November.

✼ 30 ✼

The Civil War Diary of a Quaker Conscript

At Burlington, Vermont, on the 13th of the seventh month, 1863, I was drafted. Pleasant are my recollections of the 14th. Much of that rainy day I spent in my chamber, as yet unaware of my fate, in writing and reading and in reflection to compose my mind for any event. The day and the exercise, by the blessing of the Father, brought me precious reconciliation to the will of Providence.

With ardent zeal for our Faith and the cause of our peaceable principles, and almost disgusted at the lukewarmness and unfaithfulness of very many who profess these, and considering how heavily slight crosses bore upon their shoulders, I felt to say, "Here am I, Father, for thy service. As thou will." May I trust it was He who called me and sent me forth with the consolation: "My grace is sufficient for thee." Deeply have I felt many times since that I am nothing without the companionship of the Spirit.

I was to report on the 27th. Then, loyal to our country, Wm. Lindley Dean[5] and I appeared before the Provost Marshal with a statement of our cases. We were ordered for a hearing on the 29th. On the afternoon of that

From *The Civil War Diary of Cyrus Pringle* (Pendle Hill Pamphlet 122) (Wallingford, Penn., 1962), 7–39.

day W. L. D. was rejected upon examination of the Surgeon, but my case not coming up, he remained with me, much to my strength and comfort. Sweet was his converse and long to be remembered, as we lay together that warm summer night on the straw of the barracks. By his encouragement much was my mind strengthened; my desires for a pure life, and my resolutions for good. In him and those of whom he spoke I saw the abstract beauty of Quakerism. On the next morning came Joshua M. Dean to support me and plead my case before the Board of Enrollment. On the day after, the 31st, I came before the Board. Respectfully those men listened to the exposition of our principles; and, on our representing that we looked for some relief from the President, the marshal released me for twenty days. Meanwhile appeared Lindley M. Macomber[6] and was likewise, by the kindness of the marshal, though they had received instructions from the Provost Marshal General to show such claims no partiality, released to appear on the 20th day of the eighth month.

All these days we were urged by our acquaintances to pay our commutation money; by some through well-meant kindness and sympathy; by others through interest in the war; and by others still through a belief they entertained it was our duty. But we confess a higher duty than that to country; and, asking no military protection of our Government and grateful for none, deny any obligation to support so unlawful a system, as we hold a war to be even when waged in opposition to an evil and oppressive power and ostensibly in defense of liberty, virtue, and free institutions; and, though touched by the kind interest of friends, we could not relieve their distress by a means we held even more sinful than that of serving ourselves, as by supplying money to hire a substitute we would not only be responsible for the result, but be the agents in bringing others into evil. So looking to our Father alone for help, and remembering that "Whoso loseth his life for my sake shall find it; but whoso saveth it shall lose it," we presented ourselves again before the Board, as we had promised to do when released. Being offered four days more of time, we accepted it as affording opportunity to visit our friends, and moreover as there would be more probability of meeting Peter Dakin[7] at Rutland.

Sweet was the comfort and sympathy of our friends as we visited them. There was a deep comfort, as we left them, in the thought that so many pure and pious people follow us with their love and prayers. Appearing finally before the marshal on the 24th, suits and uniforms were selected for us, and we were called upon to give receipts for them. L. M. M. was on his guard, and, being first called upon, declared he could not do so, as that would imply acceptance. Failing to come to any agreement, the matter was postponed till next morning, when we certified to the fact that the articles were "with us." Here I must make record of the kindness of the marshal, Rolla Gleason, who treated us with respect and kindness. He had spoken with respect of our Society, had given me furloughs to the amount of twenty-four days, when the marshal at Rutland considered himself restricted by his oath and duty to six days, and here appeared in person to prevent any harsh treatment of us by his sergeants, and though much against his inclinations, assisted in putting on the uniform with his own hands. We bade him farewell with grateful feelings and expressions of fear that we should not fall into as tender hands again; and amid the rain in the early morning, as the town clock tolled the hour of seven, we were driven amongst the flock that was going forth to the slaughter, down the street and into the cars for Brattleboro. Dark was the day with murk and cloud and rain; and, as we rolled down through the narrow vales of eastern Vermont, somewhat of the shadow crept into our hearts and filled them with dark apprehensions of evil fortune ahead; of long, hopeless trials; of abuse from inferior officers; of contempt from common soldiers; of patient endurance (or an attempt at this), unto an end seen only by the eye of a strong faith.

Herded into a car by ourselves, we conscripts, substitutes, and the rest, through the greater part of the day, swept over the fertile meadows along the banks of the White River and the Connecticut, through pleasant scenes that had little of delight for us. At Woodstock we were joined by the conscripts from the 1st District—altogether an inferior company from those before with us, who were honest yeomen from the northern and mountainous towns, while these were many of them substitutes from the cities.

At Brattleboro we were marched up to the camp; our knapsacks and persons searched, and any articles of citizen's dress taken from us, and then shut up in a rough board building under a guard. Here the prospect was dreary, and I felt some lack of confidence in our Father's arm, though but two days before I wrote to my dear friend, E. M. H.,—

> I go tomorrow where the din
> Of war is in the sulphurous air.
> I go the Prince of Peace to serve,
> His cross of suffering to bear.

Brattleboro. 26th, 8th month, 1863—Twenty-five or thirty caged lions roam lazily to and fro through this building hour after hour through the day. On every side without, sentries pace their slow beat, bearing loaded muskets. Men are ranging through the grounds or hanging in synods about the doors of the different buildings, apparently without a purpose. Aimless is military life, except betimes its aim is deadly. Idle life blends with violent death-struggles till the man is unmade a man; and henceforth there is little of manhood about him. Of a man he is made a soldier, which is a man-destroying machine in two senses—a thing for the prosecuting or repelling an invasion like the block of stone in the fortress or the plate of iron on the side of the Monitor. They are alike. I have tried in vain to define a different, and I see only this. The iron-clad with its gun is a bigger soldier: the more formidable in attack, the less liable to destruction in a given time; the block the most capable of resistance; both are equally obedient to officers. Or the more perfect is the soldier, the more nearly he approaches these in this respect.

Three times a day we are marched out to the mess houses for our rations. In our hands we carry a tin plate, whereon we bring back a piece of bread (sour and tough most likely), and a cup. Morning and noon a piece of meat, antique betimes, bears company with the bread. They who wish it receive in their cups two sorts of decoctions: in the morning burnt bread, or peas perhaps, steeped in water with some saccharine substance added (I dare not affirm it to be sugar). At night steeped tea extended by some other herbs probably and its pungency and acridity assuaged by the saccharine principle aforementioned. On this we have so far subsisted and, save some nauseating, comfortably. As we go out and return, on right and left and in front and rear go bayonets. Some substitutes heretofore have escaped and we are not to be neglected in our attendants. Hard beds are healthy, but I query cannot the result be defeated by the *degree*? Our mattresses are boards. Only the slight elasticity of our thin blankets breaks the fall of our flesh and bones thereon. Oh! now I praise the discipline I have received from uncarpeted floors through warm summer nights of my boyhood.

The building resounds with petty talk; jokes and laughter and swearing. Something more than that. Many of the caged lions are engaged with cards, and money changes hands freely. Some of the caged lions read, and some sleep, and so the weary day goes by.

L. M. M. and I addressed the following letter to Governor Holbrook and hired a corporal to forward it to him.

Brattleboro, Vt., 26th, 8th month, 1863.

Frederick Holbrook,
     Governor of Vermont:—
     We, the undersigned members of the Society of Friends, beg leave to represent to thee, that we were lately drafted in the 3rd Dist. of Vermont, have been forced into the army and reached the camp near this town yesterday.

That in the language of the elders of our New York Yearly Meeting, "We love our country and acknowledge with gratitude to our Heavenly Father the many blessings we have been favoured with under the government; and can feel no sympathy with any who seek its overthrow."

But that, true to well-known principles of our Society, we cannot violate our religious convictions either by complying with military requisitions or by the equivalents of this compliance—the furnishing of a substitute or payment of commutation money. That, therefore, we are brought into suffering and exposed to insult and contempt from those who have us in charge, as well as to the penalties of insubordination, though liberty of conscience is granted us by the Constitution of Vermont as well as that of the United States.

Therefore, we beg of thee as Governor of our State any assistance thou may be able to render, should it be no more than the influence of thy position interceding in our behalf.

Truly Thy Friend,
Cyrus G. Pringle.

P.S.—We are informed we are to be sent to the vicinity of Boston tomorrow.

27th—On board train to Boston. The long afternoon of yesterday passed slowly away. This morning passed by, the time of our stay in Brattleboro, and we neither saw nor heard anything of our Governor. We suppose he could not or would not help us. So as we go down to our trial we have no arm to lean upon among all men; but why dost thou complain, oh, my Soul? Seek thou that faith that will prove a buckler to thy breast, and gain for thee the protection of an arm mightier than the arms of all men.

Camp Vermont: Long Island, Boston Harbor. 28th—In the early morning damp and cool we marched down off the heights of Brattleboro to take train for this place. Once in the car the dashing young cavalry officer, who had us in charge, gave notice he had placed men through the cars, with loaded revolvers, who had orders to shoot any person attempting to escape, or jump from the window, and that any one would be shot if he even put his head out of the window. Down the beautiful valley of Connecticut, all through its broad intervales, heavy with its crops of corn or tobacco, or shaven smooth by the summer harvest; over the hard and stony counties of northern Massachusetts, through its suburbs and under the shadow of Bunker Hill Monument we came into the City of Boston, "the Hub of the Universe." Out through street after street we were marched double guarded to the wharves, where we took a small steamer for the island some six miles out in the harbor. A circumstance connected with this march is worth mentioning for its singularity: at the head of this company, like convicts (and feeling very much like such), through the City of Boston walked, with heavy hearts and down-cast eyes, two Quakers.

Here on this dry and pleasant island in the midst of the beautiful Massachusetts Bay, we have the liberty of the camp, the privilege of air and sunshine, and hay beds to sleep upon. So we went to bed last night with somewhat of gladness elevating our depressed spirits.

Here are many troops gathering daily from all the New England States except Connecticut and Rhode Island. Their white tents are dotting the green slopes and hill-tops of the island and spreading wider and wider. This is the flow of military tide here just now. The ebb went out to sea in the shape of a great shipload just as we came in, and another load will be sent before many days. All is war here. We are surrounded by the pomp and circumstance of war, and enveloped in the cloud thereof. The cloud settles down over the minds and souls of all; they cannot see beyond, nor do they try; but with the clearer eye of Christian faith I try to look beyond all this error unto Truth and Holiness immaculate: and thanks to our Father, I am favored with glimpses that are sweet consolation amid this darkness.

This is one gratification: the men with us give us their sympathy. They seem to look upon us tenderly and pitifully, and their expressions of kind wishes are warm. Although we are relieved from duty and from drill, and may lie in our tents during rain and at night, we have heard of no complaint. This is the more worthy of note as there are so few in our little (Vermont) camp. Each man comes on guard half the days. It would probably be otherwise were their hearts in the service; but I have yet to find the man in any of these camps or at any service who does not wish himself at home. Substitutes say if they knew all they know now before leaving home they would not have enlisted; and they have been but a week from their homes and have endured no hardships. Yesterday L. M. M. and I appeared before the Captain commanding this camp with a statement of our cases. He listened to us respectfully and promised to refer us to the General commanding here, General Devens; and in the meantime released us from duty. In a short time afterward he passed us in our tent, asking our names. We have not heard from him, but do not drill or stand guard; so, we suppose, his release was confirmed. At that interview a young lieutenant sneeringly told us he thought we had better throw away our scruples and fight in the service of the country; and as we told the Captain we could not accept pay, he laughed mockingly, and said he would not stay here for $13.00 per month. He gets more than a hundred, I suppose.

How beautiful seems the world on this glorious morning here by the seaside! Eastward and toward the sun, fair green isles with outlines of pure beauty are scattered over the blue bay. Along the far line of the mainland while hamlets and towns glisten in the morning sun; countless tiny waves dance in the wind that comes off shore and sparkle sunward like myriads of gems. Up the fair vault, flecked by scarcely a cloud, rolls the sun in glory. Though fair be the earth, it has come to be tainted and marred by him who was meant to be its crowning glory. Behind me on this island are crowded vile and wicked men, the murmur of whose ribaldry riseth continually like the smoke and fumes of a lower world. Oh! Father of Mercies, forgive the hard heartlessness and blindness and scarlet sins of my fellows, my brothers.

In Guard House, 31st—Yesterday morning L. M. M. and I were called upon to do fatigue duty. The day before we were asked to do some cleaning about camp and to bring water. We wished to be obliging, to appear willing to bear a hand toward that which would promote our own and our fellows' health and convenience; but as we worked we did not feel easy. Suspecting we had been assigned to such work, the more we discussed in our minds the subject, the more clearly the right way seemed open to us; and we separately came to the judgment that we must not conform to this requirement. So when the sergeant bade us "Police the streets," we asked him if he had received instructions with regard to us, and he replied we had been assigned to "Fatigue Duty." L. M. M. answered him that we could not obey. He left us immediately for the Major (Jarvis of Weathersfield, Vt.). He came back and ordered us to the Major's tent. The latter met us outside and inquired concerning the complaint he had heard of us. Upon our statement of our position, he apparently undertook to argue our whimsies, as he probably looked upon our principles, out of our heads. We replied to his points as we had ability; but he soon turned to bullying us rather than arguing with us, and would hardly let us proceed with a whole sentence. "I make some pretension to religion myself," he said; and quoted the Old Testament freely in support of war. Our terms were, submission or the guard-house. We replied we could not obey.

This island was formerly occupied by a company, who carried on the large farm it comprises and opened a great hotel as a summer resort.

The subjects of all misdemeanors, grave and small, are here confined. Those who have deserted or attempted it; those who have insulted officers and those guilty of theft, fighting, drunkenness, etc. In *most*, as in the camps, there are traces yet of manhood and of the Divine spark, but some are abandoned, dissolute. There are many here among the substitutes who were actors in the late New York riots. They show unmistakably the characteristics and sentiments of those rioters, and especially, hatred to the blacks drafted and about camp, and exhibit this in foul and profane jeers heaped upon these unoffending men at every opportunity. In justice to the blacks I must say they are superior to the whites in all their behavior.

31st P.M.—Several of us were a little time ago called out one by one to answer inquiries with regard to our offenses. We replied we could not comply with military requisitions. P. D., being last, was asked if he would die first, and replied promptly but mildly, *Yes*.

Here we are in prison in our own land for no crimes, no offense to God nor man; nay, more: we are here for obeying the commands of the Son of God and the influences of his Holy Spirit. I must look for patience in this dark day. I am troubled too much and excited and perplexed.

1st, 9th month—Oh, the horrors of the past night—I never before experienced such *sensations* and fears; and never did I feel so clearly that I had nothing but the hand of our Father to shield me from evil. Last night we three lay down together on the floor of a lower room of which we had taken possession. The others were above. We had but one blanket between us and the floor, and one over us. The other one we had lent to a wretched deserter who had skulked into our room for *relief*, being without anything of his own. We had during the day gained the respect of the fellows, and they seemed disposed to let us occupy our room in peace. I cannot say in quiet, for these caged beasts are restless, and the resonant boards of this old building speak of bedlam. The thin board partitions, the light door fastened only by a pine stick thrust into a wooden loop on the casing, seemed small protection in case of assault; but we lay down to sleep in quiet trust. But we had scarcely fallen asleep before we were awakened by the demoniac howlings and yellings of a man just brought into the next room, and allowed the liberty of the whole house. He was drunk, and further seemed to be laboring under delirium tremens. He crashed about furiously, and all the more after the guard tramped heavily in and bound him with handcuffs, and chain and ball. Again and again they left, only to return to quiet him by threats or by crushing him down to the floor and gagging him. In a couple of hours he became quiet and we got considerable sleep.

In the morning the fellow came into our room apologizing for the intrusion. He appeared a smart, fine-looking young man, restless and uneasy. P.D. has a way of disposing of intruders that is quite effectual. I have not entirely disposed of some misgivings with respect to the legitimacy of his use of the means, so he commenced reading aloud in the Bible. The fellow was impatient and noisy, but he soon settled down on the floor beside him. As he listened and talked with us the recollections of his father's house and his innocent childhood were awakened. He was the child of pious parents, taught in Sabbath School and under pure home influences till thirteen. Then he was drawn into bad company, soon after leaving home for the sea; and, since then, has served in the army and navy,—in the army in Wilson's and Hawkins's [brigades]. His was the old story of the total subjection of moral power and thralldom to evil habits and associates. He would get drunk, whenever it was in his power. It was wrong; but he could not help it. Though he was awakened and recollected his parents looking long and in vain for his return, he soon returned to camp, to his wallowing in the mire, and I fear to his path to certain perdition.

3rd—A Massachusetts major, the officer of the day, in his inspection of the guard-house came into our room today. We were lying on the floor engaged in reading and writing. He was apparently surprised at this and inquired the name of our books; and finding the Bible and Thomas à Kempis's *Imitation of Christ*, observed that they were good books. I cannot say if he knew we were Friends, but he asked us why we were in here.

Like all officers he proceeded to reason with us, and to advise us to serve, presenting no comfort if we still persisted in our course. He informed us of a young Friend, Edward W. Holway[8] of Sandwich, Mass., having been yesterday under punishment in the camp by his orders, who was today doing service about camp. He said he was not going to put his Quaker in the guardhouse, but was going to bring him to work by punishment. We were filled with deep sympathy for him and desired to cheer him by kind words as well as by the knowledge of our similar situation. We obtained permission of the Major to write to him a letter open to his inspection. "You may be sure," said E.W.H. to us at W. [Washington], "the Major did not allow it to leave his hands."

This forenoon the Lieutenant of the Day came in and acted the same part, though he was not so cool, and left expressing the hope, if we would not serve our country like men, that God would curse us. Oh, the trials from these officers! One after another comes in to relieve himself upon us. Finding us firm and not lacking in words, they usually fly into a passion and end by bullying us. How can we reason with such men? They are utterly unable to comprehend the pure Christianity and spirituality of our principles. They have long stiffened their necks in their own strength. They have stopped their ears to the voice of the Spirit, and hardened their hearts to his influences. They see no duty higher than that to country. What shall we receive at their hands?

This Major tells us we will not be tried here. Then we are to be sent into the field, and there who will deliver us but God? Ah, I have nursed in my heart a hope that I may be spared to return home. Must I cast it out and have no desire, but to do the will of my Master. It were better, even so. O, Lord, Thy will be done. Grant I may make it my chief delight and render true submission thereto.

Yesterday a little service was required of our dear L. M. M., but he insisted he could not comply. A sergeant and two privates were engaged. They coaxed and threatened him by turns, and with a determination not to be baffled took him out to perform it. Though guns were loaded he still stood firm and was soon brought back. We are happy here in guard-house—too happy, too much at ease. We should see more of the Comforter—feel more strength—if the trial were fiercer; but this is well. This is a trial of strength of patience.

6th—Yesterday we had officers again for visitors. Major J. B. Gould, 13th Massachusetts, came in with the determination of persuading us to consent to be transferred to the hospital here, he being the Provost Marshal of the island and having the power to make the transfer. He is different in being and bearing from those who have been here before. His motives were apparently those of pure kindness, and his demeanour was that of a gentleman. Though he talked with us more than an hour, he lost no part of his self-control or good humor. So by his eloquence and kindness he made more impression upon us than any before. As a Congregationalist he well knew the courts of the temple, but the Holy of Holies he had never seen and knew nothing of its secrets. He understood expediency, but is not the man to "lay down his life for my sake." He is sincere and seems to think what Major Gould believes cannot be far from right. After his attempt we remained as firm as ever. We must expect all means will be tried upon us, and no less persuasion than threats.

At the Hospital. 7th—Yesterday morning came to us Major Gould again, informing us that he had come to take us out of that dirty place, as he could not see such respectable men lying there, and was going to take us up to the hospital. We assured him we could not serve there, and asked him if he would not bring us back when we had there declared our purpose. He would not reply directly, but brought us here and left us. When the surgeon knew our determination, he was for haling us back at once; what he wanted, he said, was willing men. We sat on the sward without the hospital tents till nearly noon, for some one to take us back; when we were ordered to move into the tents and quarters assigned us in the mess-room. The Major must have interposed, demonstrating his kindness by his resolution that we should occupy and enjoy the pleasanter quarters of the hospital, certainly if serving, but none the less so if we declined. Later in the day L. M. M. and P. D. were sitting without, when he passed them and, laughing heartily, declared they were the strangest prisoners of war he ever saw. He stopped some time to talk with them and when they came in they declared him a kind and honest man.

If we interpret aright his conduct, this dangerous trial is over, and we have escaped the perplexities that his kindness and determination threw about us.

13th—Last night we received a letter from Henry Dickinson,[9] stating that the President, though sympathizing with those in our situation, felt bound by the Conscription Act, and felt liberty, in view of his oath to execute the laws, to do no more than detail us from active service to hospital duty, or to the charge of the colored refugees. For more than a week have we lain here, refusing to engage in hospital service; shall we retrace the steps of the past week? Or shall we go South as overseers of the blacks on the confiscated estates of the rebels, to act under military commanders and to report to such? What would become of our testimony and our determination to preserve ourselves clear of the guilt of this war?

P.S. We have written back to Henry Dickinson that we cannot purchase life at cost of peace of soul.

14th—We have been exceeding sorrowful since receiving advice—as we must call it—from H. D. to enter the hospital service or some similar situation. We did not look for that from him. It is not what our Friends sent us out for; nor is it what we came for. We shall feel desolate and dreary in our position, unless supported and cheered by the words of those who have at heart our best interests more than regard for our personal welfare. We walk as we feel guided by Best Wisdom. Oh, may we run and not err in the high path of Holiness.

16th—Yesterday a son-in-law of N. B. of Lynn came to see us. He was going to get passes for one or two of the Lynn Friends, that they might come over to see us today. He informed us that the sentiment of the Friends hereabouts was that we might enter the hospital without compromising our principles; and he produced a letter from W. W.[10] to S. B. to the same effect. W. W. expressed his opinion that we might do so without doing it in lieu of other service. How can we evade a fact? Does not the government both demand and accept it as in lieu of other service? Oh, the cruelest blow of all comes from our friends.

17th—Although this trial was brought upon us by our friends, their intentions were well meant. Their regard for our personal welfare and safety too much absorbs the zeal they should possess for the maintenance of the principle of the peaceableness of our Master's kingdom. An unfaithfulness to this through meekness and timidity seems manifest—too great a desire to avoid suffering at some sacrifice of principle, perhaps,—too little of placing of Faith and confidence upon the Rock of Eternal Truth.

Our friends at home, with W. D. at their head, support us; and yesterday, at the opportune moment, just as we were most distressed by the solicitations of our visitors, kind and cheering words of truth were sent us through dear C. M. P., whose love rushes out to us warm and living and just from an overflowing fountain.

I must record another work of kind attention shown us by Major Gould. Before we embarked, he came to us for a friendly visit. As we passed him on our way to the wharf he bade us Farewell and expressed a hope we should not have so hard a time as we feared. And after we were aboard the steamer, as the result of his interference on our behalf, we must believe, we were singled out from the midst of the prisoners, among whom we had been placed previous to coming aboard, and allowed the liberty of the vessel. By this are we saved much suffering, as the other prisoners were kept under close guard in a corner on the outside of the boat.

Forest City, Up The Potomac. 22nd—It was near noon, yesterday, when we turned in from sea between Cape Charles and Henry; and, running thence down across the mouth of Chesapeake Bay, alongside Old Point Comfort, dropped anchor off Fortress Monroe. The scene around us was one of beauty, though many of its adornments were the results and means of wrong. The sunshine was brighter, the verdure greener to our eyes weary of the sea, and the calm was milder and more grateful that we had so long tossed in the storm.

The anchor was soon drawn up again and the *Forest City* steamed up the James River toward Newport News, and turning to the left between the low, pine-grown banks, passed Norfolk to leave the New Hampshire detachment at Portsmouth.

Coming back to Fortress Monroe, some freight was landed; and in the calm clear light of the moon, we swung away from shore and dropping down the mouth of the river, rounded Old Point, and, going up the Chesapeake, entered the Potomac in the nighttime.

Off Shore, Alexandria. 23rd—Here we anchored last night after the main detachment was landed, and the Vermont and Massachusetts men remained on board another night. We hear we are to go right to the field, where active operations are going on. This seems hard. We have not till now given up the hope that we were not to go out into Virginia with the rest of the men, but were to be kept here at Washington. Fierce, indeed, are our trials. I am not discouraged entirely; but I am weak from want of food which

I can eat, and from sickness. I do not know how I am going to live in such way, or get to the front.

P.S. We have just landed; and I had the liberty to buy a pie of a woman hawking such things, that has strengthened me wonderfully.

Camp Near Culpeper. 25th May—My distress is too great for words; but I must overcome my disinclination to write, or this record will remain unfinished. So, with aching head and heart, I proceed.

Yesterday morning we were roused early for breakfast and for preparation for starting. After marching out of the barracks, we were first taken to the armory, where each man received a gun and its equipments and a piece of tent. We stood in line, waiting for our turn with apprehensions of coming trouble. Though we had felt free to keep with those among whom we had been placed, we could not consent to carry a gun, even though we did not intend to use it; and, from our previous experience, we knew it would go harder with us, if we took the first step in the wrong direction, though it might seem an unimportant one, and an easy and not very wrong way to avoid difficulty. So we felt decided we must decline receiving the guns. In the hurry and bustle of equipping a detachment of soldiers, one attempting to explain a position and the grounds therefor so peculiar as ours to junior, petty officers, possessing liberally the characteristics of these: pride, vanity, conceit, and an arbitrary spirit, impatience, profanity, and contempt for holy things, must needs find the opportunity a very unfavorable one.

We succeeded in giving these young officers a slight idea of what we were; and endeavored to answer their questions of why we did not pay our commutation, and avail ourselves of that provision made expressly for such; of why we had come as far as that place, etc. We realized then the unpleasant results of that practice, that had been employed with us by the successive officers into whose hands we had fallen, of shirking any responsibility, and of passing us on to the next officer above.

A council was soon holden to decide what to do with us. One proposed to place us under arrest, a sentiment we rather hoped might prevail, as it might prevent our being sent on to the front; but another, in some spite and impatience, insisted, as it was their duty to supply a gun to every man and forward him, that the guns should be put upon us, and we be made to carry them. Accordingly the equipment was buckled about us, and the straps of the guns being loosened, they were thrust over our heads and hung upon our shoulders. In this way we were urged forward through the streets of Alexandria; and, having been put upon a long train of dirt cars, were started for Culpeper. We came over a long stretch of desolated and deserted country, through battlefields of previous summers, and through many camps now lively with the work of this present campaign. Seeing, for the first time, a country made dreary by the war-blight, a country once adorned with groves and green pastures and meadows and fields of waving grain, and happy with a thousand homes, now laid with the ground, one realizes as he can in no other way something of the ruin that lies in the trail of a war. But upon these fields of Virginia, once so fair, there rests a two-fold blight, first that of slavery, now that of war. When one contrasts the face of this country with the smiling hillsides and vales of New England, he sees stamped upon it in characters so marked, none but a blind man can fail to read, the great irrefutable arguments against slavery and against war, too; and must be filled with loathing for these twin relics of barbarism, so awful in the potency of their consequences that they can change even the face of the country.

Through the heat of this long ride, we felt our total lack of water and the meagreness of our supply of food. Our thirst became so oppressive as we were marched here from Culpeper, some four miles with scarcely a halt to rest, under our heavy loads, and through the heat and deep dust of the road, that we drank water and dipped in the brooks we passed, though it was discolored with the soap the soldiers had used in washing. The guns interfered with our walking, and, slipping down, dragged with painful weight upon our shoulders. Poor P. D. fell out from exhaustion and did not come in till we had been some little time at the camp. We were taken to the 4th Vermont regiment and soon apportioned to companies. Though we waited upon the officer commanding the company in which we were placed, and endeavored to explain our situation, we were required immediately after to be present at inspection of arms. We declined, but an attempt was made to force us to obedience, first, by the officers of the company, then, by those of the regiment; but, failing to exact obedience of us, we were ordered by the colonel to be tied, and, if we made outcry, to be gagged also, and to be kept so till he gave orders for our release. After two or three hours we were relieved and left under guard; lying down on the ground in the open air, and covering ourselves with our blankets, we soon fell asleep from exhaustion, and the fatigue of the day.

This morning the officers told us we must yield. We must obey and serve. We were threatened great severities and even death. We seem perfectly at the mercy of the military power, and, more, in the hands of the inferior officers who, from their being far removed from Washington, feel less restraint from those Regulations of the Army, which are for the protection of privates from personal abuse.

26th—Yesterday my mind was much agitated: doubts and fears and forebodings seized me. I was alone, seeking a resting-place and finding none. It seemed as if God had forsaken me in this dark hour; and the Tempter whispered, that after all I might be only the victim of a delusion. My prayers for faith and strength seemed all in vain.

But this morning I enjoy peace, and feel as though I could face anything. Though I am as a lamb in the shambles, yet do I cry, "Thy will be done," and can indeed say,—

Passive to His holy will
Trust I in my Master still
Even though he slay me.

I mind me of the anxiety of our dear friends about home, and of their prayers for us.

Oh, praise be to the Lord for the peace and love and resignation that has filled my soul today! Oh, the passing beauty of holiness! There is a holy life that is above fear; it is a close communion with Christ. I pray for this continually but am not free from the shadow and the tempter. There is ever present with us the thought that perhaps we shall serve the Lord the most effectually by our death, and desire, if that be the service He requires of us, that we may be ready and resigned.

Regimental Hospital, 4th Vermont. 29th—On the evening of the 26th the Colonel came to us apologizing for the roughness with which he treated us at first, which was, as he insisted, through ignorance of our real character and position. He told us if we persisted in our course, death would probably follow; though at another time he confessed to P. D. that this would only be the extreme sentence of court-martial.

He urged us to go into the hospital, stating that this course was advised by Friends about New York. We were too well aware of such a fact to make any denial, though it was a subject of surprise to us that he should be informed of it. He pleaded with us long and earnestly, urging us with many promises of indulgence and favor and attentions we found afterwards to be untrue. He gave us till the next morning to consider the question and report our decision. In our discussion of the subject among ourselves, we were very much perplexed. If all his statements concerning the ground taken by our Society were true, we seemed to be liable, if we persisted in the course which alone seemed to us to be in accordance with Truth, to be exposed to the charge of over-zeal and fanaticism even among our own brethren. Regarding the work to be done in hospital as one of mercy and benevolence, we asked if we had any right to refuse its performance; and questioned whether we could do more good by endeavoring to bear to the end a clear testimony against war, than by laboring by word and deed among the needy in the hospitals and camps. We saw around us a rich field for usefulness in which there were scarce any laborers, and toward whose work our hands had often started involuntarily and unbidden. At last we consented to a trial, at least till we could make inquiries concerning the Colonel's allegations, and ask the counsel of our friends, reserving the privilege of returning to our former position.

At first a great load seemed rolled away from us; we rejoiced in the prospect of life again. But soon there prevailed a feeling of condemnation, as though we had sold our Master. And that first day was one of the bitterest I ever experienced. It was a time of stern conflict of soul. The voice that seemed to say, "Follow me," as I sought guidance the night before, kept pleading with me, convincing of sin, till I knew of a truth my feet had strayed from His path. The Scriptures, which the day before I could scarcely open without finding words of strength and comfort, seemed closed against me, till after a severe struggle alone in the wood to which I had retired, I consented to give up and retrace my steps in faith. But it was too late. L. M. M. wishing to make a fair, honest trial, we were brought here—P. D. being already here unwell. We feel we are erring; but scarce anything is required of us and we wait to hear from Friends.

Of these days of going down into sin, I wish to make little mention. I would that my record of such degradation be brief. We wish to come to an understanding with our friends and the Society before we move, but it does not seem that we can repress the upheavings of Truth in our hearts. We are bruised by sin.

It is with pleasure I record we have just waited upon the Colonel with an explanation of our distress of mind, requesting him to proceed with court-martial. We were kindly and tenderly received. "If you want a trial I can give it to you," he answered. The brigade has just marched out to join with the division for inspection. After that we are to have attention to our case.

P.M.—There is particular cause for congratulation in the consideration that we took this step this morning, when now we receive a letter from H. D. charging us to faithfulness.

When lately I have seen dear L. M. M. in the thoroughness and patience of his trial to perform service in hospital, his uneasiness and the intensity of his struggle as manifested by his silence and disposition to avoid the company of his friends, and seen him fail and declare to us, "I cannot stay here," I have received a new proof, and to me a strong one, because it is from the experimental knowledge of an honest man, that no Friend, who is really such, desiring to keep himself clear of complicity with this system of war and to bear a perfect testimony against it, can lawfully perform service in the hospitals of the Army in lieu of bearing arms.

3rd, 10th month—Today dawned fair and our Camp is dry again. I was asked to clean the gun I brought, and declining, was tied some two hours upon the ground.

At Washington. 6th—At first, after being informed of our declining to serve in his hospital, Colonel Foster did not appear altered in his kind regard for us. But his spleen soon became evident. At the time we asked for a trial by court-martial, and it was his duty to place us under arrest and proceed with the preferring of his charges against us. For a while he seemed to hesitate and consult his inferior officers, and among them his Chaplain. The result of the conference was our being ordered into our companies, that, separated, and with the force of the officers of a company bearing upon us, we might the more likely be subdued. Yet the Colonel assured L. M. M., interceding in my behalf, when the lieutenant commanding my company threatened force upon me, that he should not allow any personal injury. When we marched next day I was compelled to bear a gun and equipments. My associates were more fortunate, for, being asked if they would carry their guns, declined and saw no more trouble from them. The captain of the company in which P. D. was placed told him he did not believe he was ugly about it, and that he could only put him under arrest and prefer charges against him. He accordingly was taken under guard, where he lay till we left for here.

The next morning the men were busy in burnishing their arms. When I looked toward the one I had borne, yellow with rust, I trembled in the weakness of the flesh at the trial I felt impending over me. Before the Colonel was up I knocked at his tent, but was told he was asleep, though, through the opening, I saw him lying gazing at me. Although I felt I should gain no relief from him, I applied again soon after. He admitted me and, lying on his bed, inquired with cold heartlessness what I wanted. I stated to him, that I could never consent to serve, and, being under the war-power, was resigned to suffer instead all the just penalties of the law. I begged of him release from the attempts by violence to compel my obedience and service, and a trial, though likely to be made by those having no sympathy with me, yet probably in a manner conformable to law.

He replied that he had shown us all the favor he should; that he had, now, turned us over to the military power and was going to let that take its course; that is, henceforth we were to be at the mercy of the inferior officers, without appeal to law, justice, or mercy. He said he had placed us in a pleasant position, against which we could have no reasonable objection, and that we had failed to perform our agreement. He wished to deny that our consent was only temporary and conditional. He declared, furthermore, his belief, that a man who would not fight for his country did not deserve to live. I was glad to withdraw from his presence as soon as I could.

I went back to my tent and lay down for a season of retirement endeavoring to gain resignation to any event. I dreaded torture and desired strength of flesh and spirit. My trial soon came. The lieutenant called me out, and pointing to the gun that lay near by, asked if I was going to clean it. I replied to him, that I could not comply with military requisitions, and felt resigned to the consequences. "I do not ask about your feelings; I want to know if you are going to clean that gun?" "I cannot do it," was my answer. He went away, saying, "Very well," and I crawled into the tent again. Two sergeants soon called for me, and taking me a little aside, bid me lie down on my back, and stretching my limbs apart tied cords to my wrists and ankles and these to four stakes driven in the ground somewhat in the form of an X.

I was very quiet in my mind as I lay there on the ground [soaked] with the rain of the previous day, exposed to the heat of the sun and suffering keenly from the cords binding my wrists and straining my muscles. And, if

I dared the presumption, I should say that I caught a glimpse of heavenly pity. I wept, not so much from my own suffering as from sorrow that such things should be in our own country, where Justice and Freedom and Liberty of Conscience have been the annual boast of Fourth-of-July orators so many years. It seemed that our fore-fathers in the faith had wrought and suffered in vain, when the privileges they so dearly bought were so soon set aside. And I was sad, that one endeavoring to follow our dear Master should be so generally regarded as a despicable and stubborn culprit.

After something like an hour had passed, the lieutenant came with his orderly to ask me if I was ready to clean the gun. I replied to the orderly asking the question, that it could but give me pain to be asked or required to do anything I believed wrong. He repeated it to the lieutenant just behind him, who advanced and addressed me. I was favored to improve the opportunity to say to him a few things I wished. He said little; and, when I had finished, he withdrew with the others who had gathered around. About the end of another hour his orderly came and released me.

I arose and sat on the ground. I did not rise to go away. I had not where to go, nothing to do. As I sat there my heart swelled from joy from above. The consolation and sweet fruit of tribulation patiently endured. But I also grieved, that the world was so far gone astray, so cruel and blind. It seemed as if the gospel of Christ had never been preached upon earth, and the beautiful example of his life had been utterly lost sight of.

Some of the men came about me, advising me to yield, and among them one of those who had tied me down, telling me what I had already suffered was nothing to what I must yet suffer unless I yielded; that human flesh could not endure what would be put upon me. I wondered if it could be that they could force me to obedience by torture, and examined myself closely to see if they had advanced as yet one step toward the accomplishment of their purposes. Though weaker in body, I believed I found myself, through divine strength, as firm in my resolution to maintain my allegiance to my Master.

The relaxation of my nerves and muscles after having been so tensely strained left me that afternoon so weak that I could hardly walk or perform any mental exertion.[11]

I had not yet eaten the mean and scanty breakfast I had prepared, when I was ordered to pack up my things and report myself at the lieutenant's tent. I was accustomed to such orders and complied, little moved.

The lieutenant received me politely with, "Good-morning, Mr. Pringle," and desiring me to be seated, proceeded with the writing with which he was engaged. I sat down in some wonderment and sought to be quiet and prepared for any event.

"You are ordered to report to Washington," said he; "I do not know what it is for." I assured him that neither did I know. We were gathered before the Major's tent for preparation for departure. The regimental officers were there manifesting surprise and chagrin; for they could not but show both, as they looked upon us, whom the day before they were threatening to crush into submission, and attempting also to execute their threats that morning, standing out of their power and under orders from one superior to their Major Commanding E. M. As the bird uncaged, so were our hearts that morning. Short and uncertain at first were the flights of Hope. As the slave many times before us, leaving his yoke behind him, turned from the plantations of Virginia and set his face toward the far North, so we from out a grasp as close and as abundant in suffering and severity, and from without the line of bayonets that had so many weeks surrounded us, turned our backs upon the camp of the 4th Vermont and took our way over the turnpike that ran through the tented fields of Culpeper.

At the War Office we were soon admitted to an audience with the Adjutant General, Colonel Townsend, whom we found to be a very fine man, mild and kind. He referred our cases to the Secretary of War, Stanton, by whom we were ordered to report for service to Surgeon General Hammond. Here we met Isaac Newton, Commissioner of Agriculture, waiting for our arrival, and James Austin of Nantucket, expecting his son, Charles L. Austin,[12] and Edward W. Holway of Sandwich, Mass., conscripted Friends like ourselves, and ordered here from the 22nd Massachusetts.

We understand it is through the influence of Isaac Newton[13] that Friends have been able to approach the heads of Government in our behalf and to prevail with them to so great an extent. He explained to us the circumstance in which we are placed. That the Secretary of War and President sympathized with Friends in their present suffering, and would grant them full release, but that they felt themselves bound by their oaths that they would execute the laws, to carry out to its full extent the Conscription Act. That there appeared but one door of relief open—that was to parole us and allow us to go home, but subject to their call again ostensibly, though this they neither wished nor proposed to do. That the fact of Friends in the Army and refusing service had attracted public attention so that it was not expedient to parole us at present. That, therefore, we were to be sent to one of the hospitals for a short time, where it was hoped and expressly requested that we would consent to remain quiet and acquiesce, if possible, in whatever might be required of us. That our work there would be quite free from objection, being for the direct relief of the sick; and that there we would release none for active service in the field, as the nurses were hired civilians.

These requirements being so much less objectionable than we had feared, we felt relief, and consented to them. I. N. went with us himself to the Surgeon General's office, where he procured peculiar favours for us; that we should be sent to a hospital in the city, where he could see us often; and that orders should be given that nothing should interfere with our comfort, or our enjoyment of our consciences.

Thence we were sent to Medical Purveyor Abbot, who assigned us to the best hospital in the city, the Douglas Hospital.[14]

The next day after our coming here I. N. and James Austin came to add to our number E. W. H. and C. L. A., so now there are five of us instead of three. We are pleasantly situated in a room by ourselves in the upper or fourth story, and are enjoying our advantages of good quarters and tolerable food as no one can except he has been deprived of them.

8th—Today we have a pass to go out to see the city.

9th—We all went, thinking to do the whole city in a day, but before the time of our passes expired, we were glad to drag ourselves back to the rest and quiet of D.H. During the day we called upon our friend I. N. in the Patent Office. When he came to see us on the 7th, he stated he had called upon the President that afternoon to request him to release us and let us go home to our friends. The President promised to consider it over-night. Accordingly yesterday morning, as I. N. told us, he waited upon him again. He found there a woman in the greatest distress. Her son, only a boy of fifteen years and four months, having been enticed into the Army, had deserted and been sentenced to be shot the next day. As the clerks were telling her, the President was in the War Office and could not be seen, nor did they think he could attend to her case that day. I. N. found her almost wild with grief. "Do not despair, my good woman," said he, "I guess the President can be seen after a bit." He soon presented her case to the President, who exclaimed at once, "That must not be, I must look into that case, before they shoot that boy"; and telegraphed at once to have the order suspended.

I. N. judged it was not a fit time to urge our case. We feel we can afford to wait, that a life may be saved. But we long for release. We do not feel easy to remain here.

11th—Today we attended meeting held in the house of a Friend, Asa Arnold, living hear here. There were but four persons besides ourselves. E. W. H. and C. L. A. showed their copy of the charges about to have been preferred against them in court-martial before they left their regiment, to a lawyer who attended the meeting. He laughed at the Specification of Mutiny, declaring such a charge could not have been lawfully sustained against them.

The experiences of our new friends were similar to ours, except they fell among officers who usually showed them favor and rejoiced with them in their release.

13th—L. M. M. had quite an adventure yesterday. He being fireman with another was in the furnace room among three or four others, when the officer of the day, one of the surgeons, passed around on inspection. "Stand up," he ordered them, wishing to be saluted. The others arose; but by no means L. The order was repeated for his benefit, but he sat with his cap on, telling the surgeon he had supposed he was excused from such things as he was one of the Friends. Thereat the officer flew at him, exclaiming, he would take the Quaker out of him. He snatched off his cap and seizing him by the collar tried to raise him to his feet; but finding his strength insufficient and that L. was not to be frightened, he changed his purpose in his wrath and calling for the corporal of the guard had him taken to the guard-house. This was about eleven A.M. and he lay there till about six P.M., when the surgeon in charge, arriving home and hearing of it, ordered the officer of the day to go and take him out, telling him never to put another man into the guard-house while he was in charge here without consulting him. The manner of his release was very satisfactory to us, and we waited for this rather than effect it by our own efforts. We are all getting uneasy about remaining here, and if our release do not come soon, we feel we must intercede with the authorities, even if the alternative be imprisonment.

The privations I have endured since leaving home, the great tax upon my nervous strength, and my mind as well, since I have had charge of our extensive correspondence, are beginning to tell upon my health and I long for rest.

20th—We begin to feel we shall have to decline service as heretofore, unless our position is changed. I shall not say but we submit too much in not declining at once, but it has seemed most prudent at least to make suit with Government rather than provoke the hostility of their subalterns. We were ordered here with little understanding of the true state of things as they really exist here; and were advised by Friends to come and make no objections, being assured it was but for a very brief time and only a matter of form. It might not have been wrong; but as we find we do too much fill the places of soldiers (L. M. M.'s fellow fireman has just left for the field, and I am to take his place, for instance), and are clearly doing military service, we are continually oppressed by a sense of guilt, that makes our struggles earnest.

21st—I. N. has not called yet; our situation is becoming intolerable. I query if patience is justified under the circumstances. My distress of mind may be enhanced by my feeble condition of health, for today I am confined to my bed, almost too weak to get downstairs. This is owing to exposure after being heated over the furnaces.

26th—Though a week has gone by, and my cold has left me, I find I am no better, and that I am reduced very low in strength and flesh by the sickness and pain I am experiencing. Yet I still persist in going below once a day. The food I am able to get is not such as is proper.

5th, 11th month—I spend most of my time on my bed, much of it alone. And very precious to me is the nearness I am favored to attain unto the Master. Notwithstanding my situation and state, I am happy in the enjoyment of His consolations. Lately my confidence has been strong, and I think I begin to feel that our patience is soon to be rewarded with relief; insomuch that a little while ago, when dear P. D. was almost overcome with sorrow, I felt bold to comfort him with the assurance of my belief, that it would not be long so. My mind is too weak to allow of my reading much; and, though I enjoy the company of my companions a part of the time, especially in the evening, I am much alone; which affords me abundant time for meditation and waiting upon God. The fruits of this are sweet, and a recompense for affliction.

6th—Last evening E. W. H. saw I. N. particularly on my behalf, I suppose. He left at once for the President. This morning he called to inform us of his interview at the White House. The President was moved to sympathy in my behalf, when I. N. gave him a letter from one of our Friends in New York. After its perusal he exclaimed to our friend, "I want you to go and tell Stanton that it is my wish all those young men be sent home at once." He was on his way to the Secretary this morning as he called.

Later—I. N. has just called again informing us in joy that we are free. At the War Office he was urging the Secretary to consent to our paroles, when the President entered. "It is my urgent wish," said he. The Secretary yielded; the order was given, and we were released. What we had waited for so many weeks was accomplished in a few moments by a Providential ordering of circumstances.

7th—I. N. came again last evening bringing our paroles. The preliminary arrangements are being made, and we are to start this afternoon for New York.

Note. Rising from my sick-bed to undertake this journey, which lasted through the night, its fatigues overcame me, and upon my arrival in New York I was seized with delirium from which I only recovered after many weeks, through the mercy and favor of Him, who in all this trial had been our guide and strength and comfort.

⚜ 31 ⚜

Trials of a Quaker Conscientious Objector in the Confederate Army

Living near Columbia, Tenn., was one Tilghman Ross Vestal, who had been educated by Friends and had accepted their principles. . . . Southern rulers were anxious to swell the number of men who were required to "drive the

From Fernando G. Cartland, *Southern Heroes, or The Friends in War Time* (Cambridge, Mass., 1895), 316–26, and Edward Needles Wright, *Conscientious Objectors in the Civil War* (Philadelphia, 1931), 142–44.

invading Yankees from Southern soil" and establish the Confederate States as an independent government.

Tilghman Vestal had no sympathy with this movement, and was unwilling either to shed blood or to aid in having it done. But as he was of legal age he must meet the requirements of the law or suffer its penalties. He was conscripted and sent first to General Bragg's army, but as he could not be made to fight, he was sent home again. A second time he was conscripted and sent to the conscript camp at Knoxville, Tenn. From thence he was ordered to Orange Court House, Va., and assigned to the 14th Tennessee regiment, Company I.

Among his relatives were prominent Friends in North Carolina, who were interested for him and enlisted [a prominent Quaker] John B. Crenshaw's influence on his behalf; so that every effort was made to obtain his release without the payment of the $500 tax, which he was unwilling to pay or to have paid for him. A letter was written by Nereus Mendenhall to C. S. Venable in behalf of Tilghman Vestal, who was the nephew of the former, and in response C. S. Venable wrote:

> Headquarters of the Army, Virginia,
> September 24th, 1863.
>
> NEREUS MENDENHALL, New Garden, Guilford County, N.C.:
> Your letter of September 15, in behalf of your nephew, Tilghman Vestal, a private in the 14th Tennessee regiment, has been received. The general commanding has caused an investigation in his case to be made by the proper officer. This officer reports that on his refusal to do any duty whatever or to make arrangements to pay the fine imposed under the law for a discharge, compulsory means were used on the occasion referred to in your letter, and he was pricked with bayonets, but not to an extent to unfit him for duty. This proceeding was probably irregular, and as such not approved by the commanding general. But he knows but one proper mode of proceeding under the law, and that is to bring private Vestal before a court-martial for conduct prejudicial to good order and military discipline, in refusing to do duty as a soldier.
>
> The law makes but one distinction in the case of the Friends, which allows them all to escape military service by the payment of the fine imposed. This not being complied with by Tilghman Vestal, and he being sent by the authorities as a soldier to the army, the general commanding is compelled to act in this case as he would in that of any other delinquent soldier.
>
> I am, very respectfully,
> Your obedient servant,
> C. S. VENABLE, Major and Acting Colonel.

A letter from T. R. Vestal to J. B. Crenshaw, dated Orange Court House, 16th of Eleventh month, '63, says: "I have been ordered to do duty again, but have refused. Charges were then preferred against me, and I have been court-martialed. I suppose something definite will be done now. I have not heard what it is to be, neither do I have any idea. When I was court-martialed, I had three men by whom my character was attested, or at least that part of it that the men have seen since I have been in the regiment. They also stated that I had been punished, etc. My papers from the West came with a letter from General Maney or his adjutant, stating that I had been assigned to a regiment in that brigade, that he had become satisfied that I ought to be discharged, and had written to the Secretary of War about me, but did not receive any answer, and that I had been sent from that place to the conscript camp at Knoxville. These papers were filed with the charges.

Affectionately,

T.R. VESTAL."

At Orange Court House, before the above court-martial, he was sentenced to be punished until he would bear arms. The officer began promptly to use severe means, but Tilghman calmly told him that he was a Christian and could not fight. The officer knocked him down repeatedly and otherwise abused him, but as he utterly failed to induce Vestal to obey orders, he gave up and turned him over to his second officer, telling him perhaps he could make him fight. After unsuccessful attempts to overcome Vestal by knocking him down, the second officer pierced him with a bayonet, and threatened to run him through if he would not take a gun. He ran the murderous steel into Vestal's side, and then stopped to ask if he would consent to serve as a soldier. Meeting with a calm but positive refusal, he continued to wound him in other places. Seventeen times the resolute soldiers of the army pierced the unresisting soldier of Jesus Christ, and each time they met with a refusal to accede to their demands. Some of the wounds were deep, but the heroic sufferer was the victor.

Finding it impossible to make a soldier of him, they sent Vestal to Richmond, Va., where he was placed in Castle Thunder. Little attention was at first paid to his suffering condition, but some of the prisoners, having learned of his sad state and the cause of it, were touched with sympathy for him, and did what their limited means would allow for his relief. They sent petitions one after another to the authorities imploring clemency in his case. But the relief of unfortunate and suffering prisoners seemed to be no part of the business of the keepers of Southern military prisons, and they paid no heed to these petitions. Instead, they decided to be rid of Vestal by sending him farther south to Salisbury prison in North Carolina, where the prospect was that he would be speedily relieved from his suffering by death.

Tilghman Vestal, with the marks of eighteen wounds upon him, weakened and suffering by a wearisome journey, was introduced into Salisbury prison. As he was naturally a tidy person, the filthiness of the place was shocking to him. No opportunity to preserve cleanliness was allowed to the prisoners, and the more filthy and covered with vermin a prisoner became the sooner could he be taken away to help fill the long trenches dug one after another on the hillside.

On one occasion, as Vestal was endeavoring to remove the vermin from his person, which, as we have learned, it would be impossible to prevent from crawling upon him, the inhuman keeper of the prison discovered him thus employed, and with fearful oaths began to abuse him. Growing angry as he talked, the officer beat Vestal over the head until the blood ran down his shoulders upon his already wounded and sore body.

After having been confined for six weeks in this terrible place, T. R. Vestal was liberated through the instrumentality of Friends, whose strenuous efforts had hitherto been unsuccessful, and he was placed in the Friends' school at New Garden, N.C.

An account of T. R. Vestal's experiences was given [by a Confederate officer, Brigadier-General Maney] in the *Banner* of Nashville, Tenn. [1876] . . . It throws some further light on his case. [It begins:]

"I have just read in the Nashville *Banner* . . . a fragment of Governor Foote's reminiscences, headed, 'How a Quaker refused to fight.' As I am familiar with the facts and circumstances alluded to, and as the case greatly interested me at the time, I have thought it might be of some interest to your readers to go into details more than is done in Governor Foote's brief allusion to the case.

The young Quaker alluded to is Tilghman R. Vestal, who lived near Columbia, Tenn. When General Bragg's army was at Shelbyville, Tenn., young Vestal was conscripted and sent to that place. He was assigned to duty in the Fourth Tennessee regiment, commanded by Colonel Murray of Nashville. He reported to the regiment as required to do, but utterly refused to perform military duty of any character or description. Neither by threats nor persuasions could he be induced to alter his determination. The officers of the regiment were as humane as they were true and gallant, and after every effort had failed to induce Vestal to perform the duties of a soldier, they gave the matter up in despair and told him to leave and go home, which he did. But shortly thereafter another conscript officer came along, and Vestal was again duly enrolled as a conscript, and ordered to report at Bragg's headquarters. All alone and on foot Vestal went to Chattanooga and reported. By a most singular coincidence he was again assigned to the Fourth Tennessee regiment. Colonel Murray knew from his Shelbyville experience that he had a tough customer to deal with. He concluded to try the power of moral suasion, so one day he sent for Vestal to come to his quarters, and undertook to convince him from the Scriptures that he was wholly wrong in his ideas and position. But the young Quaker was rather too much for the gallant colonel in the Scripture argument, and the colonel sent for his chaplain to talk to him and convince him that he was altogether wrong in his refusal to fight or perform military duty. The chaplain came and opened the argument after this wise: 'I wouldn't give a cent for a religion that is opposed to my country.' Said Vestal: 'I wouldn't give a cent for a country that is opposed to my religion.' The argument lasted for some time, but left the young Quaker unconvinced and determined to do no military duty of any kind.

He refused to police the camp or to do the least thing that could be tortured or construed into military duty. At last Colonel Murray wholly unable to do anything with Vestal, sent him to brigade headquarters. Here he was reasoned with, and every effort was made to induce him to go and perform the duties of a soldier, but he was firm and as inflexible as the everlasting hills. He was told that if he persisted in his course he would be subjected to severe punishment, and would finally be shot for disobedience to orders. He replied that they had power to kill him, but neither the Federal nor the Confederate army possessed the power to force him to abandon his principles or prove false to his religion.

Everything that could be construed either directly or indirectly into military duty he refused most emphatically to engage in. He was only about eighteen years old. I soon became satisfied that he acted from principle, and would go to the stake or meet death in any shape it could assume, rather than swerve one particle from what he conceived to be his duty. It was the sublimest exhibition of moral courage I had ever witnessed, and it was all the more remarkable from being found in a boy of only eighteen, away from his family and friends.

I asked him one day if he had no sympathy with the contest; if he had no preference as to which side should be successful. 'Oh, yes,' he said, 'I would prefer to see the South victorious, as I live in the South and among Southern people.'

I heard a gentleman say to him: 'Vestal, did you ever exhibit any emotion in your life? Did you ever cry in your life?' 'Oh, yes,' he said, 'I have cried in my life.' 'Well,' said the gentleman, 'I would like to know what were the circumstances that caused you to cry.' 'Well, sir,' he said, 'when I left home to come here my mother cried when she told me goodby, and I cried then.' 'Yes,' said the gentleman, 'and if your mother were here now and could see how you are situated, she would tell you to take your gun and go out and do your duty as a soldier.' 'No, sir,' he quickly replied, 'the last thing my mother said to me was to be true to my religion, and I mean to do it.'

It was during his stay at Colonel Murray's headquarters that Vestal had his interview with Governor Foote. Governor Foote was at that time a member of the Confederate Congress, representing the Nashville district, and was a candidate for reëlection. The soldiers from Tennessee in the army were allowed to vote, and he was out electioneering among the soldiers. While at Colonel Murray's headquarters some one pointed out Vestal to Mr. Foote, or introduced Vestal to him as a Quaker who would not fight, when the following conversation took place between them:

Foote: 'What! young man, won't you fight? You are a stout, good-looking young man. Is it true that you refuse to fight?' Vestal: 'Yes, sir.' Foote: 'Why! you are all wrong about that. Suppose you were to marry a beautiful and accomplished young lady, and some ruffian were to come into your house and grossly insult her. Wouldn't you kill him?' Vestal: 'No, sir.' Foote, jumping from his seat in a very excited manner: 'Why! I'd kill him in a minute.' He then resumed his seat, and after surveying him a few minutes again commenced the conversation. Foote: 'Young man, you are all wrong about this matter, even from a Scriptural standpoint. When Christ was upon the earth he directed his disciples to pay tribute to Caesar. The money thus paid went into the Roman treasury and was used to carry on the wars of the Roman people.' Vestal: 'No, sir, you are mistaken about that. The temple of Janus was closed at that time, and there were no wars going on.' Foote: 'I believe he knows more about that than I do. I don't know whether the temple of Janus was closed then or not.'

Such was substantially the interview between this remarkable boy and this remarkable man. Perhaps two more opposite characters, in many particulars, never came into contact.

Vestal was ordered to Knoxville, and from there he found his way to the Virginia army, and was assigned to one of the Tennessee regiments. Here he was ordered to military duty, but firmly refused as he had done before. The brigadier in command, knowing his history, or incidents of it, ordered him to be bayonetted for disobedience to orders, and the bayonet was applied to him repeatedly. He bore it with the spirit of a martyr, and the soldiers, seeing that he would willingly die in preference to sacrificing his principles, refused to punish him further. No punishments or threats could shake the settled purpose of his soul for a moment. He was under arrest all the while. Frequently on retreats his guard would lose sight of him, but in a day or two Vestal would march up alone into camp.

He was afterwards detained in Castle Thunder for awhile, at Richmond,[15] but was finally permitted by the Secretary of War to go down to North Carolina to school, and was there when the war closed."

Petition to President Jefferson Davis [undated]

We desire respectfully to present the case of Tilman R. Vestal whose mother is a member of the Religious Society of Friends, a native of North Carolina, but now a resident of Tennessee. His father, not being a Friend, he does not come under the law allowing exemption to such, but his mother having carefully instructed him in the principles of said Society, it appears he has endeavored faithfully to maintain them. When conscribed and taken to the Western Army he was offered the privilege of the exemption Act, but declined to avail himself of it at that time, supposing that such would be the course of Friends generally. He was afterward moved to the Army of Genl.

Lee, where after having endured many trials, he was finally court-martialed and sentenced to imprisonment during the War, for declining to perform military duty. When Vestal had opportunity of communicating with friends in North Carolina Yearly Meeting of which his mother is a member, and learned that said meeting, had by Minute granted to its members the liberty of availing themselves of the law of exemption for non-combatants, he also wished to be allowed the same privilege. The case was brought by appeal before the Honl. James A. Seddon Secretary of War, who declined to allow him the privilege because he had once refused it. We hope it may be the pleasure of the President to allow said Vestal exemption on the payment of the tax, seeing that his refusal in the first instance to pay such tax arose from his separation from the body of the Society and ignorance of what action they had taken in the matter.

We would further mention that this young man is a potter by trade, and if released would be a useful member of the Community and we are sure a peaceful and law-abiding Citizen. In support of the facts above mentioned we respectfully refer to papers on file in the Office of the Adjutant General at Richmond.

Earnestly craving the guidance of best wisdom for Thee as our Ruler and submitting the above petition to thy clemency, we are respectfully—
Peter Adams   N.H.D. Wilson   C.A. Boon, Sheriff
Guilford County, N.C.   Andr. J. McAlpin,
Discharged Soldier—from 1st Regt. La. Vols.
Cyrus P. Mendenhall, President Farmers Bank
Joab Hiatt   A.P. Eckel, Mayor   James Sloan,
Major and Chf. Coms.   John A. Gilmer
Under a decision of Judge Campbell the man is entitled to exemption provided the Statements made are Correct.
(Signed)   J.H. Anderson
Capt. and E.O. 6th Dist.
James T. Morehead
Jesse H. Lindsay

From the Papers of the Office of the Confederate Adjutant General

Record of Tilman R. Vestal:
Co. I, 14 Tenn. Inf.
Appeared on Co. Muster Roll, July and Aug. 1863. Taken Aug. 12, 1863. In arrest for refusing to do duty, says he is of Quaker belief. (Sept. and Oct.) Would not draw any pay or clothing (Nov. and Dec. '63). "Imprisoned during the war for refusing to duty as a soldier by sentence of Genl. Court Martial A.N.V. Claimed to be of Quaker belief." Mar. 10, 1865. Taken oath. Trans. furnished to Phil. Pa.

Mar. 16, '64

Sp. Orders No. 63 Par. XXXIII

So much of the sentence of the military court 3 Corp. Army of Nor. Va. held Feby 6/63 as condemns Private *Tilman R. Vestal* Co. I 14 Tennessee Regt. to imprisonment for the War, is remitted & he will, accordingly, be released from confinement, & is assigned to work, during the War, with David Parr & Sons, Richmond, but without pay and allowance from the Government.

Letter fro Major H.E. Peyton, dated Headquarters Ar. N. Va. Sept. 23, 1863:

"As instructed I have made an investigation of the facts in the case of private Thos. R. Vestal—a conscript Co. I 14 Tenn. Regt. referred to in the accompanying papers from the War Dept. . . . etc."

"In compliance with the order the Col. of his Regt. had him punctured with bayonets—as stated in the enclosed letter of Vestal, but not with the severity he represents. The Surgeon present certifies that the punctures were in the fleshy part of the buttocks and *very slight* except in *two* places where the bayonet entered not *over* ½ an inch. The punishment did not at all unfit him for duty."

32

A Reluctant Conscientious Objector

When Fort Sumter was fired upon I lacked two months of being nineteen years of age. I was in perfect health and was in every way fitted for military service. A thousand times I pictured myself fighting in the ranks in the holy war against slavery. Yet when the call came I did not volunteer. But why?

I was a constant reader of the *Weekly New York Tribune* and of *The Principia*, an abolition journal edited by William Goodell of New York. Both these papers maintained a critical attitude toward the Lincoln administration. Our army was engaged in upholding slavery and in returning escaped slaves to their masters, and while the administration was engaged in seeking to effect a compromise which would result in making slavery a per-

From Katharine Macy Noyes, ed., *Jesse Macy: An Autobiography* (Springfield, Ill., 1933), 36, 41–51, 61, 76–78.

manent institution of the country, I could not be in sympathy with it. We, as Friends, were fundamentally opposed to war, but I might join the army as a noncombatant if the administration took a position which I could conscientiously endorse. . . . As seen through the columns of my abolition papers, the war was in no sense waged for the liberation of the slave. I could not support it.

Finally, at the end of the third year of the war came the Proclamation of Emancipation. I was at the time a student in the Quaker Academy at Oskaloosa. . . . A mass meeting was held to celebrate the day when the Proclamation went into effect. The Academy was soon after depleted of nearly all its men suitable for military service. I was one of the few who did not volunteer. . . . [The] men of the Academy—almost to a man—were preparing to join the army. I longed most ardently to be one of them; I believed it to be, at last, clearly, a war for the abolition of the national sin of human slavery. But if I should accept the office to which I had been appointed[16] it would mean that I could not go into the army. . . . All my associates urged me to accept. I finally decided to do so, though not with an entirely easy mind.

The Friends' School of Oskaloosa became greatly weakened and I resumed my studies [at the Academy of Iowa College] at Grinnell during the winter of 1863 and 1864. Again I was subjected to the humiliation of seeing all the able-bodied men leave for the army except myself. But my chance came in September, 1864, when a draft was ordered for the State of Iowa, and my name was drawn. My family would have had me still hold back from what seemed to me my duty. I was the only son at home and my parents were likely to need me. We were profoundly opposed to war at any and every seeming need. . . . For three hundred dollars I could secure a substitute in the army and be free for the other claims upon me. I started for Grinnell with the money in my hand.

Congress had passed a law providing that members of the Society of Friends and other religious bodies opposed to war on conscientious grounds should be permitted, in lieu of military duty, to enlist for hospital service or work among the Freedmen, or might pay the government three hundred dollars. I determined that I would enter the government service as a noncombatant, and so reported to the enrolling officers at Grinnell. Having furnished the required evidence of my membership in the Society of Friends, I was duly recorded as one enlisted in accordance with the Special Act of Congress regulating the army service of noncombatants.

Along with some twenty other drafted men I was taken to Davenport and placed in Camp McClellan to await appointment to actual duty. When the record indicating the special law under which I had enrolled was duly presented to the officer in charge, I was informed that he curtly declared, "I recognize no such law," indicating that I would be assigned to a regiment like any other soldier.

This was a notification of the beginning of trouble. I saw that it was well for me to forestall further difficulty by appealing to the superior officer and preventing the illegal assignment. I could not get a pass to visit the officer and therefore sent a written statement of my case to which I got no reply.

While at Camp McClellan the men were ordered to draw their soldier's uniform. To this I paid no attention but continued to wear my citizen's dress. A week or more later I was ordered out at night with a hundred and fifty others and put upon a train for Chicago. Next morning an officer who was passing through the car stopped and accosted me with the remark, "I don't understand your rig." I explained with considerable detail the circumstances of my enlistment and the special Act of Congress under which I had enrolled, with the exemptions to which I was thereby entitled. A few minutes later another officer appeared and addressed me as the first had done. Realizing the wisdom of brevity, I replied shortly, "I am a drafted Quaker." One of these officers was to leave us at Louisville, Kentucky. The soldiers were drawn up in line for the farewell ceremony and each one was offered a gracious handshake from the departing lieutenant. When he came to me he called out in a loud voice, "Good bye, you noncombatant, you'll keep out of the fight as long as you can, I'll bet!" I accepted this as a personal insult, for which it was plainly intended; but I stood before the speaker . . . as a peace-loving member of the Society of Friends. . . . I could not smite him in the face; I could resolve highly and firmly that if I were ever placed in a position of danger before these men who heard the jeering remark, I would show them whether I was a coward or not.

It happened a few months later that these men were strung along in the different companies of the Tenth Iowa regiment, crouching behind temporary breastworks thrown up during the night as a defense against the fire of the enemy. I took the opportunity to march the whole length of the line bolt upright with vital organs exposed to the enemy's bullets. When I reached my own Company K, the Captain said sternly, "Macy, you are in a dangerous place. Get down here by my side." The incident is generally accepted as an indication of bravery. In reality it was nothing of the sort. It was merely a foolhardy act to satisfy my own sorely wounded pride. A truly brave man would have shown his courage by carefully husbanding his strength till he could use it in exposing himself to danger in an act of real service to the army or to a fellow soldier. However, it did tend to convince the men at the time that I was not a coward.

From Louisville, Kentucky, we were hurried on to Nashville, Tennessee, and thence to Chattanooga, where we were kept more than a week. . . . It now became evident that our squad was intended to join Sherman's force, then in rapid preparation for the march to the sea.

While at Chattanooga, Company K was ordered out to draw their guns and other military equipment. For the second time I refused to obey a military order. When my name was called, one of the men undertook to explain my position, but the Captain flew into a rage and swore that I should be *compelled* to carry a gun. As the men were being marched back with their outfit, while the Captain endeavored to get them in line and I was sitting quietly in camp, one of the most popular of the members of the company, a veteran of the service who had reenlisted as a substitute for a drafted man, called to me by name. As I approached him in response to his call, he stepped out of ranks to meet me, and looking me straight in the eye, said with emphasis, "Macy, don't you draw a gun. Stand by your principles."

I was now face to face with an emergency which I had contemplated for weeks. I was at the front where discipline must absolutely be maintained. From the standpoint of the officers of my company, I was merely a common soldier like the rest. My companions who had been reading up on army discipline, were eagerly imparting to me their literary, drastic notions as to the necessity of prompt and complete obedience to every military command. "One who disobeys orders," they said, "is to be shot." Though I was probably never in a safer place in my life, yet to my ignorance and inexperience it seemed likely that my time had come.

I had endured and was still enduring a good deal of mental agony with reference to my own personal duties in respect to the war. My role as representative of a church was not in harmony with my convictions as a man. In imagination I was confronting martyrdom for opinion's sake, but without any of the consolations usually associated with the heroic assumption of the martyr's halo. I had believed that I could enter the army and fight for liberty while still remaining worthy of the Christian's name; but such action *now* I felt would be a betrayal of trust reposed in me, a sacrifice of loyalty and truth and so of true manly integrity. If I were to maintain the position that I had assumed of insubordination to military power, and so incur the extreme penalty of death, the natural inference on the part of my friends would be that I died a martyr to the pure and sacred Quaker principle of non-resistance. This would, I was sure, be a supposition contrary to fact. At the same time I was confident of having chosen a line of conduct in accordance with the best light I had and I was entirely willing to meet all consequences. At times, indeed, I looked upon my possible death as a real relief from a perplexing and intolerable situation. I felt as ready and willing to die as I had on that memorable occasion in my early boyhood, when I incurred indigestion from eating unripe paw-paws.

It was somewhat of a real disappointment that all appearance of personal danger from adherence to conviction receded.

When the Captain declared with horrid oaths that I should be *forced* to carry a gun, I felt that the issue was joined, and I knew that all the men of my company so understood it. The atmosphere was charged with the expectation that something was going to happen. I resolved to shoulder my own burden. I would have no one else involved with me as a friend or sympathizer. I refused to talk with anyone upon the subject. The Captain came around occasionally as if he were about to speak to me, yet time passed and he said nothing. Finally, when the company was ready to start upon its march to the regiment an extra gun appeared on the ground. The Captain appeared much excited. He picked up the weapon and marched along the line calling out angrily, "Where in hell is that man who has no gun?" I was standing in my place in the line in my black suit and in unobstructed view, but the officer failed to notice me, or at least did not recognize me. We had been called out late in the afternoon, to go a short distance up the hill that we might get an early start the next morning. When we were half way up the Captain suddenly saw and recognized me, but then surprised me by saying that the gun belonged to a man in the hospital who would be on hand in the morning to take it, and then he politely requested me to carry the gun temporarily for the man. Though I believed the story to be a fiction, with politeness emulating his own, I accepted the trust, bore the gun to our place of destination and deferentially returned it to the Captain.

Next morning no one appeared to take charge of the forsaken piece of arms. The Captain again requested me to carry it, explaining that he did not expect me to use it. As it was a request and not an "order" I did not positively refuse, but said calmly, "I would rather not." After studying the situation for a moment, the officer turned to another fellow and told him to take the gun and put it in the wagon. It was often said of me that I refused the order to carry a gun. I have given an exact statement of my nearest approach to such an act of military insubordination and I admit that it was pretty near. Still, strictly speaking, I was never "ordered" to bear arms.

Marching from Chattanooga to Kingston, Georgia, we there were placed under the command of Col. Henderson, of the Tenth Iowa Infantry. I assume that our Captain made a special report of my case to the Colonel and that it was far from favorable. In his address to the new men, the Colonel assured them that they should receive the same treatment as those who had been longer in the service. Referring with pride to the veterans whom he had commanded throughout the years of the war, "They ask no favors. They receive no favors," he said, and he expected to maintain the same relations to the new men. As I was the only man of the company, so far as I knew, who had entered a plea for special treatment, I accepted the Colonel's remarks as designed to apply to myself.

The men were given the privilege of choosing their own company and as far as possible their preferences were regarded. I, of course, made no choice, and, along with a few others who expressed no preferences, I was assigned to Company "K", afterwards known as Company "Q". There were, perhaps, a dozen of us. As our names were called for the purpose of identification, Colonel Henderson, who stood beside the Captain, accosted me, saying, "Is your name Macy?" "Are you a relative of the Macys of Henry County, Indiana?"

"I was born in that County," I replied, adding the names of my father and uncles.

"You are a relative of mine," he said. Looking upon the handsome man with his fine soldierly bearing, I declared myself proud to claim kinship with him. From that moment we were friends, and everything in his power to assist me in my predicament was henceforth done by my colonel.

I had already reached definite conclusions as to my line of conduct. Having been illegally assigned to military duty I would render no service at the command of army officers, except such as conformed to the law governing my entrance into the service. That is, any order pertaining to the care of the sick or disabled I would readily and gladly obey. Orders requiring other sorts of service I would not obey.

A few days after my assignment to Company K, I was detailed with others to unload horses from a train. As soon as the nature of the work was described, I broke ranks, and, as Colonel Henderson was conveniently in sight, I explained to him that I could not perform that service, and returned to my tent.

At first the preparation of food for the company was unorganized, depending upon voluntary work. Under such a plan I did more than my fair share of the daily labor. When it became organized, subject to detail, I did nothing. Captain B. was quite naturally displeased with me. He came to me one morning and explained that men were going into the woods to get fuel for our cooking and requested me to go with them. I raised the question whether this was accounted to the men as a part of their military service. He denied that it was. I suspected at the time that he was prevaricating and was in my tent pondering the question when I was called to the office by Colonel Dean, Commander of the Post, who proposed to assign me to service on a freight train plying between Chattanooga and Atlanta. I explained briefly the nature of my relation to the army and refused to accept the appointment. Colonel Dean replied, "We shall have to excuse you, Mr. Macy. We want a man on this train who, when another man insults him, can knock him down. You are excused." In the meantime the men had left for the woods, and I was saved from the necessity of deciding a troublesome question.

Nothing could be more distasteful to me than this hair-splitting analysis of the exact nature and bearing of these constantly recurring requirements.

Colonel Henderson seemed to be hopeful that as soon as he should be able to see General Smith, the Division Commander then located at Cartersville, some satisfactory settlement of my case could be made.

A few weeks later we were at Cartersville and the Colonel reported to the General. On his return from the interview I saw from his appearance that he had no favorable answer for me. My questions received only an evasive answer. There were thousands of soldiers in the Division, nearly all strangers to me. I still adhered to the policy of silence respecting my standing in the army, speaking to no one on the subject, except the officers immediately concerned, and with them as briefly as the necessities of the situation permitted. I nevertheless got the impression that the entire camp had become interested in the questions involved, some being friendly to me, others opposed. I wondered if there were among them all no other man in similar difficulties, but I heard of none. The air seemed charged with explosive conditions and I alone the cause. I determined to make effort to relieve the situation by going myself to General Smith. He was pacing to and fro in front of Headquarters. I introduced myself and began my explanation. The General was at once in a passion and interrupted me by exclaiming violently, "Nonsense, nonsense! I recognize no such principle!" I instantly turned and walked away, perceiving that I could get no hearing and must leave matters to take their course.

At last, as we were about to be severed from all communication with our friends during our long March to the Sea, a meeting of the officers of the Division was held to dispose of the irritating case. Captain B. was the medium of communication. It was proposed that I should be made company cook. I refused the appointment. Then, I should be Company Pioneer and carry an axe. That too I refused. Might I not be assigned to a place as telegrapher on signal service? Again I refused. The Captain was sent to threaten me. "We have a way in this Company of compelling men to do as they are ordered." I interrupted that it would be a powerful army, indeed, that compelled me to do a thing which I had determined not to do, and closed the conference by adding, "What I have said, I have said."

My next information as to the wishes of the military authorities who were called upon to deal with this unpretending citizen who only wanted to do his duty, came through a lieutenant who explained that no requirement would be made of me; that I would go with the company and be furnished with rations and all needful supplies. . . .

Thus ended all serious question as to my status in the army. What happened to bring the officials to so peaceful a mind I cannot say. After the war was over I was told by a member of Company K that a very large proportion of the soldiers sympathized with me in the controversy with General Smith at Cartersville and a number of them had agreed to stand together in forcible resistance in case extreme measures were instituted against me. I could not ask for treatment more uniformly respectful and friendly than that which I received from officers and men alike in Sherman's Army while on the March to the Sea.

Before my experience with the officers at Cartersville I had endeavored to make myself useful to the men who needed help. Undoubtedly this disposition was a factor in my favor in gaining exemption from military duty. . . . In addition to voluntary services of this sort, there was an understanding that in case of battle I should be given plenty of work to do. The surgeons knew that I should be subject to their orders. When we reached Savannah and I was on the point of being assigned to the regular hospital service the men of the regiment protested and our Captain assured me that the desire was universal that I should remain with the regiment. . . .

Perfect health, almost perfect weather, unlimited supplies of wholesome food, freedom from responsibility and care, moderate and agreeable exercise, the very best exercise ever yet invented for bringing all the muscles and organs of the body into play—walking, living day after day and sleeping night after night in the purest, most invigorating air, the mere consciousness of existence under such conditions was enough to make a man buoyantly, blissfully happy beyond expression! I was confident that if I should ever return home I could never consent to sleep housed up between four walls, shut away from the wild, free air of the great out-of-doors, never! . . .

Occasionally in my few waking moments as I lay under the forest pines I would overhear men of the service talking together. "What a glorious life is this! I would not have missed it for all the world!" Oh, that magnificent, free tramp of the "boys" of Sherman's Army in the glorious Southern autumn days, when I rejoiced in the fascinations of camp life and realized none of its drawbacks. It was good to be a soldier—one of Sherman's soldiers. . . .

There were a few occasions during the March when our section of the army was deployed as if to meet an enemy; but no enemy appeared. It was a strictly peaceable journey, that wonderful March. Not a gun was fired in the hearing of our regiment until we were nearing Savannah. . . .

On the morning of the twenty-first of December one of the fellows announced a prophetic dream, "I dreamed last night," he cried out, "that the rebels had left Savannah and that they crossed the river on a pontoon bridge." Sure enough, on the afternoon of that day we were allowed to break camp and rush into the city. Never, it seemed to me, was a "march" of fifteen miles covered in so short a time. The regiment was strung along for miles; only the stalwart kept in sight of the mounted officers. The last camp for me with the Tenth Iowa Infantry was in the near suburbs of Savannah.

For many months I had been longing for a recognized place in the public service and I fully expected assignment to duty by an order from Washington as soon as communication was established with Savannah. One of my Quaker friends who had entered the ranks at the same time had received an assignment to a hospital in Springfield, Illinois. But my order did not arrive, and in the meantime I besought the Army officers to assign me to duty in a Savannah hospital. It was thus that I entered the Marshal House Hospital January 14, 1865.[17] . . .

The war [had] interrupted the progress of my studies, . . . and [given] a different direction to the line of my thoughts, though I have always felt that my army experiences were a valuable part of my education.

At the close of the war I felt a lasting regret that my peculiar position in the army had been a source of annoyance to military officers whose work I regarded with sympathy and approval. I would have been willing to sacrifice my life to further the great work of saving the Union and abolishing the iniquity of slavery; but I was not clear in my mind as to the proper attitude of the Society of Friends. Each individual Quaker in North and South prayed daily for the success of the Union Army. The extreme abolition views had been considerably modified by the close of the war. They had detained me from enlistment in the army during the early years of the war, though thousands of young men from families with similar training had given their lives for the cause which I held dearer than life. Now I felt that I had done practically nothing. Many had accepted full military service, others, like myself, had passed through the momentous period in a troubled state of mind, uncertain what was the path of duty. One of my own cousins, Elwood Macy, believing when it was too late, that his own failure of duty to his country was due in large measure to the attitude of the Friends' Church, in which he had been educated, abandoned the Society and joined the Methodist Church. A similar sense of dereliction of duty led me to determine to devote the remainder of my life to some form of the work of reconstruction in the South.

I sought work among the freedmen in Missouri, intending later to enter the field of politics. But by a series of strange accidents I failed to secure a position, and in February, 1866, I resumed my studies at Grinnell. . . .

The rise of the carpetbag régime in the South drove from me all further thought of political activities in that section, and I went on to the completion of my college course at Grinnell, acting upon the general idea that a college education was a good thing in itself and as a preparation for usefulness in whatever line of public service might present itself. . . .

⚶ 33 ⚶

A Consistent War-Tax Objector

1861. 12th mo. There were many hindering considerations presented to my mind, and many arguments were used to discourage from declining to pay this tax, by Friends [Quakers] who were intrusted with the important

From *Transactions and Changes in the Society of Friends, and Incidents in the Life and Experience of Joshua Maule*. . . (Philadelphia, 1886), 222–24, 233, 234, 261, 265, 266, 271, 284, 285.

concerns of the Church, and whom I had much esteemed and would have looked to for help, instead of hindrance, in supporting the testimonies of Truth. Amid the "strife of tongues" and the abounding of reasoning, which I often thought brought darkness rather than light, it remained clear to my mind, as I endeavoured to look to the only sure guide, "the Wonderful Counsellor," that, let others do as they would, the only safe way for myself was to entirely decline paying the war tax, and leave the consequences.

Fully impressed with this feeling, I went to the County Treasurer, and informed him how I wished to pay my tax. He objected to receiving it as I requested, as he thought the law would not allow it, but he did not find any law to prohibit him from so doing. I told him I was aware that the authorities would collect the unpaid part of my tax by distraint, but that I believed it was not right for me to pay money to support war. He made many objections to complying with my wishes, all which I answered as well as I found ability. He heard me patiently and kindly, and admitted that he understood the ground of my declining to pay the war tax, and he seemed about to accede to my request when a new difficulty arose in his mind. He said "he did not know whether the law would allow him to do so; he might suffer loss or be fined, and he must consult his law-books." I saw this might unsettle the conclusion he had almost arrived at, and so increase the difficulty, and feeling more strength than when I entered his office,—for I went in weakness,—I said, if he should sustain any personal loss in the matter through being adjudged to have failed in his duty, I would be accountable to him for such loss. This seemed to be assuming a serious responsibility. I may have been in error therein, and have been censured in this particular by some Friends; but I felt satisfied at the time, and have so continued. A faithful testimony, however, subject to all that it may involve or incur, is a question of obedience rather than of dollars and cents. The Treasurer took my word in the matter, and I paid him the full year's tax, thinking it best not to avail myself of the legal privilege of paying one-half six months later. It was entered on the receipt that I had paid all my tax for 1861, except 8½ per cent., which was the part expressly named in the tax-list as for the war at that time.

1862. 1st mo., 14th. A few days since a neighbour, who frequently comes to my store, asked me to loan him a sum of money for a few days. I gave him the amount he asked for, and he then said what he wanted it for was to pay my war tax; that the delinquent tax-list had been sent to him for collection. I had not expected the unpaid tax would be collected before the expiration of the year, or till after the time fixed by law for the last payment; neither did I suppose that a man in such a position—a farmer of considerable property—would engage in such a collection, so that I was taken by surprise. I immediately told him he could not have the money for that purpose. He appeared unwilling to give me any offence or to take my property, and said he thought I would surely be willing to let him do as he intended, as he had borrowed the money. I told him I would rather have paid the Treasurer myself than have it done in this way, and that he must return the money to me. He did return it, but seemed perplexed, and to regret having undertaken to collect the tax. He said he would have to take property, and when he afterwards came for that purpose, he wished me to show him such things as I would rather he should take. I told him I would not take any part in the matter, either to help or hinder; he must take his own course. He was very respectful, and went away manifesting disappointment and uneasiness with the business he had taken in hand. I felt to rejoice that I had escaped the snare laid in borrowing the money, and had not submitted to compromise my testimony. . . .

22d. Yesterday the taxgatherer came for property to pay my war tax. He seemed embarrassed, and wished to talk with me on the subject. I felt free to converse with him, and explained the nature and ground of my declining to pay, and the view held by Friends in regard to all war. He admitted it was correct, and he believed I was acting from conscientious motives: He said "he thought it was easier for me than him." He took several pieces of goods, some of which he afterwards returned. And so what appeared at the first like a mountain of difficulty has passed comfortably away, and renewed cause remains to trust in Him who careth for all who fear and obey Him. . . .

[1862] 7th mo. Our friends Isaac and Mary Mitchell being at my house, I inquired how Friends of Flushing had fared in regard to the war tax. Isaac replied "that they had paid the whole tax without reserve." On my expressing surprise, he said "they had conferred together and reconsidered the matter after his informing me that they were decided that they could not pay it." "They had consulted Friends' writings, &c., and come to the conclusion that as this was a mixed tax, and as Friends had always paid taxes, part of which had gone to support a military establishment, it was better to pay this tax, and make no trouble about it." . . . It was a sorrowful consideration to me that leaders of the people had let fall this Christian testimony, and on the first trial of their faith, when a pecuniary sacrifice was required, had forsaken the vital principles of their profession. . . .

The question as to paying this tax came before our quarterly meeting, and there was a serious concern on the minds of some that Friends should stand faithful to our testimony against war. But this feeling was, for the most part, among those less forward in the meeting. Those who had the management of affairs had no encouragement to hold forth for any to maintain this testimony; it was far otherwise with them. They represented that the writings of early Friends justified the payment of such taxes; and while the meeting was engaged with the subject, Asa Branson declared, boldly and with an evident sense as well as tone of authority, being clerk of the meeting and a recorded minister: "We can pay the tax, but we cannot fight!" And with dark and subtle reasoning he laboured to destroy the conscientious scruples of others. Their voices were silenced, and darkness and death, spiritually, were, in my apprehension, brought over the meeting, which seemed to acquiesce in the decision of the clerk that we were at liberty to pay the hire of others engaged in war, though we could not fight ourselves. I have no doubt the sin was less with many who, without proper consideration and ignorant of the precepts and commands of Truth, went into the field of battle, than with those whose eyes had been enlightened to see the peaceable nature of the Redeemer's kingdom and were professing to uphold it, and who yet voluntarily paid the wages of the warrior, in a war that imbrued the nation in blood.[18] . . .

In the Eleventh month, 1862, I went again to pay the tax. I found a new Treasurer had been elected; he was quite respectful and civil to me, but told me decidedly he would not take any tax as I offered mine,—that is, without the war tax. We conversed freely; he stated his reasons for refusing my request, and I answered him according to the ability afforded me. . . .

* * *

Notwithstanding the . . . very little probability, if any, of my being allowed to pay the tax as I desired, I felt best satisfied to go and see the Treasurer again. . . . He received me pleasantly, and very soon inquired if [I] voted at the last election. I told him I was not at the election. He then said if I had not voted for Lincoln and to sustain the present administration he would receive my tax as I offered to pay it, and so of all the Friends who had not voted. I told him that had nothing to do with the matter in hand; he had no right to question me in regard to voting with the view of basing his action thereon. I had voted for Lincoln at his first term, and if I had voted at the last election it would have been for him; I did not desire anything of him on this ground in regard to the tax, but on the ground of Christian principle. To this he replied: "I have known you well; you are a consistent man: I will take your tax as you desire." Which he did, and that also of another Friend, which I paid in the same way. As I returned home my heart was filled with admiration of the goodness and wonder-working kindness of Him who turneth the hearts of men "as a man turneth his water-course in his field." I am satisfied it was the secret operation of Divine power that changed the strong will of this man, with whom I could have no influence; and I was convinced that he used the plea as to my voting as an excuse, when at heart he felt it was right for him to take the money as I at first requested. He did not question Friends as to their voting who afterwards paid their tax in the same way. Oh that we might learn to render unhesitating obedience to the dictates of the Spirit of Truth in our own hearts, without reasoning upon the consequences! How often a way would be made where no way at first appeared, and we be guided, though as to a hair's-breadth, in the path that would lead to comfort and true peace, both in temporal things as well as in those of higher importance!

This year, 1863, the newly-elected County Treasurer dealt moderately with me and received that part of my tax which was set down as to be applied to civil purposes. The collector distraining property for the war tax told me the amount of my bounty and war tax was one hundred and twenty-six dollars. He took a family carriage and a spring wagon, both in good repair; I paid five hundred dollars for a similar carriage and wagon to replace them. He afterwards informed me by letter that he had sold them for one hundred and sixty-six dollars, and that he had left forty dollars with the Treasurer to my credit: this I did not inquire after or claim in any way. At the time of the sale, which took place on my premises, a friendly neighbour asked me if he could do anything for me in any way to save loss on my property; but I told him he could not, and that I desired and intended to let the law take its course.

I think I was permitted throughout this transaction to experience somewhat of the feeling spoken of by early Friends when they took joyfully the spoiling of their goods. I was preserved from any desire to avert this waste of property, and for some days afterwards a feeling of peace and of sweet inward assurance of rectitude in desires and action attended my mind; and it still is renewed when I recur to the occasion. I gratefully admire how that in every step of this endeavour to bear a clean testimony, as the eye has been kept single to the true Source of help, with earnest desires to be rightly led and the will brought into subjection and true submission, strength has been afforded to meet every trial; and He who hath called to such a testimony hath not failed to verify His own words to one of the least of His creatures: "My grace is sufficient for thee." . . .

The collector of the war and bounty tax for 1865 stated that my war and bounty tax, with costs, &c., amounted to two hundred and eighty-five dollars. He went through my store and took such goods as he thought proper, —cloths, cassimeres, flannels, &c.,—leaving a list showing, as he said, the sort, quantity, and price, which showed they cost me four hundred and forty-nine dollars and thirty cents. He took them, as I was informed, to the village of Pleasant Grove, where he disposed of them by public sale. I afterwards received the following letter:

"ST. CLAIRSVILLE, July 25th, 1866.
"JOSHUA AND JACOB[19] MAULE,—Enclosed are your tax receipts for 1865, and the surplus money from the sale of the goods on the 21st. If you desire, I can send you a copy of sale lists, as I have all correct. The surplus is thirty-one dollars and thirty-five cents. I could not stop at the time I would have liked to. I did the best under the circumstances that the case would admit of, and submit myself, respectfully,
"T. J. HAWTHORNE."

I returned to the collector the money he sent me, and informed him that I understood the law did not allow of more property being sold in such cases than what satisfied the claim; that if he would return my property as it was when he took it, I would receive it, but I would not receive the money for it after passing through his hands in the manner it had.

✻ 34 ✻

A Mennonite Farmer Hires a Substitute

This was 1864, the last year of the Civil War. So many men had fallen in battle that enlistees became few. The government resorted to the draft. My brother Valentin, David Ruth, John Eicher, and I were on the list. The question of nonresistance now became very real to our family, more vital than in peacetime. By nature I was and still am no coward. But the principle of non-resistance, the main reason for our leaving Germany, had been firmly implanted by my father.[20] I had even advised members of our church who had been persuaded to join an underground organization pledged to defend the nation by the use of arms to remain loyal to the principles of our faith. (At this time the rebels were about to cross the Mississippi, a move which would have imperiled our region.) My stand was, however, strongly resented by undercover patriots. When Frederick Hecker called me a rebel and a traitor, the mob apparently threatened to hang me. But I could not be frightened into retracting my position. Later my American friends told me that American neighbors had testified to my loyalty to the Union. In this I saw the protecting hand of God.

After I had been drafted I had to settle this question with my conscience. It became clear to me that I was called to be a fighter, but not as a soldier. Several of us had agreed to pool our money ($2,000) to secure substitutes for those drafted.

My substitute, a young man from the Black Forest, Germany, Remigius Mantele, was at once sent to the front into several hard battles, but was never wounded. But after the armistice he contracted camp fever and returned home looking like a skeleton. We were able to nurse him back to health. He returned to Germany and was married, but wrote that he was not able to support himself and family. We sent him money to return with his family to America. They are now our good friends here in Halstead, Kansas.

From Christian Krehbiel, *Prairie Pioneer*, translated from the German by Elva Krehbiel Leisy (Newton, Kans., 1961), 43, 44.

⚘ 35 ⚘

Brethren and Mennonites as Exiles from the Confederate Draft

"Brethren [and Mennonites] in the South were affected by the War [through] the loss of the men of military age by emigration. . . . Some of those who attempted to escape were not so fortunate and were captured. One group of more than seventy, not all of whom were Brethren [or Mennonites] however, was captured in present-day West Virginia and taken to a prison in Richmond. Joseph Miller, who was one of the group, explained what happened" (R. E. Sappington).

In the early part of March, 1862, having been informed that all the men subject to military duty would be called to arms in a very few days, Brother David M. Miller and myself concluded to do something to keep out of the war. We heard of some Brethren and others intending to go west, and we made preparations to go too, being hurried by our wives, who feared we would be arrested and taken to the army before we got started. So we lost no time in preparation.

After traveling about twelve miles, we fell in company with about seventy others—Brethren, Mennonites and others. The conclusion among us was to cross the line to West Virginia. So with the Shenandoah Mountain before us, we proceeded, going part of the way during the night. The next day we traveled on west, and the next night we lodged at a friend's house, resting on the floor. The next day we arrived at Petersburg, W. Va. Now a good many persons came out to see us cross the South Branch of the Potomac River, it being fifty yards or more wide, and more than half our company were on foot, so that in crossing some horses had to go three trips before all had passed over the stream. It seemed to be a great curiosity for the people to see us cross the Branch and to go through the town.

Soon after passing this place came the trouble, as we then thought, but it seemed that the good Lord did not think as we did; he prepared a better way for our escape than we had marked out for ourselves. After going through Petersburg, he sent two men to cause a halt in our journey, one in front, and one in the rear. The man in front made use of some hard words, but the man in the rear was kind. We halted, and at their solicitation we

From Roger E. Sappington, ed., *The Brethren in the New Nation: A Source Book on the Development of the Church of the Brethren, 1785–1865* (Elgin, Ill., 1976), 377–82, 387.

turned back to Petersburg. They took us into a large upper room and as we passed in by the door we were asked individually whether we had any arms. When the question was put to me, I answered, "Yes." "Let us see it," said he. I showed him my New Testament, the Sword of the Spirit. He said, "that is very good; you can keep that." I do not think there were any arms found in our company, except one or two small pistols, and they were not with the Brethren. We were furnished a snack for dinner.

One brother Mennonite, who had talked of going back before we got to Petersburg, and I had encouraged him to go on, said to me. "What are you going to do now?" I replied, "Stand still and see the salvation of the Lord."

My brother, D. M. Miller, and I had near relatives in Hampshire county, about thirty miles further on, and we expected to lodge with them until we could go back home; and the Lord let us all go within a few miles of the line between the Northern and Southern armies, then turned us back by the hand of two men. How good he is; but we could not see it at that time. We wanted to go on.

We were next ordered to leave the upper room and travel south towards Franklin, the county seat of Pendleton county, West Virginia. We were guarded by eight or ten men. Not reaching Franklin that day, we lodged with Mr. Bond, where one of our company (not a brother) got away. A brother and myself had all chances to get away that night, but we had no desire to leave the brethren. The next night we lodged in the court house in Franklin, sleeping on the floor, and guarded. At this place, six or seven others, that had been captured as we were, joined our number, making in all about seventy-eight. During the night, six of us were taken out one at a time, and asked where we were going, and the reason why. We told them the truth, that we were going away only to keep from fighting, that it was contrary to our faith, and contrary to the Gospel to fight and kill our fellow-man,—entirely wrong to do so. We were not abused. At this place one brother lost his horse and his clothes.

The next day we went twenty-four miles to Monterey, the county seat of Highland county, Virginia. Then next morning we started for Staunton, Va., distant fifty-two miles. We had a barrel of crackers and a few pieces of bacon on a wagon. It took us two days to go through and over the foothills and to cross the Shenandoah Mountain; and while we were going over the mountain, one brother got away. In going up the mountain pathway on foot, some one else riding my horse along the main road, we were scattered very much. It seems that the guards had confidence in us. Brother Cool and I were walking together, and I was showing him where I was acquainted. We had got so much scattered that no one was in sight of us in front or rear. Brother Cool said, "Let us slip." I replied, "I do not feel to do so." We continued on the way till we came to an old vacant house where we lodged for the night. The officer of the guards said, "Gentlemen, I will trust to your honor tonight." Then he and the guards went away about half a mile to get their lodging. After they were gone, brother Thompson said to me, "Some of the Brethren talk about running off to-night; what do you think about it?" I said, "I do not like that." Said he, "Suppose we send for the guards?" I said, "Do so," and they were soon there, drew us into line and counted us. They had so much confidence in us that they thought we would stay without being guarded, but Satan might have made us all dishonest that night had we not been watchful of ourselves and on our guard.

The next day we went to Staunton, Augusta Co., Va., and lodged in the courthouse. We got plenty to eat. The guards were overheard saying, "Don't tell them that they have to go to Richmond to-morrow; they will not sleep well." It would have disturbed us some, if we had known it; for we did not yet know that Richmond was the place the Lord had directed us to go.

In the morning after breakfast, with some crackers in our pockets, and a little sadness in our hearts, we started on the train for Richmond, distant 120 miles, leaving our horses and saddles in the care of some one else. We were all day and part of the night on the way to Richmond. After reaching our destination, we were put into a large room in a machine house with a small stove. There was about three yards in one corner to which we had no access. The officer said, "Gentlemen, this is the best we can do for you tonight; make yourselves easy." This was the most unpleasant night for me on the trip. The weather being cool, with no fire and no bed, some of us walked nearly all night. Next morning breakfast came about 9 o'clock, but it came plentiful. We staid in that house one night only, then we were moved to a more comfortable house, and furnished with bedding and provisions.

In a day or two twelve of us were taken before Judge Baxter, and he said, "Gentlemen, I will ask you a good many questions, and if I ask any that you cannot answer, you need not say anything." He then asked many questions concerning what we had been doing during the war, and whether we had been in the service. He also asked us whether we had fed the soldiers and their families. We answered all his questions save one, and the judge was kind enough to answer that for us; which was, "Would you feed the enemy, should he come to your house?" He said, "We are commanded to feed our enemies." This was a correct answer. Before dismissing us the judge said that we would be sent home soon to work on our farms.

Just at this time the Confederate Congress was in session in Richmond, and some of the members of Congress came in to see us. Some of them wanted us to volunteer to drive teams; but we told them we left home to keep out of the war, and that we did not propose to go into the army service. Others wanted to know all about our faith, and we gave them all the information about our religious belief that we could. They also found out that twenty-five of our people were in prison in Harrisonburg, who had been arrested as we were, and that many others had gone through the lines, and we were told they got the question up in Congress, "What would we better do with these men? They raise more grain to the hand than any farmers we have, and they are nearly all laboring men, and we need them at home as much as in the Army. Would we not better make some provision for them, or they will all leave the country? If we force them into the army, they will not fight."

These things were brought to us in the guardhouse. So the question was considered in Congress, and they reached the conclusion to lay a fine on us, and send us home. The fine was fixed at five hundred dollars each. This may look like a large sum, but the Brethren at home soon sent the money to us, and we paid it, and went home. The poor brethren as well as the rich had their fine paid. It was not long after that till a good horse sold for a thousand dollars which paid two fines. This fine paid in 1862 cleared us during the war, which lasted three years more.

We were in Richmond thirty days. A few days before we left Richmond, six of us were taken before Judge Baxter again. He treated us very kindly, and expressed his sore regret that we had been kept there so long, when we should have been at home on our farms. He said the delay was on account of the press of business, and that we would soon be sent home, which came to pass. We were joyfully received at home by our families and the brethren. We were absent from home in all thirty-seven days. Our horses were kept in Staunton and put into service, but we received pay for them from the government. No money was taken from any of our company, and upon the whole we were kindly treated.

※　　※　　※

"Seventy-four men reached Richmond and were imprisoned in Castle Thunder, which was being used for political prisoners. They were interviewed, as Miller reported, by S.S. Baxter, an official of the Confederate War Department. He issued three reports. The first listed twenty-seven men who evidently were not church members and were therefore prepared to serve in the army. The second and third reports dealt with the remaining forty-seven and his recommendations regarding them" (R. E. Sappington).

Richmond, March 31, 1862.

REPORT OF S.S. BAXTER OF PRISONERS EXAMINED BY HIM

I have examined a number of persons, fugitives from Rockingham and Augusta Counties, who were arrested at Petersburg, in Hardy County. These men are all regular members in good standing in the Tunker (Dunkard) and Mennonite Churches. One of the tenets of those churches is that the law of God forbids shedding human blood in battle and this doctrine is uniformly taught to all their people. As all these persons are members in good standing in these churches and bear good characters as citizens and Christians I cannot doubt the sincerity of their declaration that they left home to avoid the draft of the militia and under the belief that by the draft they would be placed in a situation in which they would be compelled to violate their consciences. They all declare they had no intention to go to the enemy or remain with them. They all intended to return home as soon as the draft was over. Some of them had made exertions to procure substitutes. One man had sent the money to Richmond to hire a substitute. Others had done much to support the families of volunteers. Some had furnished horses to the cavalry. All of them are friendly to the South and they express a willingness to contribute all their property if necessary to establish our liberties. I am informed a law will probably pass exempting these persons from military duty on payment of a pecuniary compensation. These parties assure me all who are able will cheerfully pay this compensation. Those who are unable to make the payment will cheerfully go into service as teamsters or in any employment in which they are not required to shed blood. I recommend all persons in the annexed list be discharged on taking the oath of allegiance and agreeing to submit to the laws of Virginia and the Confederate States in all things except taking arms in war. . . .

April 2, 1862

SUPPLEMENTAL REPORT ON THE CASE OF
THE TUNKERS (DUNKARDS) AND MENNONITES.

Since my last report I have seen the copy of the law passed by the Legislature of Virginia on the 29th of March, 1862. It exempts from military duty persons prevented from bearing arms by the tenets of the church to which they belong on condition of paying $500 and 2 per cent. on the assessed value of their property, taking an oath to sustain the Confederate Government and not in any way to give aid or comfort to the enemies of the Confederate Government, with the proviso that if the person exempted is not able to pay the tax he shall be employed as teamster or in some character which will not require the actual bearing [of] arms, and surrender any arms they possess for public use. I renew my recommendation that these persons be discharged on taking the oath of allegiance and an obligation to conform to the laws of Virginia.

"*On the basis of Baxter's recommendations and of the action of the Virginia legislature on March 29, 1862, the imprisoned Brethren and Mennonites in Richmond were released after about one month in captivity. Thus, a major crisis had been overcome, since there had been a very real possibility that the group might be executed for treason*" (R. E. Sappington).

"*The Brethren in Tennessee also found it desirable to flee from their homes on occasion to escape from military service. P.R. Wrightsman was a young man during the War, and in 1864 he was drafted, according to his report*" (R. E. Sappington).

In February of 1864 I was conscripted. Learning of their coming after me, some of my neighbors, with myself, fled to the mountains in the night. With snow knee-deep, and provisions on our backs, we plodded up the mountainside.

At break of day we halted and prepared something to eat. Here we remained, in the snow-capped mountains, for a number of days. When we received word that the soldiers were coming after us, we went to the settlement, and hid until the panic of excitement passed away. I then returned home.[21]

☀ 36 ☀

Adventists Confront the Draft

Letters to the World's Crisis and Second Advent Messenger

The trial of one's faith is more precious than gold, if he *endures* the trial. So it has been, in part, with me; for I have, during the drafting excitement, published my faith at home and abroad, in the shop and store, as to what kind of weapons a *christian* should use under *all* circumstances, and what he should refuse to use under *any* circumstances. The position that our government has taken, that war is *right*, to maintain itself, and if right, that the christian should be among the first, must be *wrong*; for it is contrary to the principles of the gospel of Jesus Christ. But, the law is made, and, if "unalterable", it involves the followers of Jesus in the war, or the sufferings of the penalties of a military law;—I speak of those who, like myself, are not able to satisfy the demands of the government, either pecunarily or in person.

I was drafted. What to do I hardly knew for awhile. I consulted the brethren, for I wished to do *right* in the matter; that is, I did not wish to resist the government unscripturally. One said it was right to go; others said, "Go, but not carry the gun, dig trenches, drive team," etc.; and others said, "Take no part in it whatever, but suffer the penalties, if God wills it." My shop-mates desired to help me out, by helping me to get a substitute. To be *certain* of *doing right*, I appealed to the Lord for wisdom and direction. Soon my mind became calm and clear, I was the Lord's, and had on the

From *The World's Crisis and Second Advent Messenger* (Boston) 17, no. 24 (August 25, 1863):96, and 18, no. 6 (October 27, 1863):22.

"whole armor of God." I could not exchange that for the armor of Satan, nor lay aside the "sword of the Spirit" for the sword of blood; neither could I use both at the same time. I resolved to take no part in the war, on the principle that "the partaker is as bad as the thief." And the idea of hiring a man to kill *for* me would implicate *me* in the crime; so I refused to give even five cents for a substitute.

If I had had three hundred dollars, I could conscientiously have given it to Caesar as a last resort, to get exempt from the bloody field of carnal strife. Some tried to persuade me that it was just as bad to pay the money as to hire a substitute, as the money was for *that* purpose. The difference is great. The Lord will not hold me accountable for the mischief that money, taken from me by *force*, would do when employed by others. Caesar demands taxes of us; we pay them, according to the instruction and example of our Lord. We render unto Caesar that which is Caesar's, and Caesar hires a man to shoot his enemies for him; are we to blame? By no means. But to hire a man to fight in my place, would be like hiring a thief to *steal* in my place. Both guilty. Rather let my body be perforated with a "bushel of bullets," than to do the *least* wrong to my fellow men for the sake of escaping suffering or death! Thus I reasoned. I prayed for grace and strength to endure the trial. My Lord was with me. So with full confidence and trust in him, I went to be examined, little doubting but that I should pass, as to all appearances, being able-bodied. But for a trifling thing, of which I had never complained directly, nor was aware of, I was pronounced unfit for military duty. Thus ended my trial.

But *had* I passed examination, my mind was to keep about my work as usual, and if arrested as a deserter, and tried, to speak in my own defence as the Holy Ghost should give utterance, and preach to them the kind of *peace* that Jesus taught us. Brethren, you that are, or may be under like trial, I have written this for your comfort and consideration. Trust in the Lord and *do right*. The cause we love so well may yet demand a sacrifice; go cheerfully. Glorify God in your spirit and body which are his. Our Savior died for us; let us not refuse to die for him and his gospel's sake. Finally, brethren, one and all, fight for your country, *your* country—I mean that for which we are "seeking", and to which we are journeying as "strangers and pilgrims." God grant that the writer may meet you *in* that "better country" where all will be peace and loveliness FOREVER.

Hartford, Ct., Aug. 11th, '63   G. W. Gillespie

Having passed through this ordeal, and finding the grace of God sufficient for me, I feel like giving him the glory; and giving my brethren an account of my trial, hoping it may be [offered?], by way of suggestion or instruction, to those who may be thus called upon to go into the fight.

And I may say here, that I do not vote, fight, nor run:—not vote, because I have no precedents among gospel writers; not fight, because the apostle (Peter) was not allowed to defend even the body of the Savior with the sword; not run, because I should then be "subject to the powers that be."

As my examination was so singular, I will give it in part. I was obliged to answer the questions of the surgeons in the negative, as I had no knowledge of any cause of exemption, and this, of course, was in their favor. They, however, found a heart difficulty, and the chief surgeon (a Methodist brother, though a stranger to me) after listening closely to the action of my heart, looked me in the face, and said, "Do you have a clear conscience?"

The change from a physical to a moral examination was so sudden and unexpected as to astonish me for the moment, but it was "given me in the self-same hour what to say," and I readily answered, "I have. I am a man who fears God;" and the Surgeon added, "And escheweth evil." "Yes," said I, "so much so that I could not bear arms under any circumstances whatever."

When I had stepped along to the tables, where sat the Provost Marshal, clerks, surgeons, etc., the Marshal asked me "how much time I wanted?" I told him I wanted as much as he could give me, for there was no way for me to get clear, only to pay $300; and, said I, "I am poor and the money will come very slow and hard." The clerk said, "You are able-bodied?" "Yes, I suppose so, but I could not conscientiously bear arms." "Ah!" said the Marshal, "that's it?" "Yes."

The clerk then said to me, "You can get a substitute." "No, for that is the same as to go myself." The chief surgeon now looking up quite wise, while a smile lit up his eye, said, "Well, the government can take the money and get a substitute." "It *might* do so, but there is *no provision* into the law to carry that into effect; and furthermore, the Marshal has told me it had not been so used, but must be paid into government and he could not trace it further. I therefore calculate to pay it, if I can, as a tax; for my Master wrought a miracle when he would enforce the duty of paying taxes; and if I can pay a tax on food and raiment that the body used, of course I can pay on the body itself. My Master wrought one other miracle, when he taught his disciples that christians cannot bear arms."

On this the whole Board were silent. Thus ended my "testimony before rulers," and also "against them." I got a furlough for eight days, and some said, take this course, and some that, but almost all urged me to get a substitute. My convictions, however, were that I must pay the extreme penalty of the law, rather than do it, or fight myself.

And it is a fact worthy of note that of the many I had discussions with, out of five denominations, *not one* could be prevailed upon to offer *one gospel text* to support the "fighting", or the "substitute" theory. For my part, it was blessed to have Jesus' words, and the noble precedents in the gospel to lean on: and I prayed that the course I concluded to adopt might be stopped in season, if it was wrong.

But God lives (thank his name), and he prospered the course and the brethren gave me almost a hundred dollars, and others lent me for Christ's sake, not knowing whether I would be able to pay or not, and thus I was able to purchase my liberty, and satisfying the government, by "rendering Caesar his own," with image and superscription thereon; and if he makes a bad use of it, he is responsible; as I have no further control of it.

Query. How could the surgeon pass the sentence of "conscript" on a brother in Christ, whom he admitted somewhat unsound, and knew could not bear arms? Is it not a powerful comment upon the idea of Christians taking part in Gentile government which must be destroyed that Jesus may reign King of kings?

Concord, N.H.   John H. Dadmun

☙ 37 ❧

A Disciple of Christ Goes the Second Mile

Perhaps the only manual labor performed by Mr. Franklin[22] after he moved to Cincinnati was done in 1862. A Confederate army menaced the city, and active preparations were made for its defence. Every able-bodied man was pressed into the service and compelled to work on the entrenchments. Mr. Franklin came home from a meeting just in this crisis of affairs, and was marched to the hills back of Covington, where, with pick-axe and shovel, if he did not accomplish much for the defence of the city, he at least blistered his hands and stiffened his joints, feeding, meanwhile, on soldier's rations and resting upon the ground. He was willing to and did submit to the authorities in everything except in fighting. When the excitement was at the highest against him he was preaching in Illinois. It was reported to him that there was much threatening in the place to require him to take the oath of allegiance to the United States. "Tell them to come on with an officer," said he, smiling as if it were a capital joke. "I am willing to take the oath of allegiance to Uncle Sam every morning, if necessary."

From Joseph Franklin and J. A. Headington, *Life and Times of Benjamin Franklin* (St. Louis, Mo., 1879), 289, 290.

⚜ 38 ⚜

Christadelphians and the Draft

From Dr. John Thomas's diary, 1864

Next day, I arrived in Freeport, Stephenson County, Illinois, as one desired. 'I am more glad to see you,' said Brother Coffman, 'than I expect you are to see me.' They were disturbed in mind about the coming draft on September 19th, and were longing for my arrival in hope that I might be able to help them against the Federal provost-marshals. I told them that the Federal law exempted all who belonged to a denomination conscientiously opposed to bearing arms, on condition of paying 300 dollars, finding a substitute, or serving in the hospitals. This excluded all the *known* denominations except the Quakers; for besides this denomination, they not only proclaimed the fighting for country a Christian virtue, but were all commingled in the unhallowed and sanguinary conflict. There was, however, a denomination *not known* to the ignorance of legislative wisdom. It was relatively, very small, but, nevertheless, a denomination and a name, contrary to and distinct from all others upon earth. It comprehended all those who with Paul repudiated the use of carnal weapons; and not this only, but who, believing the gospel of the Kingdom, became constituents of the Name by being intelligently immersed into Christ Jesus their Lord. The members of this name and denomination are not politicians; they are not patriots, and take no part in the contentions of the world, which is 'the enemy of God.' Politicians, patriots, and factionists, though they may profess the theory of the truth, and have passed through the water, have not the spirit of the truth in them, and have, therefore, no scriptural claim or identity with the conscience of this name and denomination. This was their view of the matter, and met the case of these brethren in Ogle County, who have a mortal distaste for all crotchets and compromise, and refuse all identification with those who favour them. Their determination is to be shot at their own doors, rather than serve in the armies of the North and South; which to them is a degradation and defilement not to be endured by the faithful. Though these are their sentiments, they feared that in the browbeating presence of a provost-marshal's court, they might not be able to make them stand successfully against the taunts and ridicule that were sure to be

From Frank G. Jannaway, *Without the Camp: Being the Story of Why and How the Christadelphians Were Exempted from Military Service* (London, 1917), 10–12.

brought upon them. They wished therefore that I would write something that they could put into court as the ground of their claim to exemption according to the law.

It would be necessary to give the name a denominational appellative, that being so denominated, they might have wherewith to answer the inquisitors. This seemed the most difficult part of the affair, though not altogether insurmountable. The crisis had come, and something had to be done to save brethren in deed and in truth from being seized upon. . . .

I did not know a better denomination that would be given to such a class of believers than 'Brethren in Christ.' This declares their true status; and, as officials prefer words to phrases, the same fact is expressed in another form by the word *Christadelphians or Christos adelphoi—Christ's Brethren*. This matter settled to their satisfaction, I wrote for them the following certificate:-

> This is to certify that   23 and others, constitute a religious association, denominated herein for the sake of distinguishing them from all other "Names and Denominations," *Brethren in Christ*, or in one word, *Christadelphians*; and that said brethren are in fellowship with similar associations, in England, Scotland, the British provinces, New York, and other cities of the North and South—New York being for the time present the radiating centre of their testimony to the people of the current age and generation of the world.
>
> This is also to certify, that the denomination constituted of the associations or ecclesias of this Name, conscientiously opposes, and earnestly protests against "Brethren in Christ" having anything to do with politics in wordy strife, or arms-bearing in the service of the sin-powers of the world under any conceivable circumstances or conditions whatever; regarding it as a course of conduct disloyal to the Deity in Christ, their Lord and King, and perilous to their eternal welfare!
>
> This being individually and collectively the conscientious conviction of all true Christadelphians, they claim and demand the rights and privileges so considerately accorded by the Congress of the United States, in the statute made and provided for the exemption of members of a denomination conscientiously opposed to bearing arms in the service of any human government.
>
> This is also further to certify that the undersigned is the personal instrumentality by which the Christian Association aforesaid in Britain and America has been developed within the last fifteen years, and that, therefore, he knows assuredly that a conscientious, determined, and uncompromising opposition to serving in the armies of the "powers that be" is their denominational characteristic. In confirmation of this, he appeals to the definition of its position in respect of war, on page 13 of a pamphlet entitled "Yahweh Elohim," issued by the Antipas Association of Christadelphians assembling at 24, Cooper Institute, New

York, and with which he ordinarily convenes. Advocates of war and desolation are not in fellowship with them or with the undersigned.

JOHN THOMAS.[24]

NOTES

Text

1. For John Wesley Pratt's CO experiences, see "A Garrisonian Nonresistant Faces the Civil-War Draft," reprinted from Garrison's Boston journal, *The Liberator* 34, no. 14 (April 1, 1864):56, in my *Records of Conscience: Three Autobiographical Narratives by Conscientious Objectors* (York, England, 1993), 47–66. Pratt also figures in the account of Shaker Horace S. Taber's draft experiences.
2. Martin Henry Blatt, *Free Love and Anarchism: The Biography of Ezra Heywood* (Urbana, 1989), 27–35.
3. See *Memoir and Correspondence of Eliza P. Gurney*, ed. Richard F. Mott (Philadelphia, 1884), pp. 307–22. Letter dated September 4, 1864.
4. Later Pringle became well known as a botanist. "To him is credited the discovery of over a thousand new species" of plants. "He sent species all over the world and built up a herbarium of his own, still preserved at the University of Vermont, an institution . . . from which he received an honorary Doctor of Science degree." In his foreword to the reprint of Pringle's Civil War diary as a Pendle Hill pamphlet (1962), the Quaker scholar Henry J. Cadbury writes: "The incident here described is detachable from [Pringle's] main career. It is, however, a vivid, intimate human document. It has the same simplicity of style that marked his later . . . articles as a botanist, but it deals with a more inward and timeless problem of a sensitive conscience."
5. "He enrolled in the University of Vermont in 1859 but had to return to the [family] farm and the care of his widowed mother and younger brother. In literature and language and also in science he was largely self-educated." Cadbury, Foreword, *The Civil War Diary of Cyrus Pringle*, p. 3.
6. Ibid., p. 6.
7. A further example of courageous war resistance by twelve Southern Quaker COs, in this case from North Carolina, is given by Stephen M. Kohn, *Jailed for Peace: The History of American Draft Law Violators, 1658–1985* (Westport, Conn., 1986), 20, 21, reprinting from a letter from Alfred H. Love to the *Liberator*, August 21, 1863. Love reports: "Every conceivable insult and outrage was heaped upon them; they were tied up, starved and whipped. Still they remained firm to their conscientious convictions, and refused to fight. Finally, the muskets were absolutely strapped to their bodies. One of these Friends was singled out as especially obnoxious, and was whipped unmercifully. The officer in charge was lawless and brutal, and on one occasion ordered him to be shot, as an example to others. He called out a file of men to shoot him. While his executioners were drawn up before him, standing within twelve feet of their victim, the latter, raising his eyes to heaven, and elevating his hands, cried out in a loud voice: "Father, forgive them, they know not what they do." Instantly came the order to fire. But, in-

stead of obeying it, the men dropped their muskets and refused, declaring that they could not kill such a man." "The twelve objectors," writes Kohn, "were forcibly marched with the rebel army into the battle of Gettysburg. During that battle, 'they remained entirely passive' and never fired a shot. None of the Friends was injured, and all eventually were taken prisoner. Once under Northern jurisdiction, they obtained official discharges and were freed."

8. Macy later left the Quakers for the Congregationalists. Well known for his work in political science, he authored inter alia a number of books on American government. See the entry on him by Charles E. Payne in the *Dictionary of American Biography* (New York), 12:176, 177.

9. Quoted in Edward Needles Wright, *Conscientious Objectors in the Civil War* (Philadelphia, 1931), 167.

10. For the endeavors by the founder of another "new" peace sect, the Christadelphians, to obtain the Unionist authorities' acceptance of its CO exemption status, see Document 38.

11. See Roger Guion Davis, "Conscientious Cooperators: The Seventh-day Adventists and Military Service, 1860–1945" (Ph.D. diss., George Washington University, 1970), chap. 3, "Abolitionism and the Noncombatancy Debate"; and chap. 4, "From Bounties to Attempted Cooperation." Also my *Freedom from Violence: Sectarian Nonresistance from the Middle Ages to the Great War* (Toronto, 1991), chap. 21: "American Seventh-day Adventists during the Civil War." At this time there existed some uncertainty as to whether an Adventist could accept induction, provided he could enter some noncombatant branch of the army (and provided, of course, his Saturday sabbath would also be respected). Most draftees sought to obtain work in military hospitals, as American Adventist soldiers were to do in the wars of the twentieth century.

12. David Edwin Harrell, Jr., "Disciples of Christ Pacifism in Nineteenth-Century Tennessee," *Tennessee Historical Quarterly* 21, no. 3 (September 1962):263–73.

Documents

1. Elizabeth Buffum Chace (1806–1899), active in the abolitionist movement and a protagonist of women's rights, was the wife of a Quaker cotton manufacturer, Samuel Buffington Chace. A birthright New England Quaker, Mrs. Chace, like her father, Arnold Buffum, had left the Society of Friends because of what both considered its lukewarm attitude on the antislavery question. Unlike many other Garrisonian nonresistants, she remained a pacifist throughout the Civil War. For the prewar repudiation of nonviolence with respect to the slavery issue by such prominent women nonresistants as Lydia Maria Child and Angelica Grimké Weld, see Henry Mayer, *All on Fire: William Lloyd Garrison and the Abolition of Slavery* (New York, 1998), 448.

2. "Military drill in grammar schools as well as high schools and Latin schools was becoming increasingly common in . . . Massachusetts" (note by editor of Garrison's letters, W. M. Merrill).

3. "Available sources do not indicate whether Francis Jackson Garrison was excused from military drill" (Merrill's note). However, in view of Garrison's militant temperament, I am sure we would have heard from him if Frank had been forced to drill.

4. In addition to the maladies Taber's doctor and work supervisor testified that he suffered from, the community elders and the "Family nurse" also certified "that

said Taber has been blind in one eye from his early youth and that he has made frequent complaints, to at least a number of us, of the weakness of the other eye, especially when suffering from the effects of a cold."

5. W. L. D. below. Not all the acronyms used by Pringle can now be deciphered.

6. L. M. M. below.

7. P. D. below.

8. E. W. H. below.

9. H. D. below.

10. I.e., William Wood, who, along with Henry Dickinson, represented New York Quakers.

11. Simon Winchester, in his recent study *The Professor and the Madman: A Tale of Murder, Insanity, and the Making of the Oxford English Dictionary* (1998), p. 59, wrote of the punishment of "bucking" as practiced during the Civil War on recalcitrant soldiers as well as on the Quaker Cyrus Pringle: "It was a punishment so harsh as to prove often decidedly counterproductive. One general who ordered a man to be bucked for straggling found that half his company deserted in protest." Winchester describes it as "a painful ordeal . . . in which the wrists were tied tightly, the arms forced over the knees, and a stick secured beneath the arms and knees." The man was then left "in an excruciating contortion."

12. C. L. W. below.

13. I. N. below.

14. D. H. below.

15. Cartland adds (p. 326): "Brigadier-General Maney . . . was doubtless unacquainted with the imprisonment of our friend at Salisbury"—a noisome place indeed!

16. I.e., membership of the Representative Committee of the Iowa Yearly Meeting of Friends. By accepting this office in his Society Macy believed he could represent the concerns of his peers in the Yearly Meeting.

17. After continuing in army medical work at various locations, Macy received his discharge on the conclusion of the war.

18. Maule proceeds to quote at length from the writings of four prominent eighteenth-century Quakers—Thomas Story, John Churchman, John Woolman, and Job Scott—to back his view that consistent Quakers should refuse under any circumstances to pay to government money that went to support war.

19. A relative of Joshua, who took a position similar to Joshua's on the tax issue.

20. Christian Krehbiel (1832–1909) emigrated to the United States in 1851, together with his parents and siblings; they left the Palatinate so that the boys would not be conscripted as they would inevitably have been if they had remained. After the Civil War Christian became active in church work. His autobiography was written when he was seventy-five. See the entry on him by Olin Krehbiel in *The Mennonite Encyclopedia* (Scottdale, Penn.), 3 (1957):236.

21. R. E. Sappington adds (p. 387): "Wrightsman was evidently successful in escaping the pressure of the draft."

22. This Benjamin Franklin (1812–1878) was a prominent member of the Disciples of Christ. At the time of the Civil War he was editor of the *American Christian Review* (Cincinnati) and a leading proponent of an antiwar position among Disciples in the North. In 1861 he had written in his paper: "We doubt the whole business of Christians taking up arms and fighting, even if *drafted*. This is not *our country*. We are only pilgrims and sojourners here." See the entry on him by Allen C. Guelzo in the *American National Dictionary* (New York, 1999), 8:395, 396.

23. Gap in the text.
24. Dr. Thomas's followers in the South, a small group centered in Virginia, had also succeeded in gaining—qualified—exemption from the Confederate draft after petitioning for this in 1862. At that date they were known there as Nazarenes, whose identity long remained unclear. The riddle has now been solved by Michael W. Casey on the basis of meticulous research. I must thank Professor Casey for sending me a copy of his unpublished paper, "From Nazarene to Christadelphian: The Story of Pacifism in the Christadelphians."

BACKGROUND READING

Bowman, Rufus D. *The Church of the Brethren and War, 1708–1941*, 114–56. Elgin, Ill., 1944.

Brock, Peter. *Pacifism in the United States: From the Colonial Era to the First World War*, 687–866. Princeton, N.J., 1968.

Curran, Thomas F. "Pacifists, Peace Democrats, and the Politics of Perfection in the Civil War Era," *Journal of Church and State* 38, no. 3 (Summer 1996):487–505.

Nelson, Jacquelyn S. *Indiana Quakers Confront the Civil War*. Indianapolis, 1991.

Schlabach, Theron F. *Peace, Faith, Nation: Mennonites and Amish in Nineteenth-Century America*, 173–200. Scottdale, Penn., 1988.

Wright, Edward Needles. *Conscientious Objectors in the Civil War*. Philadelphia, 1931.

Printed in the United States
44220LVS00006B/73

9 780195 151220